P9-DNQ-853

ESSAYS IN THE THEORY OF ECONOMIC GROWTH

Essays in the Theory

of Economic Growth

EVSEY D. DOMAR

THE JOHNS HOPKINS UNIVERSITY

NEW YORK · OXFORD UNIVERSITY PRESS · 1957

TO THE MEMORY

OF MY DEAR FRIEND

Lt. HAROLD D. OSTERWEIL

Killed in Action in Normandy

on July 31, 1944

Acknowledgments

These essays are based on the works of two contemporary economists: Hansen and Keynes. Keynes's influence is too obvious and pervasive to require comment. To Professor Hansen I owe a great personal debt, as my teacher, supervisor, and friend. My work on growth began in his class in 1941–42 when I came across Chart 16 on page 272 of his *Fiscal Policy and Business Cycles*. The chart shows the effect of a constant stream of investment on national income. It appeared to me strange that such a stream resulted in a constant rather than a rising income, and an investigation of this puzzle resulted in the paper on the public debt (Essay II), which in turn led to the other essays.

Most of the essays were circulated before their original publication, and comments received from my friends made me rewrite whole sections. The formal references acknowledge only a small part of their contributions. I am particularly grateful to James S. Duesenberry, Richard A. Musgrave, and Mary S. Painter, members of our 'mutual aggression pact' (to steal Duesenberry's phrase), who were most helpful in the early stages of the work. None of them, of course, bears any responsibility for the content of the book.

My colleague Edith T. Penrose originally edited the Foreword and Essays I, VII, and IX, and went over the whole volume prior to its publication. The improvement in style, content, and logic as a result of her efforts was great. Her assistance can be fully appreciated only by comparing each essay as it appeared before and after her work.

Essay VI was originally edited by Faye M. Goldware, then of The Johns Hopkins University. I appreciate the very fine job she did.

Sheldon Haber, Duncan M. McDougall, and Bernard Okun, graduate students at The Johns Hopkins University, were very helpful in checking references, proofreading, and other chores.

Mr. Okun also computed the tables in Essay IX. Jean Kyle helped me with the page proofs.

I am grateful to the editors of *The American Economic Review*, *Econometrica*, *The Economic Journal*, and *The Quarterly Journal of Economics* for permission to reprint the articles originally published in these journals; to the American Philosophical Society for a grant which allowed me to complete the volume; and to my publishers for their courage in undertaking the venture and their patience in waiting for the manuscript.

My final and greatest debt is to my wife for her help, encouragement, patience, and good spirit.

E. D. D.

The Johns Hopkins University
Baltimore, Md.
January, 1957

Contents

Acknowledgments, vii

Foreword, 3

I. A Theoretical Analysis of Economic Growth, 16

II. The 'Burden of the Debt' and the National Income, 35

III. Capital Expansion, Rate of Growth, and Employment, 70

IV. Expansion and Employment, 83

V. The Problem of Capital Accumulation, 109

VI. The Effect of Foreign Investment on the Balance of Payments, 129

VII. Depreciation, Replacement, and Growth, 154

VIII. The Case for Accelerated Depreciation, 195

IX. A Soviet Model of Growth, 223

Index, 263

ESSAYS IN THE THEORY OF ECONOMIC GROWTH

Foreword

If any publication is an act of immodesty on the part of the author, a republication of essays which have already appeared in print is doubly so. I have tried to explain this away to myself, but in vain. The essays are presented here in full awareness of my offense, yet with a hope that, being collected all in one place, they will be of some use to other economists. The last—'A Soviet Model of Growth'—is free from this blemish. It has not been published before.

The nine papers are arranged in order of their original appearance, with the exception of the first one—'A Theoretical Analysis of Economic Growth'—which contains a brief survey of the field and a few general comments on subjects dealt with in the other eight. This essay, written in non-technical language, without a single formula in the text (and with only two simple ones in the notes), can serve as the introduction to the volume,[1] while a few additional and more specific comments on the background and purpose of each paper as well as some general afterthoughts are presented here. This arrangement involves some repetition, but not much.

A number of corrections of style, too unimportant to be specifically mentioned, have been made in the original texts. The several substantive changes are clearly indicated.

The essays were written over the period 1944–56.[2] They have different titles and, at first glance, deal with different subjects, but they have a unifying theme and their logical structure is almost

---

[1] It was originally presented at the 1951 meetings of the American Economic Association under the title, 'Economic Growth: An Econometric Approach.' I changed the title because the paper contains little econometrics.

[2] There are several other papers dealing with growth which I did not think appropriate for this volume. The most important of them are: 'Capital Accumulation and the End of Prosperity,' presented to the International Statistical Conference and published by the Econometric Society, *Proceedings of the International Statistical Conferences*, Vol. 5 (Washington, D. C., Sept. 6–18, 1947), pp. 307–14 and reprinted as Cowles Commission Paper, New Series, No. 33, 1951; 'Investment, Losses and Monopolies,' published in *Income, Em-*

embarrassingly similar. Each represents an application of the rate of growth as an analytical device to a specific economic problem. Two distinct methods are used. The first consists in taking a certain flow (such as national income or investment) as an independent variable, and analyzing the mutual interrelationships between this flow, other flows functionally related to it (budget deficit, investment), stocks arising from the flows (capital, national debt), flows resulting from the stocks (depreciation charges, interest payments), and flows subject to time lags (replacement as related to investment), all under conditions of growth. In the second method, the problem is expressed as a system of a few simple differential equations, the solution of which yields the rate of growth of one or another of the variables. Finally, the two methods are employed simultaneously, the solution of the second providing the rate of growth used in the first. In essays II, VI, and VIII only the first method is used; Essay IX is based on the second; the others use both.

No particular plan was followed in selecting the problems; most of them, as well as the models constructed for their solution, simply grew out of the preceding ones, and two (VI and IX) were suggested to me by friends. The transition from one model to another is sometimes accomplished with little change; on other occasions a simple model is expanded and made more complex, but the mathematics rarely leaves the haven of elementary calculus, and once the fundamental and very simple structure of the models is understood, no difficulties should be encountered. The theory of growth abounds in paradoxes, too slippery to be handled with bare hands, but I tried to minimize the use of formal mathematics and to hide most of the derivations in notes and appendixes.

ployment and Public Policy; Essays in Honor of Alvin H. Hansen (New York, 1948), pp. 33–53; 'Interrelation between Capital and Output in the American Economy,' presented to the Conference on Factors of Economic Progress held by the International Economic Association at Santa Margherita Ligure, Italy, in August-September, 1953, of which a condensed version was published in the *International Social Science Bulletin*, Vol. 6 (No. 2, 1954), pp. 236–42, and the full text in *Economic Progress, Papers and Proceedings of a Round Table held by the International Economic Association*, edited by Leon H. Dupriez (Louvain, Belgium, 1955), pp. 249–69.

A few notes, rejoinders, etc., dealing with specific essays are indicated in appropriate places.

5

It may appear strange to the present-day reader that of the nine essays, at least four (from II through V, published between 1944 and 1948) are concerned with unemployment and treat growth as a remedy for it rather than as an end in itself. This was partly due to the spirit of the times: the lessons of the Great Depression were still fresh in our minds through World War II and the subsequent inflation and prosperity. In addition, this book is the logical outcome of the work of the underconsumptionists, including Marx and particularly Keynes, though they might be surprised and not too happy with some of my results. Finally, I believe that a capitalist society (without sufficient government participation) has an inherent deflationary tendency, counteracted, but not necessarily eliminated, by technological and other changes,[3] and I doubt whether the problem of unemployment has been solved for good. Perhaps I am fighting battles long since won, but the experience of our 1956 election campaign, with both parties vying in their affection for a balanced budget and two senators introducing a constitutional amendment prohibiting deficits (except in times, of war), is not reassuring. In any case, the logical structure of the four essays is not affected by this approach, and the models can be, and have been, adapted to deal with growth as an end in itself. The last three papers were written from this point of view.

The present-day reader may also be amused (I certainly am) at the timidity with which our growth potential is treated in the four earlier essays (II through V). A potential rate of growth of a modest 2 or 3 per cent per year is discussed with numerous apologies, reservations, and what not. Whether our growth potential will be realized or dissipated in unemployment depends of course on our collective wisdom, but surely this country *can* grow at least at some 3 or 4 per cent for years to come. And yet compared to prevailing opinion, mine was optimistic.

Now for a few comments on each paper. The purpose of Essay I has already been explained. Essay II, on the burden of the national debt, is one of the simplest applications of the first of the two methods mentioned above. The essence of this paper lies not merely in a comparison between the size of the debt and of national income—

[3] Schumpeter argued that such changes are the very essence of a capitalist society which could not be capitalist without them. There is merit in this argument, but it does not solve our problem.

for absolute magnitudes obviously have little meaning in economics —but in establishing a functional relation between the debt as the dependent variable (stock) and national income as the independent one (flow), by making the deficit (i.e. the rate of change of the debt) a function of income. The ratio of the debt to income is found to be a function of the rate of growth of income (among other factors), and it is possible that a rapidly growing debt will be smaller in relation to income than a slowly growing one—a typical paradox in problems involving growth.[4]

The next two essays, III and IV, deal with investment and employment and contain much material in common. The third is rather technical, while the fourth tries to be more popular. But the overlapping is not complete, and hence both were left in.

The main purpose of these two papers was to close, or at least to narrow, the gap left in the theory of income and employment by Keynes's peculiar treatment of investment. In the short run, he took as given the productive capacity of the economy, including its stock of capital, and treated investment merely as an income-generating instrument (the multiplier effect), while ignoring its effect on capacity. In the long run, the attributes of investment were reversed: it served to augment the stock of capital, but its income-generating effects were ignored. As a result of this strange considera-tion of only one attribute of investment at a time, Keynes's short-run theory remained unnecessarily static, while his long-run analysis pushed him close to the desert of the stationary state with its investment opportunities nearly dried up by previous accumulation of capital. It is true that enlargement of capacity takes time while the multiplier effect quickly peters out, but both effects are important and the omission of either can distort one's perspective quite a bit. It is probable that here lies the explanation for many of the less enlightened passages in the *General Theory*, such as those on the future of capitalism, the euthanasia of the *rentier*, and the blessings of the Egyptian pyramids, and for Keynes's general vision of human history as a difficult and not always successful escape from an excessive propensity to save. And yet, to ignore the dual character of the investment process is quite unnecessary, since the recognition of both attributes on Keynes's own level of abstraction can be easily

---

[4] This, as well as all other conclusions given in the foreword, are subject to the qualifications stated in the respective essays.

made by means of a simple (differential) equation, the solution of which yields the rate of growth of investment and/or of national income that is required to keep the two effects of investment in balance.

This rate is shown to be the product of the propensity to save and the average productivity of investment (or in terms more commonly used today, it is the ratio of the propensity to save to the capital coefficient, the latter being the reciprocal of the productivity of investment). So the more productive investment is, that is, the less capital is required per unit of output, the faster will growth take place. Hence capital-saving rather than labor-saving devices will be more conducive to growth, a strange result in the light of our own historical experience. Perhaps this conclusion would make sense in undeveloped countries (though the mere existence of idle and semi-idle people does not provide the proper kind of labor at the proper time and place), but not ordinarily in a country like the United States. Otherwise, our road to progress would lead to Chinese hand laundries and the like. Yet no other conclusion can be wrung from the model because it treats capital as the only explicit factor of production.

I tried to avoid, rather than to solve, this difficulty by introducing a distinction between the productivity of an investment in a specific project (s), and the productivity of total investment as measured by the increment in the output of the whole economy (σ), since the latter might be affected by shifts of labor and of other factors from existing to new projects. Some such distinction is needed, but I do not think that my attempt was successful, because the model employed an inadequate production function to show what determined the difference between these two productivities. The difference was taken as given; it involved, I believe, a tautology, and judging from the reactions of my friends, must have been confusing as well. The correct alternative lay either in disregarding the difference in the hope that technological progress and the growth of population would provide a sufficient labor force to man the new plants without denuding the old, or in employing a more realistic, and a more complex, production function with an active participation of factors other than capital. In the subsequent essays I chose the easier of the two solutions, but with an ever-guilty conscience. I thought that the mere introduction of labor as another factor in a simple production function would be a rather minor improvement,[5] and that any serious attempt to make these models more realistic would require a very complex production function with a great degree of disaggregation.[6] On the whole this is true, and yet a recent article by Robert M. Solow, which appeared in print just as I was writing these lines, has shown how a growth model can be enriched by the use of a not very complex but less rigid production function.[7]

In any case, a rate of growth of output or of investment in a large and complex economy (or in any economy for that matter) which has been derived from only a few variables should not be taken too seriously.[8] The basic purpose of essays III, IV, and also V (on capital accumulation) is not to derive an empirically meaningful rate of growth, but to attempt a solution of an old problem which has appeared frequently in economic literature from Marx (more correctly, from Mandeville and Malthus, if not earlier) to and beyond Keynes, regarding the effects of capital accumulation on current investment, profit rates, and the level of income and employment. I tried to show that there exists a rate of growth of income, however vaguely defined, which if achieved will *not* lead to diminishing profit rates, scarcity of investment opportunities, chronic unemployment, and similar calamities which these writers expected, and that as far as we can now judge, this rate of growth is not beyond our physical possibilities. On the other hand, failure of the economy to grow at some approximation to such a rate will in time create idle capital resources, the presence of which will probably, though not necessarily, bring about the promised penalties. So economic salvation is not impossible; neither is it assured.

The next essay—VI—on the effects of foreign investment (suggested to me by Walter S. Salant) is similar in its logical structure to II, on the public debt. Foreign investment (including lending) is

[5] See the discussion on 'Full Capacity vs. Full Employment Growth' by D. Hamberg, Harold Pilvin, R. F. Harrod, and myself in *The Quarterly Journal of Economics*, Vol. 66 (Aug., 1952), pp. 444–9, and Vol. 67 (Nov., 1953), pp. 545–63.

[6] This was later done by Wassily Leontief in his dynamic input-output system. See his *Studies in the Structure of the American Economy* (New York, 1953).

[7] Robert M. Solow, 'A Contribution to the Theory of Economic Growth,' *The Quarterly Journal of Economics*, Vol. 70 (Feb., 1956), pp. 65–94.

[8] This warning was given in almost every essay (they are full of apologies on this and other scores), and will be repeated again at the end of this foreword.

assumed to grow at a certain rate, and the ratio between the inflow and outflow of funds is examined under several sets of conditions. The traditional view that this ratio must exceed unity in time emerges as a special, though not an implausible, case, the actual behavior of the ratio depending on the relative magnitudes of the rate of growth of foreign investment and of its yield.

The model used in this paper is somewhat more complex than the one in the debt essay, because here the independent variable is *gross* foreign investment subject not only to interest charges but to amortization as well, a welcome complication which prepared the ground for the next paper on depreciation and replacement.

In essays III, IV, and V all terms are defined net of depreciation; the latter is implicitly identified with replacement which presumably goes on continuously, but in some secret fashion outside the model itself. Such a treatment of processes which account for some 50 per cent and more of gross investment in the United States was clearly unsatisfactory, and an attempt to rectify this defect was made in Essay VII.

Essay VII—on 'Depreciation, Replacement, and Growth'—consists of two parts. The first follows the approach of essays II and VI by assuming a certain rate of growth of gross investment and then investigating the interrelations between it and replacement and depreciation. It is a typical problem of lags, flows, and stocks: replacement is related to past investment with a time lag; depreciation equals a fraction of the existing stock of capital; the latter represents the accumulation of past investments. As usual, the rate of growth plays an important role in determining the behavior of all these interrelations; in a growing economy replacement falls far short of depreciation. Their identity can no longer be taken for granted.

The second part of the paper uses this finding in the derivation of the rate of growth itself by reworking the material of essays III–V in gross terms. The emphasis is no longer (perhaps belatedly) on the elimination of unemployment, but on economic development, and the rate of growth is treated as an end in itself. Analytically, this makes little difference, but the policy implications of the change are great. No longer, for instance, is saving to be treated as a curse; it is restored to its rightful place as an important instrument of growth and development; but it is an instrument which turns against its master if left unused.[9]

Essay VII in turn provided me with a model which was easily adapted for the next problem—accelerated depreciation for tax purposes—presented in Essay VIII. The purpose of the latter was to test the usefulness of such a measure for a new and a growing firm. The results were positive: a new firm would enjoy at least a postponement of its income tax liability, while a growing one would have a lower effective tax rate. The measure could redistribute income (profits) from old or stagnant to new or growing firms.

All this seems desirable (assuming of course that growth itself is desirable), but I have examined neither the administrative aspects of this plan nor its possible abuses, particularly in connection with the treatment of capital gains under the present tax laws. There seems to be no shortage of abuses there, and I have no wish to add new ones. But these questions should be looked into by someone better versed in practical aspects of taxation than I am.

The last and previously unpublished essay on 'A Soviet Model of Growth' is based on a remarkable article by the Soviet economist G. A. Fel'dman in the journal *The Planned Economy* of 1928. Though my own work in Soviet economics has been rather amateurish, it has nevertheless been a most valuable source of ideas. The study of Soviet society is one of the very few methods available to a social scientist (as distinguished from his more fortunate laboratory colleagues) of re-examining his whole intellectual apparatus in the light of a social and economic system sufficiently different from ours to make the experiment rewarding, and yet not so different as to make it impossible. I have always felt that the Marxists, concerned as they were with the process of accumulation, should have developed some theory of growth, and when Gregory Grossman told me about Fel'dman's article (probably in 1950) my hopes were all aroused.

But at first I was disappointed. Though Fel'dman's work certainly looked impressive, both as a piece of mathematical economics and as a growth model—even as early as 1928—the similarity between his results and those since developed in the West was so

---

[9] I may point out that a reduction in the propensity to save was not advocated in the preceding essays; I argued instead for utmost efforts to utilize available savings.

striking that I failed to perceive (probably owing to the mass of mathematical detail which fills his paper) the basic difference in approach. His article therefore appeared to be of only historical interest and, not being a true antiquarian connoisseur, I put it away. Not long ago I took another look and realized that, being derived from a modified Marxist scheme, his variables are different from those we are accustomed to: instead of using the propensity to save and a single aggregate capital coefficient, he divided the whole economy into capital and consumer goods industries, each with its own coefficient, and used as his key variable the fraction of total investment that is retained by the capital goods industry in order to produce more capital goods.[10] That his results come so close to ours should only add interest to his paper.

Although Fel'dman's division of the economy into capital and consumer goods industries seems to me operationally impossible, nevertheless his model is more useful for the understanding of Soviet economic development than any of mine, be this faint praise; it also raises some interesting questions regarding the purpose of economic development in general. Finally, its use by the Soviets as an instrument of economic planning revealed its pitfalls, and not only its own. Reality, it turned out, was more than a match for a model.

So much for the individual essays. Now, the reader will ask, what do they all add up to? Do they give us a theory of growth? If he has in mind a systematic explanation of how and why some societies have developed and grown faster than others, and why some large areas have hardly developed at all, my answer must of course be negative: one can study this and similar books[11] backwards and forwards and still find no answer to that question. (If longer titles were not so clumsy, I would call this collection 'Essays in *Some Aspects* of the Theory of Growth.') More than that, by assigning the major, and almost exclusive, role to capital accumulation, these essays can give the misleading impression that it is the primary and sole cause and condition of growth, with all other factors, such as

[10] The foregoing represents my reinterpretation of his model, which is quite complicated because much of it is expressed in terms of stocks of capital in the two categories rather than of the division of current investment between them.

[11] For instance, Trygve Haavelmo's *A Study in the Theory of Economic Evolution*, Contributions to Economic Analysis, III (Amsterdam, 1954).

technological progress, labor supply, organizational skill, not to mention non-economic forces, obligingly appearing from nowhere at the proper time and place. Yet is it necessary to belabor the obvious fact that economic growth is a most complex phenomenon involving the whole structure of a society, and that capital accumulation is more an effect—almost a symptom—rather than a primary cause?

Whether a satisfactory theory of growth in the broad sense will ever be developed, I do not know. It certainly cannot be created from models only. It requires a mass of empirical work. It also requires the ability to synthesize data and ideas from all social sciences, and most of all it requires that breadth of vision and imagination and that degree of understanding which is called 'wisdom.' In short, it is a job for sages.

The function of the model-builder, i.e. the theorist in the narrow sense, is to pluck at the sage's sleeve and inquire whether one or the other pillar of his great edifice can really hold the load intended for it; to insert a steel beam here and there; to persuade the sage that the foundation be sunk deeper and the concrete reinforced (with mathematics, I presume); to tell him about new construction materials and new construction methods, and at times (not too often, I hope) even to demonstrate to him that his great design is altogether illusory. The sage's vision may be too broad to take into account small, though sometimes critical, construction details. If only Marx had had such a helper at his side!

Ideally, the sage and his two helpers—the theorist and the statistician—would all be physically one. But this is rare.[12] The temptation to double as a sage, at least part-time, is strong and hard to resist. But it is not easy to be a real sage and to avoid blind extrapolations of past events, abuse of historical parallels, mechanical applications of theory, and useless classifications, just to mention a few of the standard stocks-in-trade of would-be sages. Nor is a sage always at home with mathematics and statistics. It may be better not to insist on combining the functions and let each do his own job. In the present context, and in a more serious vein, this

[12] Marx was a great sage and a devourer of empirical data, but what a poor theorist! Schumpeter tried his hand at all three occupations, but I think he will be remembered mostly as a sage. Keynes was a better theorist than the other two, and of course a great policy-maker, but his vision as a sage was obscured by his preoccupation with immediate problems of his day. Let us not comment on any living sages.

suggests that we proceed with a revision of those parts of economic theory which do not hold true under conditions of growth.

For such a purpose our simple models are better adapted, I believe, than for any other, because so much of our traditional theory is derived from models of equal or even greater simplicity. So far it appears that growth plays an important role in problems involving time lags and interrelations between stocks and flows. This should cover a good deal of territory, including, for instance, monetary theory which is full of stocks and flows,[13] distribution of income and wealth, theory of resource allocation and particularly of investment decisions, some aspects of international trade and of public finance, as well as theory of the firm,[14] and probably quite a few others. It is also likely that growth will be found relevant in other problems not directly involving time lags and interrelations between stocks and flows; a wide range of new possibilities may open up. Perhaps a mere revision of existing theory is too modest a description of our task; new structures will be erected in the process.

All this is very theoretical. If on the one hand a model-builder is tempted to imitate a sage, on the other he itches to do something practical. The use of growth models as a practical guide to economic development is enticing, but the pitfalls are deep indeed. The rate of growth of output is expressed in our models essentially as a function of the propensity to save and the capital coefficient (in one form or another). Given only slightly optimistic, but plausible, magnitudes of these two parameters, economic development seems assured—on paper of course. Both are most heroic abstractions implying a long list of assumptions about the actual working of the economy, which these parameters, in their simple innocence, conceal. Fel'dman's story presented in the last essay is an excellent example of misuse of a model, and I have added a sort of epilogue to it in order to drive this very point home. Whether it will convince growth enthusiasts and development planners I do not know, but I have hope.

In recent times, economic growth and development have become

[13] A promising beginning was made by John G. Gurley and E. S. Shaw in 'Financial Aspects of Economic Development,' *The American Economic Review*, Vol. 45 (Sept., 1955), pp. 515–38.

[14] This work has already been started by Edith T. Penrose. See her 'Limits to the Growth and Size of Firms,' *The American Economic Review, Papers and Proceedings*, Vol. 45 (May, 1955), pp. 531–43.

the fashion of the day, and the number of books and articles entitled 'Something or Other *and* Economic Growth or Development' has risen beyond one's capacity to read. The dignity of our profession would be enhanced if it were not swept by such waves of fashion, but I cannot be expected to complain about this one. It is a hundred, or at least fifty, years overdue. Why, in spite of remarkably rapid growth, the vision of the stationary state hung so heavily over the thinking of the Great Masters of the last century, and still pre-occupies many of our contemporaries, is more than I can explain. Even my more broadminded colleagues who love growth are willing to grant her only a reprieve, but not a pardon. And yet I fail to see any indications that the world is any closer now to a stationary state than it was, say, a hundred years ago. If there has been any move-ment at all, it must surely have been away from rather than toward it. Of course, to many economists the stationary state is not a his-torical perspective, but merely an analytical device. Even so, I suspect, this device has been overworked; by now it must have become a dead weight rather than a tool.

Growth and rates of growth now appear not only in learned journals, but in political speeches, official pronouncements, news-papers, and even on television. As a goal of economic policy, growth has absorbed some of the public attention previously enjoyed by full employment. The two goals are not necessarily incompatible, but neither are they identical. At the peril of trying to pass for a sage, I would say that growth is the healthier objective not only because it implies a rising standard of living, which is obvious, but also because it thrives on saving, ingenuity, efficiency, good man-agement, hard work, and other good and puritanical virtues, while full employment may be indifferent to some and even inimical to others. An economy growing at a sufficiently rapid rate (without inflation and with the usual qualifications regarding leisure, family, motherhood, health, etc.) will enjoy full employment without worry-ing about it, but full employment can and has been known to coexist with inefficiency and stagnation. These are of course value judgments, in which an economist is not supposed to indulge too freely, and undoubtedly the mere process of growth gives rise to more strains and hardships than are realized, though not necessarily more than would be caused by stagnation. Under normal conditions the argument for and against growth could proceed leisurely, but today the argument, as a practical matter, is obsolete: when an aggressive part of the world is strongly and quite successfully committed to rapid growth the other can disregard this objective only if it is tired of its own existence as a society.

These are interesting issues, but hardly to be dealt with here. Let us turn back to theory.

I

A Theoretical Analysis of
Economic Growth*[1]

I

(In economic theory, growth has occupied an odd place: always seen around but seldom invited in. It has been either taken for granted or treated as an afterthought. In the meantime, we have cheerfully gone ahead discussing employment and investment, interest and profits, accumulation of capital, business cycles, and many other exciting problems which clearly demand the explicit use of the rate of growth, and which we have most ingeniously tried to solve in a theoretical wonderland where a positive net propensity to save is consistent with a constant stock of capital, where full employment is compatible with the traditional competitive equilibrium and capitalism with a stationary society, where every increase in the capital stock reduces investment outlets, and where the business cycle was until recently viewed as the refusal of the system to return rapidly enough to its original state of static equilibrium.

But it would be absurd to say that economic growth is a new subject. Economic historians have worked on it long and in earnest, and if it were not for their irresistible devotion to facts and scholarly caution, they might have indulged in speculative theorizing about growth, however wrong their results might have been.)(See, however, Walter Rostow's forthcoming book.)[2] Among economic the-

* [Reprinted by permission from *The American Economic Review, Papers and Proceedings*, Vol. 42 (May, 1952), pp. 479–95. The paper was presented at the December, 1951, meetings of the American Economic Association under the title of 'Economic Growth: an Econometric Approach.' I changed the title because the paper contains little econometrics.

A number of references were taken out of the text and put into notes. The notes were renumbered, and new notes and additions to old ones were bracketed.]

[1] Thanks are due to Edith T. Penrose, of The Johns Hopkins University, for giving the paper a reasonably good skin of English.

[2] [Since published as *The Process of Economic Growth* (New York, 1952).]

orists proper, particularly in ages past, growth was not neglected. Adam Smith and J. S. Mill and Marshall wrote long and thoughtful chapters about it, which, however, did not prevent the last two from developing intricate theories of resource allocation under stationary conditions. More recently we have had a whole group of writers, including Ayres, Keirstead, Wright, and of course the late Professor Schumpeter—one of the few modern economists who understood what capitalism was all about.[3] Schumpeter's writings on the subject were a bit romantic, but who of us has not admired and tried to follow the remarkable breadth of his thought in contrast to the not-too-satisfying background of saving-investment and similar controversies?

My assignment, however, deals with growth models which the program calls 'econometric,' though, to dispel any false hopes on your part, I must confess that my principal, if only periodic, bond with the econometricians consists of the eight dollars I pay each year for their incomprehensible journal. A comparison of these growth models at their present stage of development with the mature and impressive creations of our static theory calls to my mind descriptions of early mammals—frightened little creatures, entirely insignificant, who must have wandered around the legs of dinosaurs without even being noticed by them. But recent events show that this happy state of insignificance is coming to an end and, furthermore, that some of these creatures are about to expand into full-sized elephants. In economic literature, growth models, interpreted broadly, have appeared a number of times, at least as far back as Marx. Of the several schools of economics the Marxists have, I think, come closest to developing a substantial theory of economic growth, and they might have succeeded had they given less time and effort to defending their master's virtue. Some highly elaborate and interesting growth models did, however, appear in Soviet literature.[4] Among recent Western writers, Cassel, Foster and Catchings, Kalecki, Lundberg, Paul Sweezy, Harrod, Fellner, Hicks, Schelling,

---

[3] C. E. Ayres, *The Theory of Economic Progress* (Chapel Hill, N. C., 1944); B. S. Keirstead, *The Theory of Economic Change* (Toronto, 1948); David McCord Wright, *The Economics of Disturbance* (New York, 1947), *Democracy and Progress* (New York, 1948), and *Capitalism* (New York, 1951).

[4] These Soviet models are more fully developed than similar attempts made in the West, with the exception of Leontief's work discussed below. [See Essay IX.]

Tsiang, Baumol, Hawkins, Alexander, and others have done substantial work.[5] I have not tried to delve into the early growth models; it seems that we were not ready for them in any case until we had digested the consequences of the Keynesian revolution. Otherwise, it would be hard to explain the complete disregard by the profession of a growth model published by Eric Lundberg in 1937—a model not in any way inferior to Harrod's now famous creation of 1939, which in turn had to wait for almost a decade and to be repeated in his book to receive its deserved recognition.[6] The present interest in growth is not accidental; it comes on the one side from a belated awareness that in our economy full employment without growth is impossible and, on the other, from the present international conflict which makes growth a condition of survival.

Economic growth is determined by the basic structure of a society, and a comprehensive theory of growth should include physical environment, political structure, incentives, educational methods, legal framework, attitude to science, to changes, to accumulation—just to name a few. None of these could be properly taken as an independent variable, and the required system of simultaneous relationships, whether expressed in symbols or in words, would be impossibly complex and probably useless. The treatment of the subject therefore falls into two rather sharply differentiated parts: general treatises and highly simplified symbolic models, with a wide gap between. Neither approach taken by itself is satisfying. The

[5] A good bibliography of recent works on growth is given by William Fellner in his 'The Capital-Output Ratio in Dynamic Economics,' *Money, Trade, and Economic Growth; in Honor of John Henry Williams* (New York, 1951), p. 106. Here are a few additions: Gustav Cassel, *The Theory of Social Economy* (New York, 1924), pp. 34–42, and *On Quantitative Thinking in Economics* (Oxford, 1935); William T. Foster and Waddill Catchings, *Profits* (Boston and New York, 1925), and their other writings; Eric Lundberg, *Studies in the Theory of Economic Expansion* (London, 1937); Paul M. Sweezy, *The Theory of Capitalist Development* (New York, 1942); T. C. Schelling, 'Capital Growth and Equilibrium,' *The American Economic Review*, Vol. 37 (Dec., 1947), pp. 864–76; S. C. Tsiang, 'Rehabilitation of Time Dimension of Investment in Macrodynamic Analysis,' *Economica*, n.s., Vol. 16 (Aug., 1949), pp. 204–17; David Hawkins, 'Some Conditions of Macroeconomic Stability,' *Econometrica*, Vol. 16 (Oct., 1948), pp. 309–22; Sidney S. Alexander, 'The Accelerator as a Generator of Steady Growth,' *The Quarterly Journal of Economics*, Vol. 63 (May, 1949), pp. 174–97.

[6] Lundberg, op. cit.; R. F. Harrod, 'An Essay in Dynamic Theory,' *The Economic Journal*, Vol. 49 (Mar., 1939), pp. 14–33, and *Towards a Dynamic Economics* (London, 1948).

former is usually deficient in analysis, and the latter is too narrow and deceivingly exact. Both should be looked upon as the opposite ends of a bridge, the construction of which will perhaps some day give us a workable theory of growth. But if each of us starts at his own end, this need not imply a lack of understanding of the problem as a whole, even if we do not confess to the limitations of our method on every possible occasion.

II

It can be taken for granted, I believe, that we are interested neither in the growth of money income taken by itself nor in the enlargement of unutilized productive capacity. Our first step, therefore, is to provide the system with both a demand and a capacity side. Perhaps I am belaboring an obvious point, yet in pre-Keynesian days we might have dealt with the capacity side only, taking an adequate demand for granted. On the other hand, the more zealous Keynesians have been inclined to ignore the problem of capacity altogether, as if trying to justify Schumpeter's complaint that the *General Theory* was a piece of depression economics.[7] Today we cannot lose sight of either. Our problem can now be formulated as follows: assuming that output and capacity are in balance at the start, under what conditions will this balance be preserved over time, or in other words, at what rate should they grow to avoid both inflation and unemployment? This method treats economic capacity as a meaningful and measurable, though not necessarily an exact, concept. Several years ago I felt very guilty about this, but enough has been said on the subject since to make an extended apology unnecessary. The assumption that output and capacity are originally balanced is made for convenience only, though in a cyclical problem it could be quite harmful. Perhaps a slight pressure of demand on capacity would be quite healthy for a capitalist economy. These considerations can be easily taken care of. With the present speaker density on this platform, however, I suspect this journey is going to be long and arduous, so why carry excess baggage from the start?

The next step is to agree on the level of aggregation. There is nothing peculiar about growth models in this respect, and they can be made on any desired level, provided we are ready to pay for less

[7] See, for instance, Lawrence R. Klein's *Economic Fluctuations in the United States 1921–1941* (New York, 1950).

aggregation the usual penalty of increasing complexity. There exists
a model, not yet published, in which all series are broken down by
industries, and the resulting interindustrial movements are made
explicit. This is Leontief's dynamic input-output model referred to
below. Its differential equations look so forbidding, however, that
it may be just as well to leave it to the end and to start with the
usual concepts of total investment and consumption which have
become so familiar in the last fifteen years.

On the demand side we shall thus have our old friends: consumption (i.e. consumer expenditures) and investment (private capital
formation) and, of course, the government (expenditure on goods
and services). As usual, the government is the most troublesome of
the three because we have no theory of government expenditure
whatsoever. In its absence, we may dump government expenditure
on top of the other two as an exogeneous factor, merge it with
consumer expenditures (or with investment, for that matter), or
assume it away altogether. The last suggestion is certainly the most
convenient of all, and such a treatment of a troublesome factor is
richly supported by precedents in economic theory. The situation
would not be so bad if we knew something about the determination
of investment, but as will be presently indicated, here too we fail.
To have two such unreliable variables does not create any special
mathematical difficulties, but it is certainly too much for an oral
presentation. So in what follows we should either forget about the
government altogether or keep the proper adjustments in the back
of our minds.

Of the remaining two variables—investment and consumption—
we shall follow the Keynesian custom of treating investment as the
active (independent) one and of tying consumption to its tail. This
involves the use of some consumption function (or functions in case
of disaggregation)—an instrument in whose reliability our faith
seems to be subject to cycles of its own. Ever since the war, we have
felt rather gloomy about consumption functions, but a year or so
ago, Tom E. Davis, a graduate student at Hopkins, in a paper
entitled, 'Prediction and Various Consumption Functions' (presented at the meetings of the Econometric Society in Boston,
December, 1951),[8] reported that a couple of consumption functions

[8] [Since published as 'The Consumption Function as a Tool for Prediction,'
The Review of Economics and Statistics, Vol. 34 (Aug., 1952), pp. 270–77.]

originally suggested by Modigliani and Duesenberry gave excellent results when their 1929–40 regressions were extrapolated with a slight modification over the postwar years, including 1950. So now I feel quite optimistic—at least for a few more days until the 1951 figures become available. These functions when applied to a growing economy make the fraction of disposable income consumed essentially a linear function of its rate of growth. However, for our purposes any reasonably reliable consumption function will do.

All these are functions of disposable income. But to arrive at the latter, the treatment of depreciation, undistributed profits, and taxes must be settled. Depreciation can be handled either by excluding it altogether and working with net magnitudes or—more correctly—by incorporating it into the system explicitly. Undistributed profits may be made a function of total output and other variables (profit rate, utilization of capacity). This may not be too easy, and in the worst possible case they may be merged with personal savings. Taxes, of which we have quite an assortment, are less tractable, and here one appreciates once more the convenience of assuming the government away altogether. If we are essentially interested in the theory of growth rather than in its measurement, this may not be a bad idea in any case.

Attempts to derive an investment function in terms of output, profits, capital stock, interest rate, and other variables have not been successful so far, and at this stage of our knowledge it may be just as well to admit our ignorance and to treat investment as the independent variable. This will deprive us of the pleasure of having a closed mutually determined and self-propelling system like a business cycle model, capable of tracing the path which output will actually take. We shall only be able to determine the rate or rates of growth of investment and output which if maintained will bring about the balance between output and capacity.

To summarize then, the demand side of our system consists first of all of investment (or different kinds of investment), as an independent variable, and of consumption tied to it by a functional relationship via disposable income, with some provision being or not being made for the existence of government and other factors, such as depreciation. This demand side will be used in the several growth models presented here. While the exact relationship between total demand and investment need not be specified, it is important to note that an increase in demand is a function, not of the level of investment (and other things), but of an increment in investment. In other words, the rate of growth of demand is a function of the rate of growth of investment (and of other factors). But the relationship between investment and capacity is different, and this lack of symmetry is extremely important.

III

However difficult it was to express the rate of growth of the demand for goods and services in terms of a few relatively simple variables, our task on the capacity side is even more complex—and the results much less reliable. Everything is involved here: the growth of the labor force and the change in its composition, changes in hours worked, in training and skill of the workers, in amount of effort, in institutional conditions, geographical movements, accumulation of capital, and that most important and also most elusive of all variables, technological progress in the broad sense, which changes the character of labor and of capital and of everything else. The nature of these factors and of changes in them is still very imperfectly understood; nor can most of them be analyzed in isolation from the demand side, because whatever may be said about population change, investment and technological progress are undoubtedly responsive to movements in demand. But these difficulties are well known and not much will be gained by weeping over them. If our model-builders waited until these problems were solved, they would not have made that modicum of progress they have been lucky enough to achieve.

The construction of a model or of any theory, for that matter (or the writing of a novel, a short story, or a play), consists of snatching from the enormous and complex mass of facts called reality a few simple, easily manageable key points which, when put together in some cunning way, become for certain purposes a substitute for reality itself. Simplification is the heart of this process, and those who complain about the 'oversimplification' of economic theory frequently miss its objective. It is easy enough to add a few more variables, except that both the system (whether formal or not) and its results may turn out to be unmanageable. But deciding how and where to simplify and which variables to take in and which to leave out, i.e. the very essence of theorizing, always was and will remain a very subtle art.

To come back to our immediate problem. The most direct and obvious approach to an estimate of changes in capacity would consist in the use of some production function (or functions, depending on the level of aggregation desired). The work of Douglas and Cobb was quite promising in this respect, and it is regrettable that it became entangled in methodological thickets, and that no attempt has been made, at least to my knowledge, to attach it to a demand function and thus obtain the rate (or rates) of growth required to maintain the proper balance between output and capacity.[9] Recollecting that the Cobb-Douglas production function (originally applied to manufacturing) consisted of only two variables—labor and capital, with their exponents adding up to one (to achieve homogeneity)—and that technological progress was supposed to have been taken care of by a constant coefficient, you may be amazed by the courage, if not foolhardiness, of its authors; yet it is by no means the simplest model of growth. I have not worked with it myself because it appeared to me too complicated, but it probably has excellent potentialities and certainly deserves an investigation.[10]

The practical-minded economists have usually been reluctant to commit themselves to some explicit production function, such as the Cobb-Douglas, the use of which requires not only time series of labor inputs but also those of capital, or at least increments of capital, as well as the evaluation of the coefficients, all of which must have looked to them like a lot of suspicious theorizing. Instead, they have employed a very simple device which makes output a function of labor input (manhours worked), inflated by some increase in manhour productivity. Such estimates have been made on aggregate levels, at least as a first approximation; alternatively, labor inputs and increases in productivity have been computed by industries

[9] Paul H. Douglas, *The Theory of Wages* (New York, 1934); also Grace T. Gunn and Paul H. Douglas, 'The Production Function for Australian Manufacturing,' *The Quarterly Journal of Economics*, Vol. 56 (Nov., 1941), pp. 108–29. For a criticism of this approach, see Horst Mendershausen, 'On the Significance of Professor Douglas' Production Function,' *Econometrica*, Vol. 6 (Apr., 1938), pp. 143–53.

[10] [This has since been done by Robert M. Solow, 'A Contribution to the Theory of Economic Growth,' *The Quarterly Journal of Economics*, Vol. 70 (Feb., 1956), pp. 65–94.]

and then aggregated.[11] Actually we have here another production function, no less specific than Cobb-Douglas, the output being equal to labor input multiplied by a time series which is supposed to reflect the movements of all other factors: capital, technological progress, and anything else. For many practical problems, this is not the worst and is certainly the cheapest method of estimating future output; yet the assumption that changes in labor productivity derived from the past are somehow independent of the amount of investment undertaken in the period studied sometimes creates confusion, particularly when used to predict the future level of employment. An estimate of total output which is obtained by multiplying labor input by its assumed productivity is compared with total demand consisting of government expenditure, consumption, and investment calculated separately. But some amount of investment has already been implied in the assumed increase in labor productivity, and it may be questioned whether we retain the freedom of assuming a perfectly arbitrary amount of investment for the demand side, unless the period studied is extremely short. Or if we start from some amount of investment on the demand side, are we justified in assuming an independent increase in labor productivity? Perhaps it was due to the use of this method that one study predicted a gross national product (in real terms) for 1960 that was in fact reached a whole decade earlier.[12]

However great may be the practical virtues of an approach via labor productivity, it has not resulted in a model of growth as such because it is concerned only with the capacity side of the picture and remains detached from the demand side where we find neither labor force nor its productivity, but consumption, investment, and government purchases. If each new member of the labor force gave rise to a certain amount of investment, or if he came equipped with a sum of money to be spent as he pleased, we could immediately enter these facts on the demand side of the model and get the rate of growth of the labor force which would keep the demand and capacity sides in balance. Or if we could establish some relation

[11] See, for instance, E. E. Hagen and N. B. Kirkpatrick, 'The National Output at Full Employment in 1950,' *The American Economic Review*, Vol. 34 (Sept., 1944), pp. 472–500.

[12] J. Frederic Dewhurst and Associates, *America's Needs and Resources* (New York, 1947), and Robert W. Hartley, *America's Capital Requirements; Estimates for 1946–1960* (New York, 1950).

between changes in manhours worked and the community's propensity to save, a similar possibility might arise. But the way things are, on the demand side of the equation the major role is played by investment, with consumption being tied to it and government expenditures given by Congress, and on the capacity side, we have an expected increase in manhours multiplied by a productivity growth factor somehow derived from the past, without an explicit participation of investment, so that the two sides remain strangers to each other and refuse to intersect, or, more correctly, even to appear together on the same diagram. I do not mean to disparage the use of this method for many occasions; but at this moment, I do not know how to tie the two ends together so they would not be left dangling in the air.

The preceding method was deficient because investment—the active component of demand—did not appear explicitly on the capacity side. The latter, to repeat, was composed of the increment in labor input times its productivity (or productivities), in which capital accumulation and technological progress were already reflected. Suppose we reverse the roles of capital and labor and construct the capacity side of the increment in capital, i.e. of investment, times its average productivity, in which the growth of labor and technological progress have already been accounted for. From a theoretical point of view, capital is just as good a factor of production as labor; in a modern industrial society it may be more correct to speak of labor as an attachment to capital rather than the other way around. Now with investment active on both sides, the equation is complete, the curves cross, and their intersection gives the required rate of growth.

For a moment this sounds fine. Then doubts come in. Just what is meant by investment or capital accumulation in this connection and how is its productivity to be measured? Does the latter possess sufficient stability to be workable? Why has not the price mechanism been mentioned even once? Is it not a feat worthy of Don Quixote to try to express an increase in the productive capacity of a large and complex society by means of capital increments and their productivities, even if broken down by industries?

The authors of these models will, I am sure, plead guilty to most of these accusations and defend themselves on the grounds that economic theory is full of criminals like themselves. The models do involve heroic simplifications. But are they more heroic than the reduction of the whole complex of managerial decisions in an uncertain world to the intersection of marginal cost and revenue curves, which we accept so readily perhaps because we learned it in our professional childhood? We seem to have accepted the labor productivity method and it raises similar questions, notwithstanding the long experience we have had with it.

Even though capital productivity is not a new concept and has been employed in acceleration models for a long time, there is no doubt that the use of capital as *the* factor of production creates many problems that have not yet been resolved. What we want is investment which could be functionally related to an increase in productive capacity; what we get from statistics are capital expenditures as defined by the Bureau of Internal Revenue, with a few corrections. The two need not coincide, and there are many other outlays—on research, for instance—that are not classified as investment but which increase capacity. So do some government expenditures.

It is certainly not implied here that capital is the sole creator of productive capacity. In the labor models just discussed, the importance of other factors—capital, technology, etc.—was not denied, but it was assumed that their effects could be measured via the increase in labor productivity. Similarly, here we try to express the effect on capacity of all factors other than investment via the latter's productivity. The productivity of labor has increased at some 2 per cent or so per year. How has the productivity of capital behaved over the years?

From traditional theory, deeply attached to the law of diminishing returns and its corollary, the deepening of capital, we would expect a secular fall in the productivity of capital because it has increased much faster than labor. The statistical study of capital productivity is in a rather primitive stage as yet, but the information now available seems to indicate that average capital productivity for this country as a whole has not changed much over the last eighty years or so.[13] It certainly has not fallen and has possibly risen somewhat.

[13] Fellner, op. cit.; see also his paper on 'Long-Term Projections of Private Capital Formation: The Rate of Growth and Capital Coefficients,' presented to the Conference on Research in Income and Wealth, May, 1951. [Since published in *Long-Range Economic Projections*, Vol. 16 (Princeton, N. J., 1954), pp. 275–331.]

Evidently, technological progress has more than offset the insufficient growth of labor.

Our growth models do not require that capital productivity remain constant; only that its changes be known and reasonably regular. As a first approximation it may be assumed to be constant. This simplifies the mathematics enormously, but we should guard ourselves against falling into a trap similar to that set by the alleged constancy of the velocity of circulation of money some years ago. The latter also appeared quite stable and was thought to have been so deeply rooted in our institutional setting as to be immune from sudden change. You know the outcome, and what might have been a useful tool of analysis at one time certainly became an obstacle later on.

If capital productivity has remained more or less constant while investment has constituted some 10 per cent of net national income, it surely would fall if this fraction rose to 30 or 50 per cent. It is known that capital productivity varies sharply between industries, ranging from 100 per cent or higher in trade and services (on an annual basis) to between 50 and 75 per cent or so in manufacturing, and perhaps to some 10 per cent, if not lower, in housing and public utilities.[14] We may still assume its constancy for theoretical and particularly for pedagogical purposes, but for the development of a theory of economic growth and its practical applications, these variations clearly require that the aggregates be broken down into a number of industries.

Here we can take two steps at once. So far we have been essentially concerned with national income or gross national product; that is, with the production of the so-called 'final goods' for consumption and investment, with or without the addition of government purchases. But a major part of economic activity consists not in furnishing these final goods but in producing intermediate products for future production. More than that: goods do not move in one direction from the so-called 'higher' to 'lower' stages of production; there are whirlpools and cross currents where goods flow back and forth between industries. Our demand side, even if broken down by categories, will still consist of final goods, but on the capacity side these large interindustry flows of intermediate goods should be explicitly taken into account.

[14] Ibid. [See also Leontief's study (note 17), pp. 220–21.]

Such a scheme exists. It is the input-output method developed by Wassily Leontief.[15] Its essence, as you know, consists of estimating a series of inputs for each industry relative to its output, expressing these industrial interrelationships by a system of simultaneous linear equations, and solving them for any given list of final products. The method is simpler than it sounds. It is followed by every housewife preparing a dinner: given the menu and the size of the family, the quantities and assortment of inputs (which she calls ingredients) are easily determined. Fortunately, cooking does not require higher mathematics because of the absence of cross flows. A pie is made out of flour, sugar, and apples, and luckily the housewife does not have to turn around and use a part of the pie to make sugar, nor is flour made out of apples. In industry, however, steel is made out of coal, iron ore, and transportation; but coal also uses steel and transportation and the latter uses both coal and steel. This is where the simultaneous system of equations comes in.

Existing publications of Leontief's and the Bureau of Labor Statistics present static analyses of interindustrial flows;[16] they do not isolate capital formation as such and are not particularly concerned with growth. As a matter of fact, inputs of steel, machinery, or construction usually destined for capital formation do not have the normal relation to the current outputs of industries acquiring them and may distort the working of the whole system.

Suppose additions to capital stocks of the various industries are isolated and the system redesigned to include not only the flows (steel, coal, wheat, freight ton-miles) needed for the production of a given list of final goods but also the increments of capital that the enlargement of the respective capacities will demand. Here not only the flow input-output coefficients will be required but also the ratios between the outputs and the stocks of capital (in the average or

[15] Wassily W. Leontief, *The Structure of American Economy, 1919–1939* (New York, 1st ed., 1941, 2nd ed., 1951); also, 'Output, Employment, Consumption and Investment,' *The Quarterly Journal of Economics*, Vol. 58 (Feb., 1944), pp. 290–314; and his other writings. [His dynamic study has since been published. See note 17.]

[16] Jerome Cornfield, W. Duane Evans, and Marvin Hoffenberg, 'Full Employment Patterns, 1950,' reprinted from the *Monthly Labor Review*, Vol. 64 (Feb. and Mar., 1947); W. Duane Evans and Marvin Hoffenberg, 'The Interindustry Relations Study for 1947,' presented at the meetings of the Econometric Society and the American Economic Association in Boston, Dec. 26, 1951.

marginal sense) needed to produce them—the capital productivities which we met several pages ago (though Leontief and his group prefer to use their reciprocals, the capital coefficients).[17]

As a result of these changes, a system of differential (or difference) equations will emerge which should yield not only the required rate of growth of total output (which is not important here) but also the rates of growth of outputs of individual industries. This is a most noble and heroic task which requires not only skillful analysis but also an amazing amount of empirical information, frequently of a rather slippery nature. It is one thing to talk theoretically about capital and its productivity and quite a different thing to compute them in practice. One has a right to be skeptical. But Leontief's static system also met skepticism, perhaps because it made no use of our pet theoretical toys, such as elasticities of demand and supply, substitution, marginal cost, and what not, and employed instead some allegedly constant input coefficients not visibly derived from profit maximization. It is indeed the great virtue of Leontief's system that it has managed to get reasonably good results without using all these concepts and thus has shown them their proper place as servants to be called in if and when required. The construction of the dynamic system is carried on at Harvard by Leontief, Duesenberry, and their associates and they are, of course, in a better position to report on it than I am. The proof of the pudding is in its eating, and time will tell if theirs is edible. In my prejudiced and biased opinion, this is the most interesting and promising piece of research done in economics today.

IV

While empirical material is gathered, the theory of growth must go on. A frontal attack on the causes of technological progress and capital accumulation, as its two most important elements, would be the most obvious and direct approach. I have no quarrel with this method, except to find it rather difficult. Like a not-too-honest schoolboy who cannot solve his problem, I would prefer to look up the answer in the back of the book and then try to fix up the solu-

[17] Preliminary results of the Harvard Economic Research Project are given in mimeographed form in 'Estimates of the Capital Structure of American Industries, 1939' (1950). [The final results have since been published in Wassily Leontief et al., Studies in the Structure of the American Economy (New York, 1953).]

tion to satisfy the answer. Let us assume that the economy is growing. If we can learn something about its character, perhaps we shall be able to come back and get a glimpse of the causes of its growth, or at least of the conditions that should be satisfied to make this growth possible.

We start by discarding the idea of equilibrium as a state of rest to which a stable system is expected to return. (This distinguishes our approach from other dynamic models where movements of the variables are treated as deviations from some constant equilibrium magnitudes.) Our economy never returns. Its equilibrium may be said to exist if its component parts in their process of growth retain some proper relationship to each other, such as output to capital, steel to coal, costs to prices, or whatever else we are interested in. Together with static equilibrium must go out the notion that economic processes are finite—that they must 'eventually' come to an end. This idea strongly affects our discussions of deficit spending by the government, foreign lending, investment in general, to name just a few processes which are supposed to have beneficial effects while they last but bring great harm when they stop; so long as they are beneficial, they should not stop.

If the economy is in equilibrium when it grows in a certain way, the same can be said about a firm. We are interested, not in its output of today, but in the conditions under which it will increase its output tomorrow. We very definitely do not want the representative firm to be in a position of long-run static equilibrium where it has no reason to expand and hence to invest. If all our firms ever fell into this happy state, we might end up with a quarter of the labor force unemployed. The optimum allocation of resources likewise does not mean the maximum output under given conditions at a point of time but a maximum achievable rate of growth (from a given position) over time. (This statement is subject to the usual qualifications given in static analysis regarding freedom of choice between work and leisure, saving and consuming, etc.) The industrial structure most conducive to it cannot be easily described, but does anyone seriously think that perfect competition with its large number of small units—too small for research and too weak for any bold action in an uncertain world—would really maximize the rate of growth? And if it would not, perhaps a good deal of our thinking about competition and monopoly should be reconsidered.

The interest rate, so battered around by the Keynesians, may come back into its own, not as the reason for saving, which seems to be quite independent of it, nor even as the determinant of the amount invested, but perhaps again as an instrument for choosing between long-lived investments with a high coefficient per unit of output (i.e. low capital productivity) and those with a short life and a low coefficient. This may be a step back to the old Austrians, who, for all the recent criticism, might have had a better understanding of interest and capital than they have received credit for. It can be shown that investments which are durable and capital intensive may retard growth at first but accelerate it later, while those with short lives and low capital requirements will have the opposite effects. This relation between the life span of assets, their capital coefficients, and the distribution of growth over time came out of a study of capital depreciation and replacement, of which more below.

With this growth model, the Schumpeterian circular flow equilibrium, where investment and saving are absent, is also put aside, and the business cycle becomes a deviation of the economy from its equilibrium rate of growth. However little we know about causes of investment, it must be inhibited by the presence of idle capital, while the full or overfull utilization of existing capacity should act as a stimulus. This intensifies the instability. If for some reason output does not grow rapidly enough, unused capacity will develop, investment may fall off, and output will stop expanding and decline. On the other hand, a rapid growth of output presses on existing capacity and encourages investment, which in turn accelerates the growth of output and increases the pressure on capacity. It is quite paradoxical that, with a given propensity to save, to eliminate idle capital, more capital should be built, and to avoid a capital shortage, investment should be reduced.

Fortunately, we can borrow a few stabilizers from the real world, such as changes in the propensity to save, the monetary system, and others, and of course it is very lucky that investment is not solely determined by the degree to which capital stock is utilized. Technological progress, population movements, new firms, changes in tastes, etc., play an important part. It is extremely interesting to note that technological progress and other changes which, from a static point of view, appear destabilizing may indeed turn out to be the chief stabilizers of a growing economy. Thus a conclusion, correct in a static system, is wrong when applied to a growing one. There must be many such instances, and further research in the theory of growth will gradually bring them out. A few examples will be given here.

It is not true, for instance, that capital accumulation necessarily reduces the rate of profit, as believed by the classical economists, Marxists, and others. If I may indulge in a bit of simple mathematics, the average rate of profit on capital (including interest and similar payments) will tend to equal the fraction of national income going to the capitalists multiplied by the ratio between the rate of growth of income and the average propensity to save. This can be easily derived from an expression showing that the ratio of national income to capital approaches as a limit the ratio of the rate of growth to the propensity to save (given in Essay III). In the United States this ratio has not changed significantly over a long time, nor have there been any sharp changes in income distribution between capitalists and others. Hence, we should not expect any drastic fall in the average rate of profit in the secular sense. I would guess that it was and still remains somewhere around 6 per cent.[18] If American capitalism is destined to go to the dogs, it will have to be propelled there by something else.

Our next example comes from international trade. It is widely believed that the export balance of a new creditor country is gradually replaced by an import balance created by the mounting interest (and dividend) and amortization payments. In a growing economy this need not happen. The ratio between the inflow and outflow of funds is a function of the rate of growth of lending and the average rate of return received. So long as the rate of growth exceeds the rate of return, an export balance will be maintained. This is really quite obvious and it would be obvious if we did not look at foreign investment as a finite process to be terminated after three or after five years, depending upon the boldness of the author's imagination. (See Essay VI.)

My final example deals with replacement and depreciation. We are used to thinking that after the expiration of the initial period following the acquisition of the first asset, replacement and depreciation arising from a continuous stream of investments will balance, except for price changes and errors in estimating the life span of the assets. In a growing economy, however, even with constant prices and correct depreciation charges (computed according to the straight-line method), the latter will considerably exceed replacement expenditures. The ratio between them turns out to be a function of the rate of growth of gross investment multiplied by its average life span. In this country, these two magnitudes (in constant prices) may be taken to be in the vicinity of 3 per cent and thirty years respectively, with the striking result that over a period of years replacement will not exceed some 60 per cent of depreciation charges.[19]

This is not necessarily a suggestion for amending our tax laws. A rise in prices can more than eliminate this difference, though not every price rise is large enough to do it, and what about price falls? We are interested in this difference here because it shows the danger of assuming the problem of replacement and depreciation away by working with net series of income, investment, etc. If a gross capital coefficient turns out to be more meaningful than the net, which is very likely, growth models published so far will have to be reconsidered.[20]

The study of depreciation and replacement of capital goes beyond, I believe, mere bookkeeping manipulations and offers some real help in the development of a theory of growth. In addition, if we reflect on the fact that in the absence of price changes nearly two-thirds of gross capital formation in this country would be financed by depreciation charges (this fraction also being a function of the product of the rate of growth and the average life span of assets),[21] the regulation of economic growth by appropriate treatment of depre-

[19] This study, as yet unpublished, was made in the summer of 1951. It shows that after the expiration of the original m years, the ratio of replacement expenditures to depreciation charges will become and remain equal to $\dfrac{rm}{e^{rm} - 1}$, where m is the average life span of assets and r is the relative rate of growth of gross investment. [This study is presented in Essay VII.]

[20] See the preceding note.

[21] Using the symbols of note 19, the ratio of depreciation charges to gross investment, after the expiration of the first m years, will become and remain equal to $\dfrac{1 - e^{-rm}}{rm}$.

ciation charges under the income tax laws may become a practical possibility.[22]

V

These are just a few examples of the changes which even a very primitive study of growth can make in our traditional thinking, together with some hesitant suggestions for future work. I hesitate for the simple reason that I have not thought them through well enough to be reasonably sure of success. We may very well end up chasing wild geese. On the one hand, there is the problem of increasing complexity. It is not so much the formal mathematics—here the experts can be called in—but the intricacy of the answers, for this will deprive them of economic meaning. On the other hand, our results may be simply trivial. This would be sad.

And yet I think that even now these growth models, for all their simplification, abstraction, narrowness, and many other crimes, are not entirely useless for the understanding of the working of our economic system. Without any formal mathematics, if we just reflect that an increment in capacity is related (however roughly) to investment, while an increase in aggregate demand is connected with the rate of growth of investment, and that therefore a continuous growth of income, and most probably of investment, is required to keep the economy on an even keel, the nature of the capitalist system and the difficulty of its maintaining full employment year after year will become easier to understand. If we take a step further and observe that the relation between capital stock and output depends on the latter's rate of growth (and the propensity to save), and that there exists a rate of growth of income which, under existing conditions, will preserve the balance between capital and output and thus avoid excessive accumulation of capital, the theories of overinvestment and underinvestment, oversaving and undersaving, declining rate of profit, disappearing investment opportunities, and what not will fall into their proper places. Economic stabilization will become a special case of the problem of economic growth.

So much for the work on this end of the bridge. Professor Wright will probably start from the other end. Perhaps we will meet in the middle some day.

[22] It has already been applied in practice. See H. D. McGurran, 'Some Recent Developments in Canadian Taxation—Deferred Depreciation,' *National Tax Journal*, Vol. 4 (Dec., 1951), pp. 299–303. Accelerated depreciation allowed our defense plants is another case in point. [See also Essay VIII.]

II

The 'Burden of the Debt' and the National Income[*][1]

I

'Full employment after the war' has now become the subject most frequently discussed by economists. When the war is over, the level

* [Reprinted by permission from *The American Economic Review*, Vol. 34 (Dec., 1944), pp. 798–827. See also R. U. Ratchford's 'Mr. Domar's "Burden of the Debt," ' and my rejoinder in the same *Review*, Vol. 35 (June, 1945), pp. 411–18.
Since the article was published some twelve years ago, a few afterthoughts may facilitate the understanding of it.

1. The public debt and its interest charges are monetary rather than 'real' phenomena; accordingly, national (and taxable) income and its rate of growth should be expressed in money terms. Hence it was not necessary to assume a constant price level (p. 40) and to offer such profuse apologies (notes 14 and 30) for so doing. In money terms, our national income has been growing at some 4 to 5 per cent per year, rather than at the 2 to 3 per cent used in the paper. This should not be taken as an argument for solving the debt problem by means of inflation, though this has frequently happened. The real rate of growth is required for the discussion of conditions of economic growth given in Section IV, but not earlier.

2. The analysis of the debt problem as such does not call for any of the assumptions regarding the magnitudes and constancy of the marginal and average propensities to save made in the paper, except for purposes of illustration. All that is needed is a statement that a certain fraction of national income is borrowed by the government. The relation between this fraction and the propensities to save could likewise have been postponed until Section IV.

3. In the light of hindsight, an initial debt of $300 billion was a reasonable assumption; not so, however, the initial income of $130 billion. It might have also been less confusing to call the total output of goods and services national product rather than national income.

4. The performance of our economy during the last decade, the great increase in our research activities, and a faster growth of population warrant, I believe, a greater degree of optimism regarding our future rates of growth than was expressed in the paper, provided of course that our productive potential is utilized rather than dissipated in unemployment.]

[1] Thanks are due to Miss Mary Painter for her assistance in the preparation of this paper.

of employment and income will be determined to a great extent by the speed and character of the reconversion process. After that, hopes of maintaining full employment are based, for good or for ill, on the various backlogs developed during the war. But when both periods are over, the old and so painfully familiar problem of the disposal of intended savings will again appear.

It is possible that private investment will be able to absorb all savings year in and year out, or that private investment will at least fluctuate around a sufficiently high average so that deficits which may be incurred by the government in some years will be offset by surpluses made in others. Whether or not this will actually happen is a matter of opinion; it is a problem not discussed here. Instead I propose to examine the less optimistic case, when private investment is insufficient to absorb intended savings over a relatively long period of time.

Public investment financed by borrowing, though perhaps the most direct and evident, is by no means the only method of dealing with the situation. The income-generating properties of various kinds of taxation still remain to be explored;[2] the possibilities of encouraging private investment by means of various tax devices have not been sufficiently worked out either; the same can be said about plans designed to reduce the propensity to save. It will be assumed here, however, either that none of these measures can be tried, or that they have not proved sufficiently effective and that therefore a continuous policy of deficit financing must still be pursued.[3]

The theory of the multiplier and our actual experience during this war have demonstrated, I believe, that money income can be raised to any desired level if the total volume of public expenditures is sufficiently high. This view will probably be accepted also by the opponents of deficit financing. Their objections to such a policy

[2] See, however, P. A. Samuelson, 'Full Employment After the War' in *Postwar Economic Problems*, S. E. Harris, ed. (New York, 1943), p. 44; A. H. Hansen and H. S. Perloff, *State and Local Finance in the National Economy* (New York, 1944), pp. 245–6; L. A. Metzler, 'Effects of Income Redistribution,' *The Review of Economic Statistics*, Vol. 25 (Feb., 1943), pp. 49–57; B. Ruml, *National Fiscal Policy and the Two Super Budgets*, an address delivered before the Institute of Public Affairs, University of Virginia, June 27, 1941.

[3] At this stage, 'public investment financed by borrowing' and 'deficit financing' are used synonymously. The essential fact is that government absorbs the savings and spends them. The nature of these expenditures will be discussed in Section IV.

are based on several grounds, the most important being the belief that continuous government borrowing results in an ever-rising public debt, the servicing of which will require higher and higher taxes; and that the latter will eventually destroy our economy, or cause an outright repudiation of the debt.

That continuous net borrowing will result in an ever-growing public debt is evident; that, with a non-falling interest rate, the interest charges will grow is likewise true; and finally, assuming—as we shall in this paper—that all funds for payment of interest charges are to be raised by taxation,[4] there is no question that the absolute amount of taxes to be collected for that purpose will increase at the same rate. But all these *absolute* amounts do not mean much.

Whatever effects the existence and growth of the debt may have, what matters is its relation to other economic variables, such as national income, resources of the banking system, volume of private securities outstanding, and so on, the particular relation to be studied depending on the character of the problem at hand. The phrase 'burden of the debt,' if it has any meaning, evidently refers to the tax rate (or rates) which must be imposed to finance the service charges, and that the *tax rate* will rise is far from evident.

The belief that government borrowing must necessarily result in rising tax rates is so widespread both in technical and popular writings that no quantitative analysis of it has, to my knowledge, ever been made. It has been pointed out, however, particularly by Professor Hansen, that the debt problem should be studied in its relation to national income, and that with a growing national income the 'debt burden' is likely to be confined within manageable limits.[5] The proponents of deficit financing have also argued that the burden of a domestically-held debt depends to a great extent on the distribution of the debt ownership;[6] that however large the debt may be,

[4] This assumption is made both to simplify the argument and to protect the reader from shock. To many, government investment financed by borrowing sounds so bad that the thought of borrowing to pay interest charges as well is simply unbearable.

[5] A. H. Hansen and Guy Greer, 'The Federal Debt and the Future,' *Harpers Magazine*, Vol. 184 (Apr., 1942), pp. 489–500; A. H. Hansen, *Fiscal Policy and Business Cycles* (New York, 1941), pp. 135–85; 'Moulton's "The New Philosophy of Public Debt" ' in Hansen and Perloff, op. cit. pp. 285–98; and Hansen's other writings.

[6] A. H. Hansen: sources given in note 5; A. P. Lerner, 'Functional Finance and the Federal Debt,' *Social Research*, Vol. 10 (Feb., 1943), pp. 38–51; Stuart Chase, *Where's the Money Coming From?* (New York, 1943), pp. 97–110.

interest charges can still be collected because interest income constitutes a part of taxable income;[7] and finally, that a tax rate,
however high, will not deter investment if losses can be offset against
other income.[8]

No evaluation of these last three arguments will be made here.
But the issues of the debt problem will appear clearer if we adopt
the attitude of the opponents of deficit financing and treat this tax
rate as a burden, as a price for the privilege of having a higher
level of income (and employment) than would prevail without
deficit financing. We shall therefore explore the behavior of the tax
rate over time under several sets of assumptions. In addition, it will
be interesting to examine what the community gets for this payment, i.e. the net income of non-bondholders after the transfer of
interest charges to bondholders has taken place.

It is true that the existence and growth of the debt raise a number
of other problems besides the behavior of the tax rate and of the
net income of non-bondholders. I hope it will be recognized, however, that these two variables are the most important ones, and that
an analysis of their behavior will be of considerable help in the
understanding of the whole problem of the debt.

The paper is based on several dynamic models which are developed mathematically. All mathematics, however, is concentrated in
the Mathematical Appendix and only the final results are given in
the text. As in most investigations of this character, certain simplifying assumptions will have to be made, but ways of modifying them
will become apparent as the argument proceeds.

II

The burden of the debt, or the average tax rate covering the
interest charges, equals, roughly speaking, the ratio of the interest
charges to income; or the ratio of the debt to income multiplied by
the interest rate paid on bonds.[9] *It will be assumed that this interest*

---

[7] Lerner, op. cit.; S. E. Harris, 'Postwar Public Debt' in *Postwar Economic
Problems* edited by him (New York, 1943), pp. 169–85. Unfortunately both
Lerner and Harris assumed arbitrary magnitudes of the debt and income
without any analysis of their interrelationship.

[8] Lerner, op. cit. For a more elaborate analysis of the effects of loss offset,
see E. D. Domar and R. A. Musgrave, 'Proportional Income Taxation and Risk-
Taking,' *The Quarterly Journal of Economics*, Vol. 58 (May, 1944), pp. 388–422.

[9] Though not quite correct, this statement will do for the time being. A more

rate is a given constant (*i*). If we now want to find the effects of deficit financing on the tax rate, we should examine its effects on the magnitude of the debt and of the national income.

The effect of borrowing on the debt is somewhat complex and will be taken up in Section III. At this stage we can only record the obvious fact that continuous net borrowing will of course result in an ever-increasing debt. Indeed, this point has never been overlooked in the numerous writings on the subject.

The other relevant fact—that deficit financing may have some effect on income—has received a different treatment. Opponents of deficit financing often disregard it completely, or imply, without any evidence, that income will not rise as fast as the debt. On the other hand, we sometimes get the incorrect impression that it is sufficient for the government to spend, say, $100, and the national income will *rise* by $300 or $400, depending on the magnitude of the multiplier. If this were really so, there would be no debt problem at all: it would certainly pay us to *raise* the national income by $300 at the expense of some $2 increase in interest charges.[10]

A clear distinction should be made between *levels* of investment expenditures and income and *increments* in investment expenditures and income. With a given average propensity to save, the level of national income will be a multiple of the level of investment expenditures (public or private). Similarly, with a given marginal propensity to save, an increment in national income will be a multiple of an increment in investment expenditures. But neither of these two statements tells anything about the relation between the *level* of investment expenditures and an *increment* in income.

It should be emphasized that the stimulating effects of a given increment in expenditures tend to disappear quite soon, unless, of course, one believes in pump-priming, which does not at present find many proponents. Pump-priming aside, an increase in national income of, say, $300 produced by an increase in investment expenditures of, say, $100 will presently disappear and income will fall back to its former level. But the public debt (if investment expenditures are financed by government borrowing) has permanently increased (by $100), and so have interest charges (by $2). This is the source

---

correct one will be given on p. 41.

[10] That is, 2 per cent of the $100 borrowed.

of the debt problem. If the national income is to be maintained at the new level, new amounts must be spent.[11]

In order to simplify the problem, *it will be assumed that the community's average and marginal propensities to save are equal and constant.*[12] Under this assumption, national income will be simply a multiple of investment expenditures, and the two series will behave in exactly the same manner.[13] To maintain a *constant* level of income it is sufficient to have a *constant* stream of investment expenditures, public and private, but to achieve a *rising* income, total investment expenditures must also be *rising*. Thus, if it is desired that income should rise at a constant absolute rate, total investment expenditures must also rise at a constant absolute rate; or if income is to rise at a constant relative rate, investment expenditures must also rise at a constant relative rate; and so on. In other words, by regulating the total investment expenditures, national income can be made to behave in any desired manner.

All this refers to *money* income. Nothing has been said so far about *real* income. Whether or not real income will follow the movements of money income depends on a number of circumstances which will be discussed briefly in Section IV. But it will greatly simplify our analysis if *we now assume that the price level remains constant* (whatever that means over long periods of time), *so that changes in money income and in real income are the same.*[14]

[11] That this is so can be easily demonstrated by means of algebra, a numerical table, or a chart. For a good example, see A. H. Hansen, *Fiscal Policy and Business Cycles* (New York, 1941), Chart 16, p. 272. It was from this chart that the present paper originated.

[12] This would be a bad assumption in any cyclical problem. It may be quite reasonable, however, in an analysis of a secular problem such as ours. More about it will be said in Section IV.

[13] This of course follows from the definition of the propensity to save. Using I for investment, Y for income and λ for propensity to save, we have $Y = I \cdot \frac{1}{\lambda}$

so that if $I = f(t)$ where t is time, $Y = f(t) \cdot \frac{1}{\lambda}$.

[14] It is well to recognize that the assumption of a constant price level considerably reduces the quality of the analysis. As a matter of fact, in three out of the four cases to be analyzed (1, 2, and 4), a constant price level is unlikely to be maintained. But the purpose of this paper is to study the debt problem in its bearing on deficit financing. It therefore appears worth while to sacrifice some theoretical completeness in order to bring out clearly the essence of the problem. I do not think that the validity of the final conclusions is thereby impaired.

Before proceeding to the actual analysis of our problem, two other questions have to be settled. The first refers to the distinction between national income and taxable income. Without getting into current controversies, it will be sufficient to define *national income* as the sum of all wages, salaries, dividends, etc., paid out plus undistributed corporate profits, but excluding interest paid on the public debt. *Taxable income* will be defined as the national income *plus* interest receipts on the public debt, since interest receipts are also subject to taxation. It will be assumed that service charges are raised by means of a proportional income tax imposed on the total taxable income (without any exemptions), so that the tax rate will equal the ratio of interest charges to taxable income, it being understood that taxes levied for other purposes than to service the debt have already been subtracted in arriving at this definition of national income.[15]

Since no mathematical derivations are given in the text, it will be necessary to construct numerical tables to demonstrate the argument. It must be made perfectly clear that these tables are given as an illustration only and do not represent any attempt to forecast. They cover a period of 300 years not because I expect deficit financing, in the accepted sense of the terms, to last that long, but simply to convey the notion of a long period of time.

To construct the tables, the parameters used must be given numerical values. We may just as well try to take reasonable magnitudes.

Let the debt at the beginning of the 'experiment' = $300 billion, the national income at the beginning of the 'experiment' = $130 billion, the interest rate of the debt, i, = 2 per cent.

In addition, a decision must be made with regard to the magnitude of government borrowing. To do this, we must have some idea about the community's propensity to save. An examination of Professor Kuznets's estimates shows that over the period 1879–1928 net capital formation constituted about 13 per cent of national income (in 1929 prices). This percentage appears to have been remarkably stable, with a slight downward trend; in the decade 1919–28 it was

[15] Disposable income after taxes will equal taxable income minus tax collections, i.e. national income, since interest charges equal tax collections. It appears reasonable to apply the propensity to save to *disposable* income, and the fact that it equals national income considerably simplifies the mathematics of the problem.

about 10.6 per cent.[16] There may be serious objections against this kind of approach to an estimate of a future secular propensity to save under conditions of full employment, but it is a question which cannot be discussed here. I shall assume that the propensity to save will be 12 per cent. How this 12 per cent will be divided between private and public investment is again a matter of guesswork. It can just as well be assumed that they share in it equally. In other words, the fraction of national income borrowed by the government, to be indicated by α, will be assumed to equal 6 per cent.[17]

III

All preliminaries having been disposed of, a direct attack on the problem can now be made, which is to find out what the tax rate and other variables will be when national income is made to behave in a given manner.[18] Theoretically, there is an infinite number of patterns which the national income may be assumed to follow, but only the simplest ones will be considered here. It is clear that, in a problem of this type, it is more meaningful to express the growth of income in relative rather than absolute terms, and a function with a constant relative rate of growth will occupy the center of the discussion (Case 3).[19] But it may also be interesting to examine situations where income is held constant (Case 1), or is increasing at a constant absolute rate (Case 2). Finally, a variable percentage of income

[16] It may be well argued that non-deflated series should be used. Numerically, the difference is very small, and there is no need to elaborate this point any further here. Source: Simon Kuznets, an unpublished revision of Table 2 in *Uses of National Income in Peace and War* (New York, National Bureau of Economic Research, Occasional Paper 6, 1942), p. 31.

[17] Some remarks about a rising propensity to save and a rising α will be made in Section IV. In addition, a variable percentage of national income borrowed by the government is discussed in Case 4 (The War Model) below.

By referring to the Mathematical Appendix, the reader can easily construct other tables based on different numerical magnitudes of the parameters.

[18] As stated above, national income is made to behave in a given manner by regulating the volume of investment expenditures. Investment expenditures are the independent variable. This must be borne in mind, because the discussion in this section might give the misleading impression that national income is the independent variable.

[19] From a realistic point of view, a function with a slowly declining relative rate of growth would probably be more significant. This paper being but a first step in an analysis of this type, I thought it better to make no use of the more complex functions. A declining relative rate of growth is, however, discussed in Section IV.

borrowed by the government is analyzed in the so-called 'War Model' (Case 4).

Case 1. National Income Remains Constant

Since the government keeps borrowing an α fraction of national income, it is evident that the debt will increase at a constant absolute rate. The ratio of the debt to national income will therefore grow without limit and the tax rate will asymptotically approach 100 per cent.[20] The net income after taxes of non-bondholders will approach zero. The picture is rather dismal.

Actually, it takes quite a long time before conditions become really bad, depending of course on the magnitude of the parameters. As shown in Table I, after 50 years the tax rate is only about 10 per cent, and it takes almost 250 years to bring it to 25 per cent. But there is something inherently odd about an economy with a continuous stream of investment expenditures and a stationary national income. There are at least two explanations:

(1) Investment expenditures do not result in a higher per man-hour productivity, and there is no increase in the number of man-hours worked. It is doubtful whether these expenditures should be called *investment* in the first place. But such a situation is not incompatible with full employment, if the level of national income is sufficiently high.

(2) As a result of investment expenditures, productivity per manhour rises, but there is a continuously falling number of man-hours worked. It may mean an ever-shortening work-week. Under present institutional conditions, it is more likely to mean ever-increasing unemployment. Together with the ever-rising tax rate, it would combine the bleakest prophecies of both Karl Marx and the *Wall Street Journal*.[21]

[20] It may appear strange that the tax rate does not go beyond 100 per cent, in view of the fact that the ratio of the debt to income increases without limit. But the tax rate is the ratio of the interest charges to the *taxable* income, and as the debt and therefore the interest charges grow, taxable income increases as well. It is on this fact that Harris and Lerner based their defense of a large public debt, as already mentioned in note 7.

[21] There is of course a third possibility, namely, a falling price level, so that the real income would be actually rising. Such a case would exclude neither increasing productivity nor full employment. It is worth further study. What really matters is the fact that an ever-increasing share of the national income goes to bondholders. This raises grave doubts as to the advisability of fiscal and price policies resulting in a constant money and a rising real national income.

To repeat, continuous government borrowing not accompanied by a rising national income results in an ever, though slowly, rising debt burden in addition to the other possible economic dislocations already mentioned. How long such a policy can be pursued is a

TABLE I.—THE TAX RATE AND THE RATIO OF THE DEBT TO NATIONAL INCOME WHEN NATIONAL INCOME REMAINS CONSTANT

Original debt   = $300 billion α = 6 per cent
Original income = $130 billion i = 2 per cent

Years	Tax Rate Per Cent	Ratio of Debt to National Income
0	4.41	2.31
1	4.52	2.37
2	4.63	2.43
3	4.74	2.49
4	4.85	2.55
5	4.96	2.61
10	5.50	2.91
15	6.03	3.21
20	6.56	3.51
25	7.08	3.81
30	7.60	4.11
40	8.61	4.71
50	9.60	5.31
75	11.98	6.81
100	14.25	8.31
125	16.40	9.81
150	18.44	11.31
175	20.40	12.81
200	22.25	14.31
225	24.02	15.81
250	25.71	17.31
275	27.33	18.81
300	28.88	20.31
At the limit	100.00	Infinitely large

matter of conjecture. It will be shown in Cases 2 and 3, however, that the difficulty lies not in deficit financing as such, but in its failure to raise national income. To have a rising income, investment expenditures (public and private) must not remain constant, but must increase.

Case 2. National Income Increases at a Constant Absolute Rate

As the fraction of income borrowed (α) is constant, by assumption, and the income grows at a constant absolute rate, the annual deficits become larger and larger, so that the debt itself grows at an accelerated absolute rate.[22] Therefore the ratio of the debt to national income will rise without limit, and the tax rate will again approach 100 per cent.

It is of course evident that in the present case the absolute magnitude of income is larger than it was in Case 1. It is equally evident that a more rapidly growing income will, with our assumptions, result in a larger debt. We might therefore expect that the tax rate (and the ratio of the debt to income) will be the greater the more rapidly income rises. Actually, exactly the opposite holds true.

Table II compares the tax rates resulting from a constant income (as in Case 1) and from income rising at 5 and 10 billion dollars per year, respectively. After 50 years, the tax rate equals 9.6 per cent when income is constant, 5.3 per cent when it rises at 5 billions per year, and only 4.4 per cent when the rate of growth equals 10 billions. It takes about 280 years to raise the tax rate to 15 per cent when income increases at 10 billions per year, and only 110 years when it remains constant. And in general, it can easily be shown[23] that *the faster income rises the lower will be the tax rate*, even though a more rapidly rising income results in a larger absolute magnitude of the debt. This point will be taken up again in Case 3 and in Section IV.

It is still true, however, that we are confronted with an ever-rising tax rate. It could therefore be expected that the net income after taxes of non-bondholders would gradually approach zero as it did in Case 1. But this growth of the tax rate is more than offset by the ever-rising national income, so that the net income of non-bondholders after taxes approaches a very high asymptote.[24] It therefore follows that non-bondholders will be much better off than they were

[22] Mathematically speaking, this means that while national income is linear, the debt, being a function of the integral of income, is a quadratic. See Mathematical Appendix.

[23] See Mathematical Appendix.

[24] This asymptote is given by the expression $\dfrac{2b}{\alpha i}$ where b is the absolute rate of increase of the national income, and i is the interest rate paid on the debt.

at the beginning of the experiment, in spite of the rising tax rate. But it is doubtful, nevertheless, whether an economy with an ever-rising tax rate levied for the sole purpose of paying interest on the

TABLE II.—A COMPARISON OF TAX RATES WHEN NATIONAL INCOME REMAINS CONSTANT AND INCREASES AT $5 BILLION AND $10 BILLION PER YEAR (IN PERCENTAGES)

Original debt = $300 billion

Original income = $130 billion

α = 6 per cent

i = 2 per cent

Years	Constant Income	Income Increasing at $5 Billion per Year	Income Increasing at $10 Billion per Year
0	4.41	4.41	4.41
1	4.52	4.36	4.22
2	4.63	4.32	4.06
3	4.74	4.29	3.92
4	4.85	4.26	3.80
5	4.96	4.24	3.71
10	5.50	4.18	3.43
15	6.03	4.22	3.35
20	6.56	4.29	3.37
25	7.08	4.42	3.47
30	7.60	4.56	3.61
40	8.61	4.91	3.96
50	9.60	5.31	4.37
75	11.98	6.41	5.52
100	14.25	7.57	6.74
125	16.40	8.75	7.95
150	18.44	9.92	9.16
175	20.40	11.08	10.35
200	22.25	12.21	11.54
225	24.02	13.33	12.33
250	25.71	14.42	13.77
275	27.33	15.49	14.86
300	28.88	16.53	15.92
At the limit	100.00	100.00	100.00

debt will be able to escape serious economic and social difficulties which may possibly lead to a repudiation of the debt.

What is the nature of the economy described in this model? We see that larger and larger absolute amounts are invested (publicly and privately), but in spite of this, national income rises only by the *same* amount. The explanation of this phenomenon is practically the same as in Case 1:

(1) Investment fails to raise productivity per manhour sufficiently to allow the national income to grow faster; neither is there a sufficient rise in the number of manhours worked. In other words, the result is a diminishing productivity of investment which may be due to the wasteful character of investment expenditures, or to a lack of new technological improvements.[25]

(2) Productivity per manhour rises sufficiently, but there is a continuous decline in the number of manhours worked. This may mean more voluntary leisure or more unemployment.

If it is unemployment that prevents national income from rising faster (e.g. at a constant relative rate), the remedy is simple (at least in theory): investment expenditures should proceed at a faster rate. But if productivity per manhour fails to advance sufficiently, the situation is more serious. This question will be taken up in Section IV.

Case 3. National Income Increases at a Constant Relative Rate

Since Case 3 is the most important model, the major part of the subsequent discussion refers to it. Use will be made here of three symbols, two of which have already been introduced:

α—fraction of national income borrowed,

i—interest rate paid on bonds,

and

r—relative annual rate of growth of income.

To understand the relationship between the debt and income in this case, it is necessary to make use of the following two propositions *on which the whole analysis rests:*

1. If a variable Q is the sum of q_1, q_2, q_3, q_4, . . . and so on, each of which is larger than the preceding one by a fraction r, then the addition of more and more q's makes Q itself increase at a rate approaching r.

2. If any two variables increase at the same relative rate, the ratio between them remains constant.

---

[25] Productivity of investment as used in this paper refers to an increment in *national income* due to a given investment, and not to return over cost received or expected by an investor, which forms the essence of Keynes's marginal efficiency of capital and allied concepts.

Mathematically, both propositions can be proved very simply.[26] The non-mathematical reader can construct numerical tables and plot the results on semi-logarithmic paper. He will find that as time goes on, his sum, whose components grow at a constant relative rate, will look more and more like a straight line, i.e. its rate of growth will approach a constant. If he plots two functions growing at the some constant rate, they will be represented by two *parallel* straight lines.

Now, according to our assumption, national income grows at a constant relative rate of r. Since every year a constant fraction (α) of that income is being borrowed, it is clear that the deficits also grow at the rate of r per year. The total debt is simply the sum of all the deficits. Therefore, according to the first proposition, the rate of growth of the debt itself will also approach r, and according to the

---

[26] *The first proposition:*

A proof not involving the use of calculus: as stated in the text, let

$$Q = a + a(1 + r) + a(1 + r)^2 + \cdots + a(1 + r)^t,$$

where a is the original value of Q, r is the relative rate of increase, and t indicates the number of years. We have here a geometric progression in which $(1 + r)$ is the common ratio. Its sum is

$$Q = \frac{a[(1 + r)^{t+1} - 1]}{r}.$$

As t increases, Q approaches the expression

$$\frac{a}{r}(1 + r)^{t+1},$$

which increases at the rate of r per year.

The reader familiar with calculus can use a continuous function. If

$$\frac{dQ}{dt} = ae^{rt}$$

over the interval from 0 to t, then

$$Q = a \int_0^t e^{rt}dt = \frac{a}{r}(e^{rt} - 1),$$

which increases at a rate approaching r as t becomes large.

The second proposition:

Any two variables increasing at the same rate r can be expressed as $a_1(1 + r)^t$ and $a_2(1 + r)^t$ (or $a_1 e^{rt}$ and $a_2 e^{rt}$), where a_1 and a_2 are constants. Their ratio equals $\frac{a_1}{a_2}$ which is also constant.

Gustav Cassel applied these principles to the relationship between capital and income. See his *On Quantitative Thinking in Economics* (Oxford, 1935), p. 24.

second proposition, *the ratio between the debt and the national income will approach a constant.* This conclusion presents a striking contrast to the results obtained in Cases 1 and 2 where the ratio of the debt to income increased without limit.

CHART I.—THE BEHAVIOR OF THE TAX RATE WHEN NATIONAL INCOME INCREASES AT A CONSTANT RELATIVE RATE

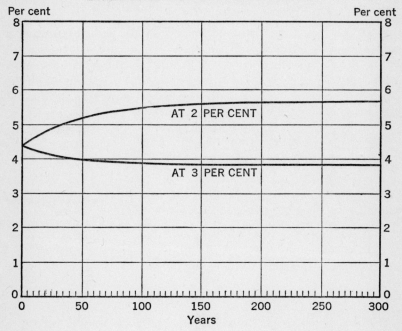

It is shown in the Mathematical Appendix that the constant which the ratio of the debt to income approaches equals the simple expression

(1) $$\frac{\alpha}{r}.$$

Similarly, the average tax rate approaches the limit expressed by

(2) $$\frac{i}{\dfrac{r}{\alpha} + i}.$$

To obtain some idea of the magnitudes of these two expressions, numerical values must be given to r. We shall experiment with $r = 2$ per cent and $r = 3$ per cent.[27]

The ratio of the debt to national income will approach 3 when $r = 2$ per cent, and 2 when $r = 3$ per cent. The tax rate will approach 5.7 per cent and 3.9 per cent with $r = 2$ and 3 per cent respectively. These figures and the examination of expressions (1) and (2)

TABLE III.—THE BEHAVIOR OF THE TAX RATE WHEN NATIONAL INCOME
INCREASES AT A CONSTANT RELATIVE RATE (IN PERCENTAGES)

Original debt = $300 billion $\alpha = 6$ per cent
Original income = $130 billion $i = 2$ per cent

Years	$r = 2$ Per Cent	$r = 3$ Per Cent
0	4.41	4.41
1	4.44	4.40
2	4.46	4.38
3	4.49	4.36
4	4.51	4.35
5	4.53	4.33
10	4.64	4.27
15	4.74	4.21
20	4.82	4.16
25	4.91	4.11
30	4.98	4.08
40	5.10	4.02
50	5.21	3.97
75	5.39	3.91
100	5.49	3.87
125	5.56	3.86
150	5.60	3.85
175	5.62	3.85
200	5.64	3.85
225	5.65	3.85
250	5.65	3.85
275	5.66	3.85
300	5.66	3.85
At the limit	5.71	3.85

again show that *the greater is the rate of growth of income, the lower will be the tax rate, even though a more rapidly rising income results in a larger absolute magnitude of the debt.*

[27] A brief discussion of what r was in the past and may be expected to be in the future is presented in Section IV and in Appendix B.

The net income of non-bondholders after taxes will also grow at a rate approaching r.

We thus see that, in spite of continuous government borrowing, the tax rate does not rise indefinitely but approaches a fairly reasonable limit. Even if private (net) investment disappears altogether, and the government has to borrow all the 12 per cent of income that the community desires to save, the tax rate will approach only 10.7 per cent and 7.4 per cent with r equal to 2 per cent and 3 per cent respectively.

Table III and Chart I show the behavior of the tax rate over time with $r = 2$ and 3 per cent. It is interesting to note that when $r = 2$ per cent, the tax rate approaches its asymptote from below up; while with $r = 3$ per cent, the corresponding asymptote is reached by a downward movement.[28] The latter is true because the ratio of the debt to income $300/130 = 2.3$ assumed here at the beginning of the experiment is larger than the final ratio which equals 2; some doubt is, therefore, thrown on the soundness of the assumption that α will equal only 6 per cent. Evidently, greater fractions of national income were borrowed in the past, especially in periods of war.[29] It is of course hoped that the future will be free of wars. Still, it may be interesting to inquire what will happen to the variables if wars or other similar emergencies occur. This brings us to Case 4.

Case 4. The War Model

The amount of guesswork involved in the preceding three cases is negligible compared with the degree of imagination required from here on. Probably the best thing to do is to present a very dark picture and then find relief in the thought that the future will not be as bad as that.

[28] In general, the movement will be up or down depending on whether the original magnitude of the debt is smaller or larger than $Y \cdot \frac{\alpha}{r}$.

[29] Strictly speaking this means that the ratio of the debt to income $\frac{300}{130}$ is inconsistent with the assumed magnitude of $\frac{\alpha}{r} = \frac{6 \text{ per cent}}{3 \text{ per cent}} = 2$. If we retain the $\frac{300}{130}$ ratio, we should change, α, r, or both. As will be shown in Section IV and Appendix B, 3 per cent is a reasonable estimate of the rate of growth of the (real) national income in the past. Therefore the magnitude of α should be raised.

Accordingly, let us assume that the future will consist of alternating periods of 25 years of peace (p) and 5 years of war (w); let the fractions of income borrowed be 6 per cent (α) in peacetime, and 50 per cent (β) during the war; and finally let the national income continue to grow at 2 per cent (r) per year.[30]

It can be easily shown by means of a table or a semi-logarithmic chart that the debt will grow very fast during wartime and more slowly in peacetime, but that *its average rate of growth will still approach r. Therefore the average tax rate will again approach a constant.*[31]

Actually the behavior of the tax rate is more complex. As shown in Table IV and Chart II, it fluctuates between two curves, reaching a maximum at the end of each war period and then going down to its minimum at the end of each peace period. With the parameters used, the limits of these maxima and minima are:

$$\begin{array}{ll} \text{Maximum} & \text{13.25 per cent} \\ \text{Minimum} & \text{10.42 per cent[32]} \end{array}$$

The ratio of the debt to national income will fluctuate in a similar

---

[30] This statement represents a drastic simplification of the problem. In particular, objections can be raised against our assumption of a constant price level, which is unlikely to prevail during these alternating periods of war and peace. During the wars, money income will probably rise much faster than at the rate of 2 per cent per year. But we can treat the 2 per cent rate as representing a long-run trend, to which the parameters apply. A comparison of methods of financing the last and the present wars (both in this country and in Great Britain) would indicate a movement toward less reliance on borrowing; hence, the 50 per cent of income assumed to be borrowed during future wars is probably too high. If, however, this fraction is applied to the trend rather than to the actual money income, it will appear more reasonable.

The reader may also wonder whether an economy engaged in such frequent wars can expect to have a steadily rising income. This remains an interesting question.

[31] This statement will become clearer if we assume that the government borrows a β fraction (e.g. 50 per cent) of national income *every* year. Then the tax rate, as given by (2), will approach $\dfrac{i}{\dfrac{r}{\beta}+i}$ which is a constant. Since the actual fraction of income borrowed is smaller than β the ratio of the debt to income must be below $\dfrac{i}{\dfrac{r}{\beta}+i}$.

[32] The formulas for these expressions are too complex to be reproduced here. See Mathematical Appendix.

manner, its maximum and minimum values approaching 7.64 and 5.82.

Since the tax rate and the ratio of the debt to income continue to fluctuate between their maximum and minimum values, it may be interesting to inquire what limits their *average* magnitudes

CHART II.—THE BEHAVIOR OF THE TAX RATE IN THE WAR MODEL

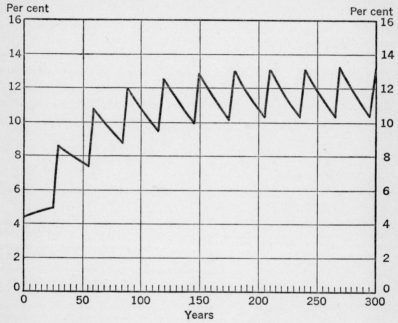

approach.[33] The latter are given by the expressions:

$$(3) \qquad \text{Average ratio of debt to income} = \frac{\sigma}{r} = 6.67;$$

$$(4) \qquad \text{Average tax rate} = \frac{i}{\dfrac{r}{\sigma} + i} = 11.76 \text{ per cent;}[34]$$

where

$$(5) \qquad \sigma = \frac{\alpha p + \beta w}{p + w} = \frac{.06 \times 25 + .50 \times 5}{25 + 5} = 13.33 \text{ per cent,}$$

i.e. σ is the weighted average of fractions of income borrowed.

[33] I am referring to simple arithmetic averages of actual tax rates (and ratios of debt to income) over the whole period of time.

[34] For a minor qualification of this formula see Mathematical Appendix.

TABLE IV.—THE BEHAVIOR OF THE TAX RATE IN THE WAR MODEL

Original debt = $300 billion $r = 2$ per cent
Original income = $130 billion $i = 2$ per cent

Years	Tax Rate Per Cent
0	4.41
1 peace time	4.44
2 peace time	4.46
3 peace time	4.48
4 peace time	4.51
5 peace time	4.53
25 end of peace	4.91
30 end of war	8.61
55 end of peace	7.48
60 end of war	10.77
85 end of peace	8.83
90 end of war	11.91
115 end of peace	9.55
120 end of war	12.52
145 end of peace	9.94
150 end of war	12.85
175 end of peace	10.16
180 end of war	13.04
205 end of peace	10.28
210 end of war	13.13
235 end of peace	10.34
240 end of war	13.19
265 end of peace	10.37
270 end of war	13.22
295 end of peace	10.39
300 end of war	13.24
At the limit	
end of war	13.25
end of peace	10.42
average	11.76

It is evident that the expressions (3) and (4) are identical with (1) and (2), respectively, except that α is replaced by σ. This fact makes the results obtained in Case 3 much more general. *It is no longer necessary that a constant fraction of income be borrowed every year. Variable fractions can be borrowed, and the α of Case 3 can then be treated as their weighted average.*

Whether the average tax rate of 11.8 per cent can still be regarded as 'reasonable' is a matter of opinion. Those who expect it to ruin the economy should remember that more than half of it is due to government borrowing to finance the wars; as shown in Case 3, peacetime deficit financing resulted in a tax rate of only 5.8 per cent. But it is a curious fact that those who have been most vociferous against government borrowing to achieve a high level of income

CHART III.—A COMPARISON OF TAX RATES IN MODELS 1–4

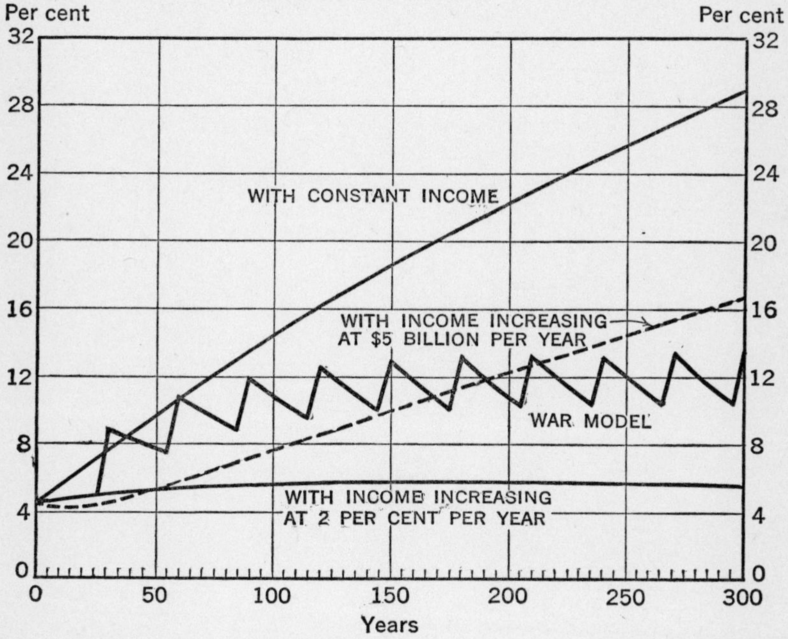

and employment in peacetime have also opposed higher taxes during the present war!

Chart II has important implications for post-war fiscal policy. To repeat, the tax rate reaches its maximum at the end of the war, and then gradually declines during the peace period, *in spite of the fact that the government does not stop borrowing and the debt itself continues to rise.*[35] Now, some economic and political circles are burning with a desire to reduce the debt burden after the war. They recognize no

[35] It is true, however, that the fraction of income borrowed does fall after the end of the war.

other method of achieving their goal than by reducing the absolute size of the debt; that the government must stop borrowing is of course taken for granted. They should beware, however, lest the policies they advocate exert such a depressing effect on the national income as to result in an actually heavier debt burden, even though a part of the debt is repaid.

Finally, it may be worth while to compare the several tax rates obtained from the four cases discussed. In Case 1 income is held constant; in Case 2 it rises at 5 billion dollars per year; in Cases 3 and 4, at 2 per cent. Such a comparison is presented in Chart III. It reveals the interesting fact that a constant relative rate of growth of income is such a powerful force that we could engage in a 5-year war every thirty years and eventually come out with a lower tax rate than would be the case in continuous peace, but with the national income rising at a constant *absolute* rate!

IV

In Cases 3 and 4 of the preceding section, we have established that when national income grows at a relative rate of r per year, the result at the limit is

$$(6) \qquad \text{Ratio of debt to income} = \frac{\alpha}{r},$$

and

$$(7) \qquad \text{Tax rate} = \frac{i}{\dfrac{r}{\alpha} + i},$$

where α can be interpreted either as a constant fraction of national income borrowed, or as a weighted average of variable fractions actually borrowed. As expression (7) for the tax rate looks rather complicated, it will be convenient—for purposes of exposition—to use an approximation to it, according to which

$$(8) \qquad \text{Tax rate} = \frac{\alpha}{r}\, i.\,[36]$$

[36] This expression is derived from (7) by omitting i from the denominator, since i is apt to be quite small relative to $\dfrac{r}{\alpha}$. By this simplification we are in fact assuming that interest on the debt is exempt from taxation. But numerically speaking, the mistake thus made is quite small and will be more than compensated for by convenience in exposition.

The reader is reminded that a constant price level is assumed as before, so that movements of money income and real income are identical.

Expression (8) clearly shows that the burden of the debt is directly proportional to α and i and inversely to r. If the burden is to be light (with given α and i), there must be a rapidly rising income. *The problem of the debt burden is a problem of an expanding national income.* How can a rapidly rising income be achieved?

If this question were asked in the pre-Keynesian era, the answer would be given in terms of manhours worked, productivity, and other *real* factors. Since the appearance of the *General Theory*, analysis has run in terms of investment expenditures, the multiplier, and other *monetary* considerations. Actually, there is no conflict in these two approaches: they simply state two sides of the same problem.

The real productive powers of the economy establish the ceiling beyond which real national income, at any given time, cannot go, but whether or not it will reach this ceiling depends on the volume of expenditures actually made. If a rising income is desired, there must be both rising expenditures and rising productive capacity.

As explained in Section II, national income will grow at a constant relative rate if and only if investment expenditures grow at the same rate (provided, of course, that the propensity to save remains constant). Since a stated fraction of these expenditures is assumed to be made by the government out of borrowed funds, it follows that deficits must also grow at the same relative rate. In absolute terms, the deficits must grow at an accelerated rate. It is horrifying to many to watch the public debt grow at an accelerated rate;[37] such a growth, however, is the only one which (with constant α and i) will *not* result in a rising burden of the debt.

From now on the heroic assumption is made that the stream of monetary expenditures will always be sufficient to maintain the national income at the maximum level established by the productive forces of the country. The growth of income will then be determined by the growth of these productive forces. The behavior of the latter in the past and their expected rate of growth in the future represent an important and interesting subject which can be but briefly

[37] 'Government spending tends to be like a drug, in that it takes larger and larger doses to get results, and all the time debt and taxes get higher and higher,' National City Bank, *Economic Conditions* (Jan., 1944), p. 11.

touched upon here. As a matter of fact, available past estimates refer to actually realized real income, and it can hardly be asserted that productive resources were always fully utilized even before the collapse of 1929.

Appendix B presents rates of growth of real national income for several countries, but the data are so fragmentary that not much reliance can be placed on them. For the United States, there are, fortunately, Professor Kuznets's estimates going back to 1879, which are presented in Table V. Over the whole period 1879–1928, total and per capita income grew at 3.3 and 1.5 per cent per year, respectively.[38] It is hard to form a definite opinion about their secular trend, because up to 1919 the estimates are presented only by (overlapping) decades, and the comparison between 1919 and 1929 is not very meaningful in view of the difficulty of measuring real output in a year like 1919. The general impression one gets from these figures is that there may have been some slackening of the rate of growth of total income, and possibly also of per capita income, though the performance of both rates in the twenties appears to have been extremely encouraging. Not much can be said about the period after 1929, because real output during the thirties had certainly little to do with productive powers. Also, there has been so much controversy about the measurement of real income during the present war years that it is better to postpone judgment. Estimates obtained from the U. S. Commerce Department show that, in the thirteen years 1929–42, total and per capita real income increased at an average rate of 3.4 and 2.6 per cent, respectively. Finally, there are estimates by the National Industrial Conference Board going back to 1799; these are also given in Appendix B.

The rate at which real output can be expected to grow in the future is a question about which a present-day economist has amazingly little to say. The problem of making full use of available productive capacity (except for the last few years when the war

[38] In regard to *money* income over the period 1879–1928, Professor Kuznets's estimates place the rates of growth of total and per capita income at 5.0 and 3.2 per cent, respectively. A comparison of these rates with the 3.3 and 1.5 per cent at which total and per capita *real* income was growing indicates that the price level rose at an average of 1.7 per cent.

Since the burden of the debt depends on the rate of growth of money income, a secular rise in prices will lighten the burden. In this paper it was agreed, however, to maintain a constant price level.

offered a solution) has been so challenging that not much attention has been devoted to the problem of long-run expansion. Indeed, one hesitates to talk about the expansion of productive powers when unemployment still looms as the most pressing post-war problem.

TABLE V.—PERCENTAGE RATES OF GROWTH OF REAL NATIONAL INCOME IN
THE UNITED STATES, 1879–1929 (1929 PRICES)[a]

Period	Total	Per Capita
Annual averages by decades[b]		
1884–1894	2.8	0.7
1894–1909	4.2	2.4
1909–1914	3.1	1.5
1884–1914	3.6	1.7
1914–1919	1.8	0.4
1919–1924	2.9	1.5
1914–1924	2.4	0.9
1884–1924	3.3	1.5
Annual estimates		
1919–1923	5.4	3.7
1923–1929	3.5	2.1
1919–1929	4.2	2.7

Source: Simon Kuznets, op. cit., and *National Income and Its Composition,
1919–1938*, Vol. I (New York, 1941), p. 147.

[a] All rates were computed exponentially by comparing the corresponding magnitudes at the beginning and end of each period.

[b] Each year represents the mid-point of a decade. For instance, 1884 indicates the average magnitude for the decade 1879–88; 1924, the period 1919–28; and so on.

In general it appears very unlikely that national income, or any economic series for that matter, can grow indefinitely at some constant relative rate.[39] The rate of growth achieved in the United States in the period 1879–1928 was due to technological improvements, growth of the labor force, and the discovery of new resources. Whether much reliance can be placed on resources still to be dis-

[39] For instance, one cent invested at 2 per cent 1944 years ago would amount now to something like 768,000 billion dollars.

covered is hard to say. It is true, however, that improved technological methods find new applications for known resources and thus may have the same effect as an actual discovery of new ones. The rate of growth of population has been slackening ever since about 1850, and the various estimates of future population growth predict a practically stationary if not declining population by 1980. Under these conditions, a 3 per cent rate of growth of real income may be too much to hope for, but a 2 per cent rate for the next 50 or even 100 years can probably be well defended.

We have to recognize that the main, and later on the only, propelling force in the economy will be technological improvements which should result in an ever-rising productivity per manhour. Only technological improvements can offset the diminishing productivity of investment which would be caused by the insufficient growth of the labor force and of natural resources. Whether new inventions will be forthcoming in sufficient numbers and whether they will be applied fast enough is hard to tell; one often gets the impression that the scientific age is just beginning, and that once monetary problems are solved, technological advance will proceed at a tremendous rate. On the other hand, one also cannot escape the impression that certain institutional developments, particularly the growth of huge corporations and monopolies, are not conducive to rapid technological change, and that the mere assurance of an adequate effective demand will not solve the whole problem. A thorough reform of the whole process of industrial research and particularly of the application of inventions may be needed as well.

It thus follows that, if it is desired to have national income grow at a given rate, two conditions must be satisfied:

1. The total volume of monetary expenditures, public and private, must grow at the same rate;

2. Of the total volume of these expenditures, a sufficient amount should be directed toward increasing the efficiency of production, in order that the required volume of monetary expenditures could take place without a rise in prices.

Since government is absorbing a part of savings, it is of course desirable that its expenditures be productive. This productivity has nothing to do, however, with such questions as whether or not the assets constructed make a direct contribution to the federal treasury or are self-liquidating. As a matter of fact, the term 'investment expenditures' may be misleading, because it is too closely associated with steel and concrete.[40] If healthier people are more productive, expenditures on public health satisfy these requirements. The same holds true for expenditures on education, research, flood control, resource development, and so on. Finally, if institutional forces prevent the government from spending money on anything but leaf-raking, it should still absorb the savings unused by private enterprise and spend them on leaf-raking, relying on private investment to raise the efficiency of production, rather than do nothing at all and thus create a shortage of monetary expenditures and unemployment.[41] Of course, national income would be able to advance at a higher rate if governmental expenditures were productive in our sense. In 1940 total private and public expenditures on industrial and scientific research in the United States were less than 500 million dollars. What would be the result if this amount were doubled, tripled, or multiplied ten times? Indeed, large-scale governmental participation in industrial and scientific research could become one of the major propelling forces in the economy.[42]

It is possible, or even likely, that, in spite of all these efforts, national income will grow at a *decreasing* relative rate. Several possibilities should now be examined:

(a) The fall in the rate of growth is accompanied, or rather

[40] A substantial part of efficiency-raising expenditures is usually treated as current costs, and does not appear under the heading of capital formation or investment.

[41] It is an interesting question whether private investment would be able to take place at all in an economy characterized by a chronic shortage of monetary expenditures.

[42] Expenditures on industrial research made by private business in 1940 amounted to about 300 million dollars. To this should be added some 50 millions spent by universities; the latter figure includes their expenditures on research in social sciences as well. The figures for federal expenditures on scientific and industrial research in 1940 are not available; in 1938, they amounted to some 52 millions, the largest share going to the Department of Agriculture. See U. S. National Resources Committee, *Research—A National Resource, Vol. I—Relation of the Federal Government to Research* (Washington, 1938); U. S. National Resources Planning Board, *Research—A National Resource, Vol. II— Industrial Research* (Washington, 1941).

Since the beginning of the war, federal expenditures on research, particularly in the fields connected with the war effort, have shown a marked increase. A bill recently introduced by Senator Kilgore would authorize an annual appropriation of 250 millions on subsidies to various research organizations and on direct research by the federal government. The amount is rather small, but may prove to be a good beginning.

caused, by a declining propensity to save. The public prefers to consume a greater share of its income; therefore, a smaller fraction is invested, and income cannot grow as fast as it otherwise would. If the decline in the propensity to save and therefore in α is proportional to that in r, the burden of the debt $\dfrac{\alpha}{r} i$ remains unchanged. If, however, r suffers a greater proportional decline than α, we have the next case (b).

(b) r declines while the propensity to save and α remain constant, or at least do not decline as fast (proportionally) as r. The result is a genuine diminishing productivity of investment: further investments of the same fraction of national income result in smaller and smaller relative increases in income. Under these conditions, whether the investment be made by private enterprise or by the government, it is impossible to pay a constant rate of return on the investment without increasing indefinitely the relative share of the national income going to property owners. If such a course is regarded as impossible or undesirable, the rate of return on the amounts invested must go down as well. This would mean in the case under discussion here that the interest rate on bonds must be continuously reduced.[43]

All of this discussion, with the exception of the case (a) just considered, was based on the assumption that over a period of time α remained constant. It will be worth while to examine the not improbable case when α increases, i.e. when the government borrows an increasing fraction of national income. There are again several possibilities:

(c) α remains a constant fraction of the propensity to save, but the propensity to save itself rises. In other words, a larger fraction of national income is invested. If so, the rate of growth may also increase and thus leave the burden of the debt, $\dfrac{\alpha}{r} i$, unchanged. If, on the other hand, r does not rise—or at least does not rise as fast (proportionally) as α—the result is diminishing productivity of investment already discussed under (b).

(d) The propensity to save remains constant, but α increases. In other words, a larger fraction of total savings is absorbed by the

---

[43] It is very amusing that those who appear most worried about the burden of the debt are usually least willing to advocate a lower interest rate on the debt!

government and a smaller one by private business. As the propensity to save remains constant, there is no reason to expect an increase in r. Therefore, the ratio $\frac{\alpha}{r} i$ and, hence, the burden of the debt will increase.

On the face of it, such a development appears quite unfavorable, since it was agreed to regard the debt burden as an evil which should be minimized. It is presumably an evil because a part of the national income has to be taken from the public and given to bondholders. But if interest charges on the public debt are treated in this manner, a question arises why other forms of property income should be treated differently. After all, in peacetime society has a choice (at least in theory) of having its investment undertaken by the government or by private business. In the first case, a fixed return is given to the bondholders, and presumably neither the interest nor the principal is subject to default. In the second case, society promises the investors nothing, but allows them, subject to certain rules, to get whatever they can. Which method will result in a more rapidly rising national income is a question on which many opinions have been expressed but few, if any, studies ever undertaken. Nor has any serious attempt been made (at least to my knowledge) to analyze the possible changes in the magnitude of property income produced by a replacement of private investment by government investment. Too often has it been implicitly assumed that interest on government bonds is necessarily a net *addition* to other property income, rather than a *substitution* for other forms of property income; or, in other words, that investment by government, rather than by private business, must increase the magnitude of income going to property owners. Since this may or may not be true, there is no ground as yet for asserting that government investment raises the 'burden' of the total, public and private, debt, that it increases the concentration of wealth and income, that it accelerates the growth of the *rentier* class, or that it raises the community's propensity to save—thus creating new difficulties all of which would be absent if the investment were done solely by private business.

There is also the question whether the transfer of income to property owners by means of taxation is more or less 'painful' to the public or disturbing to the economy than a transfer of an equal amount by means of higher prices or lower wages.

The whole problem needs further study.

It is hoped that this paper has shown that the problem of the debt burden is essentially a problem of achieving a growing national income. A rising income is of course desired on general grounds, but in addition to its many other advantages it also solves the most important aspects of the problem of the debt. The faster income grows, the lighter will be the burden of the debt.

In order to have a growing income there must be, first of all, a rising volume of monetary expenditures. Secondly, there must be an actual growth in productive powers in order to allow the increasing stream of expenditures to take place without a rise in prices.

* * * *

When post-war fiscal policy is discussed, the public debt and its burden loom in the eyes of many economists and laymen as the greatest obstacle to all good things on earth. The remedy suggested is always the reduction of the absolute size of the debt or at least the prevention of its further growth. If all the people and organizations who work and study, write articles and make speeches, worry and spend sleepless nights—all for fear of the debt—could forget about it for a while and spend even half their efforts trying to find ways of achieving a growing national income, their contribution to the benefit and welfare of humanity—and to the solution of the debt problem—would be far greater.

MATHEMATICAL APPENDIX

LIST OF SYMBOLS

Y = national income;

D = public debt;

$U = Di$ = interest charges on the debt;

$T = Y + U$ = taxable income;

$\dfrac{U}{T}$ = tax rate;

$Y' = Y\left(1 - \dfrac{U}{T}\right)$ = net income of non-bondholders after the payment of taxes;

a = national income at the beginning of the 'experiment';
α = fraction of national income borrowed by the government;
i = interest rate paid on the debt;
b = absolute annual rate of growth of national income (in Case 2);
r = relative annual rate of growth of national income (in Cases 3 and 4);
t = time (in years).

Case 1

$$Y = a;$$
$$D = D_0 + \alpha a t;$$
(1) $$\frac{D}{Y} = \frac{D_0}{a} + \alpha t;$$
(2) $$\lim_{t \to \infty} \frac{D}{Y} = \infty;$$
$$\frac{U}{T} = \frac{Di}{Y + Di} = \frac{1}{\frac{Y}{Di} + 1};$$
(3) $$\lim_{t \to \infty} \frac{U}{T} = 1 = 100 \text{ per cent};$$
(4) $$\lim_{t \to \infty} Y' = Y\left(1 - \lim_{t \to \infty} \frac{U}{T}\right) = 0.$$

Case 2

$$Y = a + bt;$$
$$D = D_0 + \alpha \int_0^t (a + bt)dt = D_0 + \alpha t\left(a + \frac{b}{2}t\right);$$
(5) $$\frac{D}{Y} = \frac{D_0 + \alpha t\left(a + \frac{b}{2}t\right)}{a + bt};$$
(6) $$\lim_{t \to \infty} \frac{D}{Y} = \infty;$$
(7) $$\lim_{t \to \infty} \frac{U}{T} = 1 = 100 \text{ per cent};$$
$$Y' = Y\left(1 - \frac{U}{T}\right) = \frac{Y^2}{Y + U};$$
(8) $$\lim_{t \to \infty} Y' = \frac{2b}{\alpha i}.$$

It can be readily shown from (5) that $\dfrac{D_1}{Y_1} < \dfrac{D_2}{Y_2}$ if $b_1 > b_2$, other parameters remaining the same. This also holds true for $\dfrac{U}{T}$.

Case 3

$$Y = ae^{rt};$$

$$D = D_0 + \alpha a \int_0^t e^{rt}dt = D_0 + \frac{\alpha a}{r}(e^{rt} - 1);$$

(9) $$\frac{D}{Y} = \frac{D_0}{ae^{rt}} + \frac{\alpha}{r}(1 - e^{-rt});$$

(10) $$\underset{t \to \infty}{\text{Lim}}\ \frac{D}{Y} = \frac{\alpha}{r};$$

(11) $$\underset{t \to \infty}{\text{Lim}}\ \frac{U}{T} = \frac{i}{\dfrac{r}{\alpha} + i}.$$

Case 4. The 'War Model'

List of Additional Symbols

p = length of the 'peace' period;

α = fraction of national income borrowed during the 'peace' period;

w = length of the 'war' period;

β = fraction of national income borrowed during the 'war' period;

$\sigma = \dfrac{\alpha p + \beta w}{p + w}$ = the average fraction of national income borrowed.

Only the final results are given here.

(12)   Maximum $\underset{t \to \infty}{\text{Lim}}\ \dfrac{D}{Y} = \dfrac{\alpha + Ke^{rp}}{r};$

(13)   Minimum $\underset{t \to \infty}{\text{Lim}}\ \dfrac{D}{Y} = \dfrac{\alpha + K}{r};$

(14)   where $K = \dfrac{(\beta - \alpha)(e^{rw} - 1)}{e^{(p+w)r} - 1};$

(15)   Average $\underset{t \to \infty}{\text{Lim}}\ \dfrac{D}{Y} = \dfrac{\sigma}{r};$

(16)   Maximum $\underset{t \to \infty}{\text{Lim}}\ \dfrac{U}{T} = \dfrac{(\alpha + Ke^{rp})i}{r + (\alpha + Ke^{rp})i};$

(17)   Minimum $\underset{t \to \infty}{\text{Lim}}\ \dfrac{U}{T} = \dfrac{(\alpha + K)i}{r + (\alpha + K)i};$

$$(18) \qquad \text{Average} \qquad \lim_{t \to \infty} \frac{U}{T} = \frac{i}{\dfrac{r}{\sigma} + i}.$$

In expressions (15) and (18) a simple arithmetic average is used. The expression (18) is actually an approximation of the true value of Aver. $\lim\limits_{t \to \infty} \dfrac{U}{T}$. It can be shown that the difference between them is likely to be very small and that (18) always overstates the true magnitude of Aver. $\lim\limits_{t \to \infty} \dfrac{U}{T}$.

APPENDIX B

By Mary Painter

Table VI is presented here merely as an illustration: the data are not sufficiently comparable and are too fragmentary to warrant a more serious use. Definitions and accuracy of measurement vary from country to country. In addition, some figures were deflated by a cost-of-living index, while an index of wholesale prices had to be used for others. The relatively low rates of growth obtained for Germany may be due to the fact that a wholesale price index was used as a deflator.[44]

Sources of the figures for each country and the deflator used to get real income are given below.

Australia—Income, deflated by an index of prices of consumption and investment goods: Colin Clark and J. G. Crawford, *The National Income of Australia* (Sydney and London, 1938), p. 65. Investment: Clark, *The Conditions of Economic Progress* (London, 1940), p. 406.

Canada—Income, deflated by index of cost-of-living: *The Monthly Review of Business Statistics* (April, 1943). Population: *The Canada Year Book*, 1940 and 1942.

Germany—Income figures, deflated by wholesale price index: *Das Deutsche Volkseinkommen vor und nach dem Kriege*, bearbeitet im Statischen Reichsamt, 1931, p. 68. Savings, as a percentage of in-

---

[44] The period 1891–1913 was one of rising prices, and wholesale prices were rising faster than the cost of living. For instance, during this period the wholesale price index in England rose by 26.6 per cent, while the rise in the cost-of-living index was only 17 per cent. It is very likely that if the national income in Germany were deflated by a cost-of-living index, it would show a higher rate of growth than given in the table. Such an index, however, was not available.

TABLE VI.—PERCENTAGE RATES OF GROWTH OF REAL INCOME, TOTAL AND PER CAPITA, IN VARIOUS COUNTRIES[a]

Country	Period	Rate of Increase of Total Real Income	Rate of Increase of Per Capita Real Income	Percentage of Income Invested (Current Prices)
Australia	1901-03–1928-29	3.0	1.1	
	1921-22–1928-29	4.6	3.6	
	1901-03–1937-38	2.6	1.0	
	1921-22–1937-38	2.8	1.9	8.8[b]
Canada	1919 –1929	3.6	1.7	
	1919 –1940	2.5	1.0	
Germany	1891 –1913	1.8	0.5	18.0
Great Britain	1880 –1891-95	3.4	2.6	
	1891-95–1913	1.5	0.6	11.1
Hungary	1925-26–1936-37	1.9	1.2	4.8
Japan	1919 –1936	3.9	2.5	
New Zealand	1926 –1940	3.0	2.0	
Sweden	1913 –1930	2.3	1.8	11.2
	1922 –1930	2.9	2.6	10.5
United States N.I.C.B.[c]	1799 –1859	3.6	0.6	
	1879 –1929	3.2	1.4	
	1799 –1929	3.3	0.8	
Kuznets[d]	1884 –1924	3.3	1.5	13.3
	1919 –1929	4.2	2.7	10.8
U. S. Dept. of Commerce	1929 –1942	3.4	2.6	6.3

[a] All rates were computed exponentially by comparing the corresponding magnitudes at the beginning and at the end of each period.

[b] Average for years 1928–29 through 1937–38.

[c] National Industrial Conference Board.

[d] See Table V.

come: Leon Goldenberg, *Income and Savings in France 1871–1914* (unpublished), p. 139.

Great Britain—Income, deflated by cost-of-living index: A. L. Bowley, *Wages and Income Since 1860* (Cambridge, 1937), p. 94. Savings as percentage of income: Leon Goldenberg, *Income and Savings in France 1871–1914* (unpublished), p. 145.

Hungary—All figures: Matthias Matolcsy and Stephen Varga, *The National Income of Hungary* (London, 1938), pp. 68*ff*. The deflator used was a comprehensive price index.

Japan—Income, in current prices: *Mitsubishi Economic Research Bureau Monthly Circular* (April, 1937), p. 12. Deflated by index of wholesale prices: the *Federal Reserve Bulletin*. Population: *Japan Yearbook*, 1937.

New Zealand—Income, in fiscal years: *New Zealand Official Yearbook*, 1937, 1938, and 1943, interpolated to calendar years and deflated by index of retail prices from same source. Population: *Official Yearbook*.

Sweden—All figures: E. Lindahl, E. Dahlgren, and K. Koch, *National Income of Sweden 1861–1930* (London, 1937). The deflator was a cost-of-living index.

United States—N.I.C.B. figures: Income, deflated by an index of the general price level: Robert F. Martin, *National Income in the United States, 1799–1938*, National Industrial Conference Board, Inc. (New York, 1939), p. 6.

Kuznets's figures: Income deflated by a comprehensive price index. See Table V, p. 59.

U. S. Department of Commerce figures: Income, deflated by comprehensive price index: National Income Unit of the Bureau of Foreign and Domestic Commerce.

III

Capital Expansion, Rate of Growth, and Employment*[1]

I

Introduction

This paper deals with a problem that is both old and new—the relation between capital accumulation and employment. In economic literature it has been discussed a number of times, the most notable contribution belonging to Marx. More recently, it was brought forth by Keynes and his followers.

A thorough analysis of the economic aspects of capital accumulation is a tremendous job. The only way in which the problem can be examined at all in a short paper like this is by isolating it from the general economic structure and introducing a number of simplifying assumptions. Some of them are not entirely necessary and, as the argument progresses, the reader will see how they can be modified or removed.

The following assumptions and definitions should be noted at the start: (a) there is a constant general price level; (b) no lags are present; (c) savings and investment refer to the income of the same

* [Reprinted by permission from *Econometrica*, Vol. 14 (Apr., 1946), pp. 137–47. Essay IV presents much of the discussion of this paper in a less technical language, but lacks its mathematical derivations.

As indicated in the Foreword, I am not quite happy with the concepts used here. A concurrent reading of the relevant part of the Foreword (pp. 6–8) is recommended.]

[1] This is a summary of a paper presented before a joint session of the Econometric Society and the American Statistical Association in Cleveland on Jan. 24, 1946. Many thanks for help and criticism go to my fellow members of the 'Little Seminar': Paul Baran, Svend Laursen, Lloyd A. Metzler, Richard A. Musgrave, Mary S. Painter, Melvin W. Reder, Tibor Scitovsky, Alfred Sherrard, Mary Wise Smelker, Merlin Smelker, and most of all to James S. Duesenberry.

period; (d) both are net of depreciation; (e) depreciation is not measured by historical costs, but by the cost of replacing the depreciated asset by another one of the same productive capacity;[2] (f) productive capacity of an asset or of the whole economy is a measurable concept.

The last assumption, on which (e) also depends, is not at all safe. Productive capacity, whether of a certain piece of capital equipment or of the whole economy, depends not only on physical and technical factors, but also on the whole complex of economic and institutional conditions, such as distribution of income, consumers' preferences, relative wage rates, relative prices, and the structure of industry, many of which are in turn affected by the behavior of the variables analyzed here. We shall nevertheless assume all these conditions to be given, and shall mean by the productive capacity of an economy its total output when its labor force is fully employed in some conventional sense.[3]

The economy will be said to be in equilibrium when its productive capacity P equals its national income Y. Our first task is to discover the conditions under which this equilibrium can be maintained, or more precisely, the rate of growth at which the economy must expand in order to remain in a continuous state of full employment.

II

The Problem of Growth

The idea that the preservation of full employment in a capitalist economy requires a growing income goes back (in one form or another) at least to Marx. It has been fully recognized in numerous

[2] If the original machine worth $1,000 and producing 100 units is replaced by another one worth also $1,000, but producing 120 units, only $833.33 will be regarded as replacement, and the remaining $166.67 as new investment. A similar correction is made when the new machine costs more or less than the original one. The treatment of depreciation, particularly when accompanied by sharp technological and price changes, presents an extremely difficult problem. It is quite possible that our approach, while convenient for present purposes, may give rise to serious difficulties in the future. [No distinction is made in this paper between replacement and depreciation. This distinction is developed in Essay VII.]

[3] It is undoubtedly possible to work out a more precise definition of productive capacity, but I prefer to leave the matter open, because a more precise definition is not entirely necessary in this paper and can be worked out as and when

studies (recently made in Washington and elsewhere) of the magnitude of gross national product needed to maintain full employment. But though the various authors come to different numerical results, they all approach their problem from the point of view of the size of the labor force. The labor force (manhours worked) and its productivity are supposed to increase according to one formula or another, and if full employment is to be maintained, national income must grow at the combined rate. For practical relatively short-run purposes this is a good method, but its analytical merits are not high, because it presents a theoretically incomplete system: since an increase in labor force or in its productivity only raises productive capacity and does not by itself generate income (similar to that produced by investment), the demand side of the equation is missing. Nor is the difficulty disposed of by Mr. Kalecki's method according to which capital should increase proportionally to the increase in labor force and its productivity.[4] As Mrs. Robinson well remarked, 'The rate of increase in productivity of labor is not something given by Nature.'[5] Labor productivity is not a function of technological progress in the abstract, but technological progress embodied in capital goods, and the amount of capital goods in general. Even without technological progress, capital accumulation increases labor productivity, at least to a certain point, both because more capital is used per workman in each industry and because there is a shift of labor to industries that use more capital and can afford to pay a higher wage. So if labor productivity is affected by capital accumulation, the formula that the latter should proceed at the same rate as the former (and as the increase in labor force) is not as helpful as it appears.

The standard Keynesian system does not provide the tools for deriving the equilibrium rate of growth. Growth is entirely absent

---

needed. [In the original version of the paper, productive capacity of an economy was defined as 'its total output when all productive factors are fully employed.' I have changed the definition because it contradicted the meaning in which the concept of productive capacity was used throughout the paper. This important correction was suggested by Edith T. Penrose.]

[4] See his essay, 'Three Ways to Full Employment' in *The Economics of Full Employment* (Oxford, 1944), p. 47, and also his 'Full Employment by Stimulating Private Investment?' in *Oxford Economic Papers*, No. 7 (Mar., 1945), pp. 83–92.

[5] See her review of *The Economics of Full Employment*, *The Economic Journal*, Vol. 55 (Apr., 1945), p. 79.

from it because it is not concerned with changes in productive capacity. This approach permits the assumption that employment is a function of national income (and the wage unit), an assumption which can be justified for short periods of time, but which will result in serious errors over a period of a few years. Clearly, a full employment level of income of five years ago would create considerable unemployment today. *We shall assume instead that employment is a function of the ratio of national income to productive capacity.* While this approach seems to me to be superior to that of Keynes, it should be looked upon as a second approximation rather than a final solution: it does not allow us to separate unused capacity into idle machines and idle men; depending upon the circumstances, the same ratio of income to capacity may yield different fractions of the labor force employed.

Because investment in the Keynesian system is merely an instrument for generating income, the system does not take into account the extremely essential, elementary, and well-known fact that investment also increases productive capacity.[6] This *dual* character of the investment process makes the approach to the equilibrium rate of growth from the investment (capital) point of view more promising: if investment both increases productive capacity and generates income, it provides us with *both* sides of the equation the solution of which may yield the required rate of growth.

Let investment proceed at the rate I per year, and let s be the ratio of the productive capacity net of depreciation (net value added) of the new projects to capital invested in them (I).[7] The net annual potential output of these projects will then be equal to Is. But the productive capacity of the whole economy may increase by a smaller amount, because the operations of these new projects may involve a transfer of labor (and other factors) from other plants, whose productive capacity is therefore reduced.[8] We shall define σ, the

[6] Whether every dollar invested increases productive capacity is essentially a matter of definition. It can safely be said that investment taken as a whole certainly does. To make this statement hold in regard to residential housing, imputed rent should be included in the national income. See also note 19.

[7] The use of the word 'project' does not imply that investment is done by the government, or that it is always made in new undertakings. I am using 'project' (in the absence of a better term) because investment can mean the act of investing and the result of the act.

[8] I am disregarding the external economies and diseconomies of the older plants due to the operation of the new projects.

potential social average investment productivity, as

(1)
$$\sigma = \frac{\dfrac{dP}{dt}}{I}.$$

The following characteristics of σ should be noted:

1. It does not imply that factors of production other than capital and technology remain constant. On the contrary, its magnitude depends to a very great extent on technological progress. It would be more correct to say that σ refers to an increase in capacity accompanying rather than caused by investment.

2. σ refers to the increase in *potential* capacity. Whether or not this potential increase results in a larger income depends on the behavior of expenditures.

3. σ is concerned with the increase in productive capacity of the whole society, and not with the rate of return derived or expected from investment. Therefore σ is not affected directly by changes in distribution of income.

4. s is the maximum that σ can attain. The difference between them will depend on the magnitude of the rate of investment on the one hand, and on the growth of other factors, such as labor and natural resources, and on technological progress on the other. A misdirection of investment will also produce a difference between s and σ.

We shall make the heroic assumption that s and σ are constant. From (1) it follows that

(2)
$$\frac{dP}{dt} = I\sigma.$$

It is important to note that, with a given σ, dP/dt is a function of I, and not of dI/dt. Whether dI/dt is positive or negative, dP/dt is always positive so long as σ and I are positive.

Expression (2) showing the increase in productive capacity is essentially the supply side of our system. On the demand side we have the multiplier theory, too familiar to need any comment, except for an emphasis on the obvious but often forgotten fact that with any given marginal propensity to save, dY/dt *is a function not of I, but of dI/dt*. Indicating the marginal propensity to save by α, and assuming it to be constant,[9] we have the simple relationship that

(3)
$$\frac{dY}{dt} = \frac{dI}{dt}\frac{1}{\alpha}.$$

Let the economy be in an equilibrium position so that[10]

(4)
$$P_0 = Y_0.$$

To retain the equilibrium position, we must have

(5)
$$\frac{dP}{dt} = \frac{dY}{dt}.$$

Substituting (2) and (3) into (5) we obtain our fundamental equation

(6)
$$I\sigma = \frac{dI}{dt}\frac{1}{\alpha},$$

the solution of which gives

(7)
$$I = I_0 e^{\alpha\sigma t}.$$

$\alpha\sigma$ is the equilibrium rate of growth. So long as it remains constant, *the maintenance of full employment requires investment to grow at a constant relative or compound interest rate.*

If, as a crude estimate, α is taken at 12 per cent and σ at some 30 per cent, the equilibrium rate of growth will be some 3.6 per cent per year.[10a]

[9] Over the period 1879–1941 the average propensity to save (ratio of net capital formation to national income) was fairly constant and approximately equal to some 12 per cent. See Simon Kuznets, *National Product Since 1869*, National Bureau of Economic Research (mimeographed, 1945), p. II-89 [since published under the same title (New York, 1946), p. 119] and the *Survey of Current Business*, Vol. 22 (May, 1942), and Vol. 24 (Apr., 1944). In a cyclical problem the assumption of a constant propensity to save would be very bad. Since we are interested here in a secular problem of maintaining continuous full employment, this assumption is not too dangerous.

[10] The problem can be also worked out for the case when $P_0 > Y_0$.

[10a] After this paper was sent to the printer, I found a very interesting article by E. H. Stern, 'Capital Requirements in Progressive Economies,' *Economica*, n.s., Vol. 12 (Aug., 1945), pp. 163–71, in which the relation between capital and output in the U.S. during 1879–1929 is expressed (in billions of dollars) as *capital* = 3.274 *income* − 3.55. My estimates gave roughly similar results. This would place *s* around 30 per cent, though this figure should be raised to account for the underutilization of capital during a part of that period. It is also not clear how the junking process (see below) was reflected in these figures.

The average rate of growth of real national income over the period 1879–1941 was some 3.3 per cent. See Table V and Appendix B of Essay II.

The reader will now see that the assumption of constant α and σ is not entirely necessary, and that the whole problem can be worked out with variable α and σ.

III

The Effects of Growth

Our next problem is to explore what happens when investment does grow at some constant percentage rate r, which, however, is not necessarily equal to the equilibrium rate $\alpha\sigma$. It will be necessary to introduce two additional concepts: average propensity to save I/Y and the average ratio of productive capacity to capital P/K. To simplify the problem, we shall assume that

1. $I/Y = \alpha$, so that the average propensity to save is equal to the marginal.

2. $P/K = s$, i.e. the ratio of productive capacity to capital for the whole economy is equal to that of the new investment projects.

We shall consider first the special simple case $\sigma = s$, and then the more general case when $\sigma < s$.[11]

Case 1: $\sigma = s$. Since $I = I_0 e^{rt}$, capital, being the sum of all net investments, equals

$$(8) \qquad K = K_0 + I_0 \int_0^t e^{rt}dt = K_0 + \frac{I_0}{r}(e^{rt} - 1).$$

As t becomes large, K will approach the expression

$$(9) \qquad \frac{I_0}{r}e^{rt},$$

so that capital will also grow at a rate approaching r.

As $Y = (1/\alpha)I_0 e^{rt}$, the ratio of income to capital is

$$(10) \qquad \frac{Y}{K} = \frac{\dfrac{1}{\alpha}I_0 e^{rt}}{K_0 + \dfrac{I_0}{r}(e^{rt} - 1)},$$

[11] It is also possible that, owing to capital-saving inventions in existing plants, $\sigma > s$. Formally this case can be excluded by falling back on the definition of depreciation given in note 2. This, however, is not a very happy solution, but the approach used in this paper will hardly offer a better one. I think, however, that α in our society is sufficiently high to make $\sigma > s$ in a continuous state of full employment more an exception than a rule.

and

(11)
$$\lim_{t \to \infty} \frac{Y}{K} = \frac{r}{\alpha}.$$

Thus so long as r and α remain constant (or change in the same proportion) no 'deepening' of capital takes place. This, roughly speaking, was the situation in the United States over the last seventy years or so prior to World War II.

Substituting $K = P/s$ into (11) we obtain

(12)
$$\lim_{t \to \infty} \frac{Y}{P} = \frac{r}{\alpha s}.$$

Since in the present case $\sigma = s$,

(13)
$$\lim_{t \to \infty} \frac{Y}{P} = \frac{r}{\alpha \sigma}.$$

The expression

(14)
$$\theta = \frac{r}{\alpha \sigma}$$

may be called the *coefficient of utilization*. When the economy grows at the equilibrium rate, so that $r = \alpha \sigma$, $\theta = 100$ per cent and productive capacity is fully utilized. But as r falls below $\alpha \sigma$, a fraction of capacity $(1 - \theta)$ is gradually left unused.[12] *Thus the failure of the economy to grow at the required rate creates unused capacity and unemployment.*

Case 2: $\sigma < s$. As investment proceeds at the rate I, new projects with a productive capacity of Is are built. Since the productive capacity of the whole economy increases only by $I\sigma$, it follows that somewhere in the economy (not excluding the new projects) productive capacity is reduced by $I(s - \sigma)$. Therefore every year an amount of capital equal to $I(s - \sigma)/s$ becomes useless.

The problem can now be approached from two points of view. The amounts $I(s - \sigma)/s$ can be looked upon as capital losses, which are not taken into account in calculating income and investment.[13] In this case, I still indicates the rate of net investment, and all other

[12] It should be noted that if r, α, and σ are constant, θ is also a constant. Even though the economy fails to grow at the required rate, the relative disparity between its capacity and income does not become wider, because its capital also grows not at the $\alpha \sigma$ but at the r rate.

[13] These losses are not necessarily losses in the accounting sense. See note 14.

symbols retain their old meaning, except that capital has to be redefined as the integral of investment *minus* capital losses: every year chunks of capital (over and above depreciation) are written off and junked. The annual addition to capital will then be

$$(15) \qquad \frac{dK}{dt} = I - \frac{I(s - \sigma)}{s} = I\frac{\sigma}{s},$$

and

$$(16) \qquad K = K_0 + I_0\frac{\sigma}{s}\int_0^t e^{rt}dt = K_0 + I_0\frac{\sigma}{sr}(e^{rt} - 1).$$

Also,

$$(17) \qquad \lim_{t\to\infty}\frac{Y}{K} = \frac{r}{\alpha}\cdot\frac{s}{\sigma},$$

and

$$(18) \qquad \lim_{t\to\infty}\frac{Y}{P} = \frac{r}{\alpha\sigma},$$

which is exactly the same result we had in (13).

The second approach consists in treating the amounts $I(s - \sigma)/s$ not as capital losses but as a special allowance for obsolescence. Net investment would then have to be defined not as I, but as $I\sigma/s$. Other symbols would have to be redefined accordingly, and the whole problem could then be reworked in the same way as on pp. 76–7.

In a sense the choice between these two methods is a matter of bookkeeping; depending upon the character of the problem in hand, one or the other can be used, though I suspect that the second method can easily become misleading. The nature of the process will be the same whichever method is used. The fact is that, owing to a difference between s and σ, the construction of new investment projects makes certain assets (not excluding the new projects them-selves) useless, because under the new conditions brought about by changes in demand, or a rise in the wage rates, or both, the products of these assets cannot be sold.[14] As stated on p. 73 the difference

[14] To be strictly true, the statement in the text would require considerable divisibility of capital assets. In the absence of such divisibility, the expression 'junking' should not be taken too literally.

The fact that these assets may still be operated to some extent or that their products are sold at lower prices or that both these conditions exist does not invalidate our argument, because σ, being expressed in real terms, will be higher than it would be if the assets were left completely unused.

between s and σ is created either by misdirection of investment or by the lack of balance between the propensity to save on the one hand, and the growth of labor, discovery of natural resources, and technological progress on the other. So long as mistakes are made or this lack of balance exists, the junking process is inevitable.

From a social point of view, the junking process is not necessarily undesirable. In this country, where saving involves little hardship, it may be perfectly justified. But it may present a serious obstacle to the achievement of full employment, because the owners of capital assets headed for the junk pile will try to avoid the losses. So long as they confine themselves to changes in their accounting practices, no special consequences will follow. But it is more likely that they will try to accumulate larger reserves either by reducing their own consumption or by charging higher prices (or paying lower wages). As a result, the total propensity to save may rise. This will be exactly the opposite measure from what is needed to avoid the junking process, and will of course lead to greater trouble, though I am not prepared to say to what extent capital owners will succeed in passing on these losses.

In so far as they are able to control new investment, they will try to avoid losses by postponing it. Consequently, the rate of growth may well be depressed below the required $\alpha\sigma$, and unused capacity will develop. Our present model does not allow us to separate unused capacity into idle capital and idle men, though most likely both will be present.[15] For humanitarian reasons we are more concerned with unemployed men. But *unemployed capital is extremely important, because its presence inhibits new investment.*[16] It presents a grave danger to a full employment equilibrium in a capitalist society.

IV

Guaranteed Growth of Income

In the preceding sections it was shown that a state of full employment can be maintained if investment and income grow at an annual

[15] The presence of unemployed men may be obscured by inefficient utilization of labor, as in agriculture.

[16] It is true that a given capital owner may often have a hard time distinguishing between capital idle because of $\sigma < s$, and capital idle because of $r < \alpha\sigma$. The first kind of idleness, however, is relatively permanent, and cannot be corrected by greater expenditures, while the second is temporary (it is hoped) and is due to poor fiscal and monetary policies.

rate $\alpha\sigma$. The question now arises as to what extent the argument can be reversed: suppose income is guaranteed to grow at the $\alpha\sigma$ rate; will that call forth sufficient investment to generate the needed income?

We are concerned here with a situation where spontaneous investment (i.e. investment made in response to changes in technique, shifts in consumers' preferences, discovery of new resources, etc.) is not sufficient, and therefore a certain amount of induced investment (made in response to a rise in income) is also required.[17] To simplify the argument, let us assume that spontaneous investment is absent altogether. It should also be made clear that the problem is treated from a theoretical point of view, without considering the numerous practical questions that the income guarantee would raise.

If an economy starts from an equilibrium position, an expected rise in income of $Y\alpha\sigma$ will require an investment equal to $Y\alpha\sigma/s$. As before, two cases have to be considered.

1. If σ is equal or reasonably close to s, the resulting amount of investment of $Y\alpha$ will equal the volume of savings that will be made at that level of income, and equilibrium will be maintained.[18] *Thus a mere guarantee of a rise in income* (if taken seriously by the investors) *will actually generate enough investment and income to make the guarantee good without necessarily resorting to a government deficit.*

2. If σ is appreciably below s, investment will probably fall short of savings and equilibrium will be destroyed. The difficulty arises because a full employment rate of investment in the face of a $\sigma < s$ makes the junking process (discussed above) inevitable, while a mere guarantee of a rise in income, as a general rule, lacks the instrument to force the capital owners to discard their equipment. They will simply invest $Y\alpha\sigma/s$ instead of $Y\alpha$. Only if in the economy as a whole there is a considerable number of products the demand for which is highly elastic with respect to income, and a good number of others the demand for which is negatively elastic with respect to income, will a larger amount than $Y\alpha\sigma/s$ be invested and a corresponding amount of capital junked. Of course, if the rise in income is accompanied by shifts in consumers' preferences, the appearance

---

[17] Cf. Alvin H. Hansen, *Fiscal Policy and Business Cycles* (New York, 1944), Part Three, and particularly p. 297.

[18] There is a slight error in the magnitudes in the text because of the use of discontinuous functions.

of new products, aggressive competition, and other changes, the junking process will be speeded up, but if these changes do take place they may give rise to spontaneous investment of their own and the guaranteed *rise* in income will not be important. Still, the assurance of a high and rising income is undoubtedly one of the best methods for encouraging investment.

As explained before, a substantial difference between s and σ simply indicates that with the available labor force and the current progress of technology, the maintenance of full employment under a given α requires the accumulation of capital at a faster rate than it can be used. As a general rule, this applies equally well to both private and public investment, though there may be special cases when, owing to the development of particular consumers' preferences (e.g. for vacations), or to technological reasons (e.g. need for power), or to institutional conditions (as in urban redevelopment), considerable need for public investment still exists.[19]

I am not prepared to say whether we already are or shall soon be faced with a serious difference between s and σ, though I doubt that it was an important problem in the past, except perhaps for the short boom years. My own guess is that we shall be more concerned with the disparity between $\alpha\sigma$ and r, that is, with the failure of income to grow at the required rate.

If, however, the difference between σ and s becomes serious and inhibits investment, or if the junking process proceeds at a faster rate than is deemed socially desirable, the society will have at its disposal two not mutually exclusive methods: (1) the reduction of the propensity to save, or (2) the speeding up of technological progress. I hope that the main emphasis will be placed on the latter.

* * * *

This paper attempted to analyze the relation between investment, rate of growth, and employment. The analysis was carried out on a

[19] As soon as the government enters the picture we find ourselves in a maze of definitional problems. From the point of view of this paper, saving and investment should be understood in reference to the whole economy, including the government, and not to its private sector only. But which government expenditures should be regarded as investment? The difficulty is present in the private sector as well, except that there we can take refuge in formal definitions, which cannot be well applied to government. I leave the question open. Certainly, investment need not be limited to inventories, steel, and concrete.

very abstract and simplified level—a procedure which may be justified at the beginning of an investigation, but which must be corrected later on. In general, there is no such a thing as an absolutely good or bad assumption: what may be safe in one kind of a problem can become fatal in another. Of the several assumptions made here, that regarding depreciation is likely to cause the greatest difficulties, but it is by no means the only one. I hope to develop the whole subject further at a later date.

The central theme of the paper was *the rate of growth*, a concept which has been little used in economic theory, and in which I put much faith as an extremely useful instrument of economic analysis. One does not have to be a Keynesian to believe that employment is somehow dependent on national income, and that national income has something to do with investment. But as soon as investment comes in, growth cannot be left out, because for an individual firm investment may mean *more* capital and *less* labor, but for the economy as a whole (as a general case) investment means *more* capital and *not less* labor. If both are to be profitably employed, a *growth* of income must take place.

IV

Expansion and Employment[1]

'A slow sort of a country,' said the Queen. 'Now, *here*, you see, it takes all the running *you* can do, to keep in the same place. If you want to get somewhere else, you must run at least twice as fast as that.'

Lewis Carroll: *Through the Looking Glass*

In these days of labor shortages and inflation, a paper dealing with the conditions of full employment and with the threat of deflation may well appear out of place. Its publication now is due partly to a two-year lag between the first draft and the final copy; also to the widely held belief that the present inflation is a temporary phenomenon, and that once it is over, the old problem of deflation and unemployment may possibly appear before us again.

* * * *

Our comfortable belief in the efficacy of Say's Law has been badly shaken in the last fifteen years. Both events and discussions have shown that supply does not automatically create its own demand. A part of income generated by the productive process may not be returned to it; this part may be saved and hoarded. As Keynes put it, 'Unemployment develops . . . because people want the moon; men cannot be employed when the object of desire (i.e. money) is something which cannot be produced. . . . '[2] The core of the problem then is the public's desire to hoard. If no hoarding takes place, employment can presumably be maintained.

This sounds perfectly straight and simple; and yet it leaves some-

---

[1] [Reprinted by permission from *The American Economic Review*, Vol. 37 (Mar., 1947), pp. 34–55. The mathematical derivations on which this paper is based are given in greater detail in Essay III. As indicated in the Foreword, I am not quite happy with the concepts used here. A concurrent reading of the relevant part of the Foreword (pp. 6–8) is recommended.]

[2] John M. Keynes, *The General Theory of Employment Interest and Money* (New York, 1936), p. 235.

thing unexplained. Granted that absence of hoarding is a *necessary* condition for the maintenance of full employment, is it also a *sufficient* condition? Is the absence of hoarding *all* that is necessary for the avoidance of unemployment? This is the impression *The General Theory* gives. And yet, on a different plane, we have some notions about an increasing productive capacity which must somehow be utilized if unemployment is to be avoided. Will a mere absence of hoarding assure such a utilization? Will not a continuous increase in expenditures (and possibly in the money supply) be necessary in order to achieve this goal?

The present paper deals with this problem. It attempts to find the conditions needed for the maintenance of full employment over a period of time, or more exactly, *the rate of growth of national income* which the maintenance of full employment requires. This rate of growth is analyzed in Section I. Section II is essentially a digression on some conceptual questions and alternative approaches. It may be omitted by the busy reader. Section III is concerned with the *dual* character of the investment process; that is, with the fact that investment not only generates income but also increases productive capacity. Therefore the effects of investment on employment are less certain and more complex than is usually supposed. In Section IV a few examples from existing literature on the subject are given, and Section V contains some concluding remarks. The most essential parts of the paper are presented in Sections I and III.

As in many papers of this kind, a number of simplifying assumptions are made. Most of them will become apparent during the discussion. Two may be noted at the outset. First, events take place simultaneously, without any lags. Second, income, investment, and saving are defined in the *net* sense, i.e. exclusive of depreciation. The latter is understood to refer to the cost of replacement of the depreciated asset by another one of *equal* productive capacity.[2a] These assumptions are not entirely essential to the argument. The discussion could be carried out with lags, and, if desired, in gross terms or with a different concept of depreciation. Some suggestions along these lines are made in Section II. But it is better to begin with as simple a statement of the problem as possible, bearing in mind of course the nature of assumptions made.

[2a] [No distinction is made in this essay between replacement and depreciation. See Essay VII.]

I

The Rate of Growth

It is perfectly clear that the requirement that income paid out should be returned to the productive process, or that savings be equal to investment, or other expressions of the same idea, are simply formulas for maintaining the existing level of income. If underemployment was present yesterday, it would still remain today. If yesterday's income was at a full employment level, that *income level* would be retained today. It may no longer, however, correspond to full employment.

Let yesterday's full employment income equal an annual rate of 150 billion dollars, and let the average propensity to save equal, say, 10 per cent. If now 15 billions are annually invested, one might expect full employment to be maintained. But during this process, capital equipment of the economy will have increased by an annual rate of 15 billions—for after all, investment *is* the formation of capital.[3] Therefore, the productive capacity of the economy has also increased.

The effects of this increase on employment will depend on whether or not *real income* has also increased. Since money income has remained, as assumed, at the 150 billion annual level, an increase in real income can be brought about only by a corresponding fall in the general price level. This indeed has been the traditional approach to problems of this kind, an approach which we shall have to reject for the following reasons:

1. The presence of considerable monopolistic elements (in industry and labor) in our economy makes unrealistic the assumption that a falling *general* price level could be achieved without interfering with full employment. This of course does not exclude *relative* price changes. As a matter of fact, if industries subject to faster-

[3] The identification of investment with capital formation is reasonably safe in a private economy where only a small part of resources is disposed of by the government. When this part becomes substantial, complications arise. This question will be taken up again in Section II. Meanwhile, we shall disregard it and divide total national income, irrespective of source, into investment (i.e. capital formation) and consumption.

The term 'national income' is understood here in a broad sense, as total output minus depreciation. Perhaps 'net national product' would be more appropriate for our purposes.

than-average technological progress do not reduce their prices to some extent, a constant general price level cannot be maintained.

2. For an economy saddled with a large public debt and potentially faced (in peacetime) with serious employment problems, a falling price level is in itself undesirable.

3. With a constant propensity to save and a given rate of real investment, a falling price level can bring about larger real income only in the special cases where prices of consumers' goods fall more rapidly than those of investment goods.[3a]

4. Finally, the assumption of a falling general price level would obscure—and I believe quite unnecessarily—the main subject we are concerned with here.

For these reasons, a *constant general price level* is assumed throughout this paper. But, from a theoretical point of view, this is a convenience rather than a necessity. The discussion could be carried on with a falling or a rising price level.

To come back to the increase in capacity. If both money and real national income thus remain fixed at the 150 billion annual level, the creation of the new capital equipment will have one or more of the following effects: (1) The new capital remains unused; (2) The new capital is used at the expense of previously constructed capital, whose labor and/or markets the new capital has taken away; (3) The new capital is substituted for labor (and possibly for other factors).

The first case represents a waste of resources. That capital need not have been constructed in the first place. The second case—the substitution of new capital for existing capital (before the latter is worn out, since investment is defined here in the net sense)—takes place all the time and, in reasonable magnitudes, is both unavoidable and desirable in a free dynamic society. It is when this substitution proceeds on a rather large scale that it can become socially wasteful; also, losses sustained or expected by capital owners will make them oppose new investment—a serious danger for an economy with considerable monopolistic elements.

Finally, capital may be substituted for labor. If this substitution results in a *voluntary* reduction in the labor force or in the length of the work week, no objections can be raised. Such a process has of

[3a] [This paragraph was rewritten to make its meaning clearer.]

course been going on for many years. But in our economy it is very likely that at least a part of this substitution–if carried on at an extensive scale—will be involuntary, so that the result will be unemployment.

The tools used in this paper do not allow us to distinguish between these three effects of capital formation, though, as will appear later, our concepts are so defined that a voluntary reduction in the number of manhours worked is excluded. In general, it is not unreasonable to assume that in most cases all three effects will be present (though not in constant proportions), and that capital formation not accompanied by an increase in income will result in unemployed capital and labor.

These problems do not arise in the standard Keynesian system because it is not concerned with changes in capacity. It can therefore assume that employment is a function of national income, an assumption which admittedly can be justified only over short periods of time. Clearly, the full employment income of 1941 could not maintain full employment today. While Keynes's approach—the treatment of employment as a function of income—is a reasonable first approximation, we shall go a step further and assume instead that *the fraction of labor force employed is a function of the ratio between national income and productive capacity.* This should be an improvement, but we must admit the difficulties of determining productive capacity, both conceptually and statistically. These are obvious and need not be elaborated. We shall mean by productive capacity the total output of the economy at what is usually called full employment (with due allowance for frictional and seasonal unemployment), such factors as consumers' preferences, price and wage structures, intensity of competition, and so on being given.

The answer to the problem of unemployment lies of course in a growing income. If after capital equipment has increased by (an annual rate of) 15 billions an income of 150 billions leaves some capacity unused, then a higher magnitude of income can be found—say 155 or 160 billions—which will do the job. There is nothing novel or startling about this conclusion. The idea that a capitalist economy needs growth goes back, in one form or another, at least to Marx. The trouble really is that the idea of growth is too easily taken for granted. It is always treated as an afterthought, to be added to one's speech or article if requested, but very seldom incorporated in its body. Even then it is regarded as a function of some abstract technological progress which somehow results in increasing productivity per manhour, and which takes place quite independently of capital formation. And yet, our help in the industrialization of undeveloped countries will take the form not only of supplying technical advice and textbooks, but also of actual machinery and goods. Certainly the 80 odd billion dollars of net capital formation created in the United States in the period 1919–29 had a considerable effect on our productive capacity.[4]

A change in productive capacity of a country is a function of changes in its natural resources (discovery of new ones or depletion of others), in its labor force (more correctly, manhours available), in capital, and in the state of technique.[5] Since changes in natural resources and technique are very difficult concepts, we can express changes in total capacity via changes in the quantity and productivity of labor or of capital. The traditional approach builds around labor. Several recent studies have computed the magnitude of total output at full employment as a product of the expected labor force (subdivided into several classes) and its expected average productivity (in each class).[6] This procedure does not imply that the other three factors (natural resources, technology, and capital) remain constant; rather that their variations are all reflected in the changes in the productivity of labor.

It is also possible to put capital in the center of the stage and to estimate variations in total capacity by measuring the changes in the quantity of capital and in its productivity, the latter reflecting changes currently taking place in natural resources, technology, and the labor force. From a practical point of view, the labor approach has obvious advantages, at least in some problems, because labor is a more homogeneous and easily measurable factor. But from a theoretical point of view, the capital approach is more promising and for this reason: the appearance of an extra workman or his decision to work longer hours *only* increases productive capacity without, however, generating any income. But the construction of

[4] This figure, in 1929 prices, is taken from Simon Kuznets, *National Income and Its Composition, 1919–1938*, Vol. I (New York, 1941), p. 269. The actual figure is 79.1 billion dollars.
[5] Taking other conditions listed on p. 87 as given.
[6] See for instance E. E. Hagen and N. B. Kirkpatrick, 'The National Output at Full Employment in 1950,' *The American Economic Review*, Vol. 34 (Sept., 1944), pp. 472–500.

a new factory has a *dual* effect: *it increases productive capacity and it generates income.*

The emphasis on this dual character of the investment process is the essence of the approach in this paper to the problem of employment. If investment increases productive capacity and also creates income, what should be the magnitude of investment, or at what rate should it grow, in order to make the increase in income equal to that of productive capacity?[7] Couldn't an equation be set up, one side of which would represent the increase (or the rate of increase) of productive capacity, and the other side that of income, and the solution of which would yield the required *rate of growth?*

We shall attempt to set up such an equation. It will be first expressed in symbolic form, and later illustrated by a numerical example.

Let investment proceed at an annual rate of I, and let annual productive capacity (net value added) per dollar of newly created capital be equal on the average to s. Thus if it requires, say, 3 dollars of capital to produce (in terms of annual net value added) one dollar of output, s will equal one-third or 33.3 per cent per year. It is not meant that s is the same in all firms or industries. It depends of course on the nature of capital constructed and on many other factors. Its treatment here as a given magnitude is a simplification which can be readily dispensed with.

The productive capacity of I dollars invested will thus be Is dollars per year. But it is possible that the operation of new capital will take place, at least to some extent, at the expense of previously constructed plants, with which the new capital will compete both for markets and for factors of production (mainly labor). If as a result, the output of existing plants must be curtailed, it would be useless to assert that the productive capacity of the *whole economy* has increased by Is dollars per year.[8] It has actually increased by a smaller amount which will be indicated by $I\sigma$.[9] The symbol σ indicates what may be called the *potential social average productivity of investment.* Such a long name calls for an explanation.

[7] This statement of the problem presupposes that full employment has already been reached and must only be maintained. With a small extra effort we could begin with a situation where some unemployment originally existed.

[8] These comparisons must of course be made at a full employment level of national income. See also pp. 94–6.

[9] We are disregarding here external economies obtained by existing plants from the newly constructed ones.

1. As stated above, σ is concerned with the increase in productive capacity of the whole society and not with the productive capacity per dollar invested in the new plants taken by themselves, that is, with s. A difference between s and σ indicates a certain misdirection of investment, or—more important—that investment proceeds at too rapid a rate as compared with the growth of labor and the progress of technology. This question will be taken up again in Section II.

2. σ should not be confused with other related concepts, such as the traditional marginal productivity of capital. These concepts are usually based on a *ceteris paribus* assumption regarding the quantity of other factors and the state of technique. It should be emphasized that the use of σ does not imply in the least that labor, natural resources, and technology remain fixed. It would be more correct therefore to say that σ indicates the increase in productive capacity which *accompanies*, rather than which is caused by, each dollar invested.

3. For our purposes, the most important property of σ is its *potential character*. It deals not with an increase in national income but with that of the *productive potential* of the economy. A high σ indicates that the economy is *capable* of increasing its output relatively fast. But whether this increased capacity will actually result in greater output or greater unemployment, depends on the behavior of money income.

The expression $I\sigma$ is the supply side of our system; it is the increase in output which the economy *can* produce. On the demand side we have the multiplier theory, too familiar to need any elaboration, except for the emphasis on the obvious but often forgotten fact that, with any given marginal propensity to save, to be indicated by α, an increase in national income is not a function of investment, but of the *increment* in investment. If investment today, however large, is equal to that of yesterday, national income of today will be just equal and not any larger than that of yesterday. All this is obvious, and is stressed here to underline the lack of symmetry between the effects of investment on productive capacity and on national income.

Let investment increase at an absolute annual rate of ΔI (e.g. by two billions per year), and let the corresponding absolute annual increase in income be indicated by ΔY. We have then

$$(1) \qquad\qquad \Delta Y = \Delta I \, \frac{1}{\alpha},$$

where $\frac{1}{\alpha}$ is of course the multiplier.

Let us now assume that the economy is in a position of a full employment equilibrium, so that its national income equals its productive capacity.[10] To retain this position, income and capacity should increase at the same rate. The annual increase in potential capacity equals $I\sigma$. The annual increase in actual income is expressed by $\Delta I(1/\alpha)$. Our objective is to make them equal. This gives us the fundamental equation

$$(2) \qquad\qquad \Delta I \, \frac{1}{\alpha} = I\sigma.$$

To solve this equation, we multiply both sides by α and divide by I, obtaining

$$(3) \qquad\qquad \frac{\Delta I}{I} = \alpha\sigma.$$

The left side of expression (3) is the absolute annual increase (or the absolute rate of growth) in investment—ΔI—divided by the volume of investment itself; or in other words, it is the relative increase in investment, or the annual relative rate of growth of investment. Thus the maintenance of full employment requires that investment grow at the annual relative rate of $\alpha\sigma$.

So much for investment. We shall now assume that the marginal and average propensities to save are equal and constant, i.e. that income is a constant multiple of investment. Therefore income must also grow at the same annual relative rate of $\alpha\sigma$.[10a]

To summarize, the maintenance of a continuous state of full employment requires that *investment and income grow at a constant annual relative (or compound interest) rate* equal to the product of the

[10] See note 7.

[10a] [This paragraph was rewritten. In the original text only the marginal propensity to save was assumed to be constant. But for income and investment to grow at the same relative rate, the average propensity to save must be constant and hence equal to the marginal. In the remaining part of the paper, the word 'marginal' before propensity to save has been deleted.

A model in which the marginal and average propensities to save are different is presented in Essay IX.]

propensity to save and the average (to put it briefly) productivity of investment.[11]

This result can be made clearer by a numerical example. Let $\sigma = 25$ per cent per year, $\alpha = 12$ per cent, and $Y = 150$ billions per year. If full employment is to be maintained, an amount equal to $150 \times \dfrac{12}{100}$ should be invested. This will raise productive capacity by the amount invested times σ, i.e. by $150 \times \dfrac{12}{100} \times \dfrac{25}{100}$, and national income will have to rise by the same annual amount. But the relative rise in income will equal the absolute increase divided by the income itself, i.e.

$$(4) \qquad \frac{150 \times \dfrac{12}{100} \times \dfrac{25}{100}}{150} = \frac{12}{100} \times \frac{25}{100} = \alpha\sigma = 3 \text{ per cent.}$$

These results were obtained on the assumption that α, the propensity to save, and σ, the average productivity of investment, remain constant. The reader can see that this assumption is not necessary for the argument, and that the whole problem can be easily reworked with variable α and σ. Some remarks about a changing α are made on pp. 100–101.

The expression (3) indicates (in a very simplified manner) conditions needed for the maintenance of full employment over a period of time. It shows that it is not sufficient, in Keynesian terms, that savings of yesterday be invested today, or, as it is often expressed, that investment offset savings. Investment of today must always exceed savings of yesterday. A mere absence of hoarding will not do. An injection of new money (or dishoarding) must take place every day. Moreover, this injection must proceed, in absolute terms, at an accelerated rate. The economy must continuously expand.[11a]

---

[11] The careful reader may be disturbed by the lack of clear distinction between increments and rates of growth here and elsewhere in the text. If some confusion exists, it is due to my attempt to express these concepts in non-mathematical form. Actually they all should be stated in terms of rates of growth (derivatives in respect to time). See Essay III.

[11a] After this paper was sent to the printer, I happened to stumble on an article by R. F. Harrod, published in 1939, which contained a number of ideas similar to those presented here. 'An Essay in Dynamic Theory,' *The Economic Journal*, Vol. 49 (Mar., 1939), pp. 14–33.

II

The Argument Re-examined

The busy reader is urged to omit this section and proceed directly to Section III. The present section is really a long footnote which re-examines the concepts and suggests some alternative approaches. Its purpose is, on the one hand, to indicate the essential limitations of the preceding discussion, and on the other, to offer a few suggestions which may be of interest to others working in this field.

It was established in Section I that the maintenance of full employment requires income and investment to grow at an annual relative rate equal to $\alpha\sigma$. The meaning of this result will naturally depend on those of α and σ. Unfortunately neither of them is devoid of ambiguity.

The propensity to save—α—is a relatively simple concept in a private economy where only a small part of resources is handled by the government. National income can be divided, without too much trouble, into investment and consumption, even though it is true that the basis for this distinction is often purely formal.[12] But on the whole it sounds quite reasonable to say that if the propensity to save is α, then an α fraction of income is saved by the public and invested in income-producing assets.

When a substantial part of the economy's resources is disposed of by the government, two interpretations of the propensity to save, or of savings and investment in general, appear possible. The first is to continue dividing the total output, whether produced by government or by private business, into consumption and investment. This method is implicitly followed in this paper. But a question arises regarding the meaning and stability of α. It makes sense to say that the public (or a person) saves, in accordance with the size of its income, habits, expectations, etc., a certain (not necessarily constant) fraction of its disposable income (i.e. after income and social security taxes), but can a similar statement be made regarding total national income, a good part of which is not placed at the disposal of the public? Also it is difficult to divide government expenditures into consumption and investment.

[12] Thanks are due to George Jaszi for his persistent efforts to enlighten me on this subject. The division of national income into investment and consumption is really a more difficult task than my text might imply.

Another method would limit α to disposable income only, and then provide for government expenditures separately. It would be necessary then to find out the effects of these expenditures on productive capacity.

Depreciation raises another problem. Since all terms are net, the meaning and magnitude of α will also depend on those of depreciation, irrespective of the choice between the above two methods. Depreciation has been defined here (see p. 84) as the cost of replacing a worn-out asset by another one with an equal productive capacity. While this approach is about as bad or as good as any other, the difficulty still remains that businesses ordinarily do not use this definition, and therefore arrive at a different estimate of their net incomes, which in turn determine their propensity to save.

I do not have ready answers to these questions, though I do not consider them insurmountable. I am mentioning them here in order to indicate the limitations of the present argument and obstacles that will have to be overcome if a more exact analysis is to be undertaken.

Even more ambiguous is σ. It springs from s which has already been used, in one form or another, in economic literature, particularly in connection with the acceleration principle.[13] Here it indicates the annual amount of income (net value added) which can be produced by a dollar of newly created capital. It varies of course among firms and industries, and also in space and time, though a study recently made seems to indicate that it has been quite stable, at least in the United States and Great Britain, over the last 70 years or so.[14] Whether s has or has not been relatively constant is not essential for our discussion. The real question is whether such a concept has meaning, whether it makes sense to say that a given economy or a plant has a certain capacity. Traditional economic thinking would, I fear, be against such an approach. Unfortunately, it is impossible to discuss this question here. I believe that our actual

[13] See for instance Paul A. Samuelson, 'Interactions between the Multiplier Analysis and the Principle of Acceleration,' *The Review of Economic Statistics*, Vol. 21 (May, 1939), pp. 75–8 [reprinted in The American Economic Association, *Readings in Business Cycle Theory* (Philadelphia, 1944), pp. 261–9]; also R. F. Harrod, *The Trade Cycle* (Oxford, 1936). These authors, however, used not the ratio of income to capital, but of consumption to capital, or rather the reciprocal of this ratio.

[14] See Ernest H. Stern, 'Capital Requirements in Progressive Economies,' *Economica*, n.s., Vol. 12 (Aug., 1945), pp. 163–71.

experience during the last depression and World War II, as well as a number of empirical studies, show that productive capacity, both of a plant and of the whole economy, is a meaningful concept, though this capacity, as well as the magnitude of s, should be treated as a *range* rather than as a single number.

In some problems s may be interpreted as the minimum annual output (net value added) per dollar invested which will make the investment worth undertaking. If this output falls below s, the investor suffers a loss or at least a disappointment, and may be unwilling to replace the asset after it has depreciated.

All these doubts apply to σ even more than to s. As explained above, σ differs from s in that it indicates the annual increment in capacity of the *whole economy* per dollar invested, rather than of the newly created capital taken by itself. Differences between s and σ may occur for the following reasons:

1. New plants are not operated to capacity because they are unable to find a market for their products.

2. Old plants reduce their output because their markets are captured by new plants.

As productive capacity has no meaning except in relation to consumers' preferences, in both of the above cases productive capacity of the country is increased by a smaller amount than that of the new plants; in the limiting case it is not increased at all, and $\sigma = 0$, however high s may be. But it must be made clear that the test of whether or not σ is below s can be made only under conditions (actual or assumed) of full employment. If markets are not large enough because of insufficiency of effective demand due to unemployment, it cannot yet be concluded that σ is below s.

3. The first two cases can occur irrespective of the volume of current investment. A more important case arises when investment proceeds at such a rapid rate that a shortage of other factors relative to capital develops. New plants may be unable to get enough labor, or more likely, labor (and other factors) is transferred to new plants from previously constructed ones, whose capacity therefore declines. In its actual manifestation, case 3 can hardly be separated from cases 1 and 2, because to the individual firm affected the difference between s and σ takes the form of a cost-price disparity. The reason why we are trying to separate the first two cases from the third lies in the bearing of this distinction on practical policy. The first two

cases arise from an error of judgment on the part of investors (past or present) which is, at least to some extent, unavoidable and not undesirable. The struggle for markets and the replacement of weaker (or older) firms and industries by stronger (or newer) ones is the essence of progress in a capitalist society. The third case, on the other hand, may result from poor fiscal or monetary policy. It constitutes an attempt to invest too much, to build more capital than the economy can utilize even at full employment. Such a situation can develop if an economy with a high propensity to save tries to maintain full employment by investing all its savings in capital goods. But it should be made clear that the expressions 'too much capital' or 'high propensity to save' are used in a relative sense—in comparison with the growth of other factors, that is, natural resources, labor, and technology.

The use of σ certainly does not imply that these factors remain fixed. As a matter of fact, it would be very interesting to explore the use of a more complex function as the right side of expression (2) instead of $I\sigma$, a function in which the growth of labor, natural resources, and technology would be presented explicitly, rather than through their effects on σ.[15] I did not attempt it because I wanted to express the idea of growth in the simplest possible manner. One must also remember that in the application of mathematics to economic problems, diminishing returns appear rapidly, and that the construction of complex models requires so many specific assumptions as to narrow down their applicability.

And yet it may be interesting to take a step in another direction, namely to introduce lags. In this paper both the multiplier effect and the increase in capacity are supposed to take place simultaneously and without any lag. Actually, the multiplier may take some time to work itself out, and certainly the construction of a capital asset takes time. For secular problems these lags are not likely to be of great importance, but they may play an essential role over the cycle. We shall return to this question below.

Finally, it is possible to approach the problem of growth from a different point of view. It was established here that the rate of growth required for a full employment equilibrium, to be indicated

---

[15] Some work along these lines has been done by J. Tinbergen. See his 'Zur Theorie der langfristigen Wirtschaftsentwicklung,' *Weltwirtschaftliches Archiv*, Vol. 55 (May, 1942), pp. 511–49.

by r, is

(5) $$r = \alpha\sigma,$$

so that if α and σ are given, the rate of growth is determined. But the equation (5) can also be solved for α in terms of r and σ, and for σ in terms of r and α. Thus if it is believed that r should be treated as given (for instance by technological progress), and if it is also decided to keep σ at a certain level, perhaps not too far from s, then it is possible to interpret $\alpha = r/\sigma$, as that propensity to save which can be maintained without causing either inflation or unemployment. This approach was used by Ernest Stern in his statistical study of capital requirements of the United Kingdom, the United States, and the Union of South Africa.[16] I also understand from Tibor Scitovsky that he used the same approach in a study not yet published.

It is also possible to treat r and α as given and then determine what $\sigma = r/\alpha$ would have to be. Each approach has its own advantages and the choice depends of course on the nature of the problem in hand. The essential point to be noticed is the relationship between these three variables r, α, and σ, and the fact that if any two of them are given, the value of the third needed for the maintenance of full employment is determined; and if its actual value differs from the required one, inflation in some cases and unused capacity and unemployment in others will develop.

III

The Dual Nature of the Investment Process

We shall continue the discussion of growth by returning to expression (2) above,

(2) $$\Delta I \frac{1}{\alpha} = \overline{I\sigma},$$

which is fundamental to our whole analysis. As a matter of fact, the statement of the problem in this form (2) appears to me at least as important as its actual solution expressed in (3). To repeat, the left side of the equation shows the annual increment in national income and is the demand side; while the right represents the

[16] Stern, op. cit.

annual increase in productive capacity and is the supply side. Alternatively, the left may be called the 'multiplier side,' and the right, the 'σ side.'

The fact that investment appears on both sides of the equation is most important for our purposes; that is, it has a *dual effect:* on the left side it generates income via the multiplier effect; and on the right side it increases productive capacity—the σ effect. The explicit recognition of this dual character of investment could undoubtedly save much argument and confusion. Unless some special assumptions are made, the discussion of the effects of investment on profits, income, employment, etc., cannot be legitimately confined to one side only. For the generation of income and the enlargement of productive capacity often have diametrically opposed effects, and the outcome in each particular case depends on the special circumstances involved.[17]

Analyzing expression (2) further, we notice that even though investment is present on both sides, it does not take the same form. On the σ side we have the *amount* of investment; but on the multiplier side we have not the amount of investment but its annual increment, or its absolute *rate of increase.*

The amount of investment (always in the net sense) may remain constant, or it may go up or down, but so long as it remains positive (and except for the rare case when $\sigma \leqq 0$) productive capacity increases. But if income is to rise as well, it is not enough that just any amount be invested: *an increase in income is not a function of the amount invested; it is the function of the increment of investment.* Thus the whole body of investment, so to speak, increases productive capacity, but only its very top—the increment—increases national income.

In this probably lies the explanation why inflations have been so rare in our economy in peacetime, and why even in relatively prosperous periods a certain degree of underemployment has usually

---

[17] The effects of labor-saving machinery on employment of labor is a good case in point. Some economists, particularly those connected with the labor movement, insist that such machines displace labor and create unemployment. Their opponents are equally sure that the introduction of labor-saving devices reduces costs and generates income, thus increasing employment. Both sides cite ample empirical evidence to prove their contentions, and neither side is wrong. But each presents an incomplete picture from which no definite conclusion can be derived.

been present. Indeed, it is difficult enough to keep investment at some reasonably high level year after year, but the requirement that it always be rising is not likely to be met for any considerable length of time.

Now, if investment and therefore income do not grow at the required rate, unused capacity develops. Capital and labor become idle. It may not be apparent why investment, by increasing productive capacity, creates unemployment of labor. Indeed, as was argued on pp. 86–7, this need not always be the case. Suppose national income remains constant or rises very slowly while new houses are being built. It is possible that new houses will be rented out at the expense of older buildings and that no larger rents will be paid than before; or that the new houses will stand wholly or partly vacant with no change in rents.[18] But it is also possible, and indeed very probable, that the complete or partial utilization of the new buildings, which are usually better than the old ones, will require the payment of larger rents, with the result that less income will be left for the purchase of, say, clothing—thus causing unemployment in the clothing trades. So the substitution of capital for labor need not take the obvious form of labor-saving machinery; it may be equally effective in a more circuitous way.

The unemployment of men is considered harmful for obvious reasons. But idle buildings and machinery, though not arousing our humanitarian instincts, can be harmful because their presence inhibits new investment. Why build a new factory when existing ones are working at half capacity? It is certainly not necessary to be dogmatic and assert that no plant or house should ever be allowed to stand idle, and that as soon as unused capacity develops the economy plunges into a depression. There is no need, nor is it possible or desirable, to guarantee that every piece of capital ever constructed will be fully utilized until it is worn out. When population moves from Oklahoma to California, some buildings in Oklahoma will stand idle; or when plastics replace leather in women's handbags, the leather industry may suffer. Such changes form the very life of a free dynamic society, and should not be interfered with. The point is that there should be no vacant houses while

---

[18] It is worth noticing that in both cases the construction of the new houses represents a misdirection of resources, at least to some extent. But a complete avoidance of such misdirection is impossible and even undesirable.

prospective tenants are present but cannot afford to live in them because of unemployment due to insufficient growth of income and investment.

The extent to which unused capacity, present or expected, inhibits new investment greatly depends on the structure of industry and the character of the economy in general. The more atomistic it is, the stronger is competition, the more subject it is to territorial, technological, and other changes, the smaller is the effect of unused capacity on new investment. One firm may have an idle plant, while another in the same industry builds a new one; steel may be depressed while plastics are expanding. It is when an industry is more or less monopolized, or when several industries are financially connected, that unused capacity presents a particularly serious threat to new investment.

Strictly speaking, our discussion so far, including equation (2), has been based on the assumption that α remained constant. If α varies within the time period concerned, the relation between investment and income becomes more involved. What the left side of the equation (2) requires is that *income* increase; and investment must grow only in so far as its growth is necessary for the growth of income. So if α declines sufficiently fast, a growing income can be achieved with a constant or even falling investment. In the United States, years of declining α have evidently been offset by others of rising α, because available information indicates that over the seventy years or so before World War II the fraction of income saved was reasonably constant, possibly with a slight downward trend.[19] Therefore, in the absence of direct government interference, it would seem better not to count too much on a falling α, at least for the time being.

In general, a high α presents a serious danger to the maintenance of full employment, because investment may fail to grow at the required high rate, or will be physically unable to do so without creating a substantial difference between s and σ. This difference indicates that some capital assets become unprofitable and their owners suffer losses or at least disappointments (see pp. 95–6). Space does not permit me to develop this idea at greater length

[19] See Simon Kuznets, *National Product since 1869*, National Bureau of Economic Research (mimeographed, 1945), p. II-89 [since published under the same title (New York, 1946), p. 119]. I do not mean that we must always assume a constant α; rather that we lack sufficient evidence to rely on a falling one.

here.[20] But it must be emphasized that what matters is not the magnitude of α taken by itself, but its relation to the growth of labor, natural resources, and technology. Thus a country with new resources, a rapidly growing population, and developing technology is able to digest, so to speak, a relatively large α, while absence or at least a very slow growth of these factors makes a high α a most serious obstacle to full employment.[21] But the problem can be attacked not only by lowering α, but also by speeding up the rate of technological progress, the latter solution being much more to my taste. It must be remembered, however, that technological progress makes it *possible* for the economy to grow, without guaranteeing that this growth will be realized.

In a private capitalist society where α cannot be readily changed, a higher level of income and employment at any given time can be achieved only through increased investment. But investment, as an employment-creating instrument, is a mixed blessing because of its σ effect. The economy finds itself in a serious dilemma: if sufficient investment is not forthcoming today, unemployment will be here today. But if enough is invested today, still more will be needed tomorrow.

It is a remarkable characteristic of a private capitalist economy that while, on the whole, unemployment is a function of the difference between its actual income and its productive capacity, the standard measure, i.e. investment, directed toward raising national income also enlarges productive capacity. It is very likely that the increase in national income will be greater than that of capacity, but the whole problem is that the increase in income is temporary and presently peters out (the usual multiplier effect), while capacity has been increased for good. As far as unemployment is concerned, investment is at the same time a cure for the disease and the cause of even greater ills in the future.[22]

[20] See Essay III.
[21] Cf. Alvin H. Hansen, *Fiscal Policy and Business Cycles* (New York, 1941), particularly Part IV.
[22] That income-generating effects of investment are temporary and that new and larger amounts must be spent to maintain full employment has been mentioned in economic and popular literature a number of times. Particular use has been made of this fact by opponents of so-called deficit financing, who treat government expenditures as a 'shot in the arm' which must be administered at an ever-increasing dose. What they fail to realize is that exactly the same holds true for private investment.

IV

An Economic Excursion

It may be worth while to browse through the works of several economists of different schools of thought to see their treatment of the σ and of the multiplier effects of investment. I do not intend to make an exhaustive study, but just to present a few examples.

Thus in Marshall's *Principles* capital and investment are looked upon as productive instruments (the σ effect), with little being said about monetary (that is, income or price) effects of investment.[23] The same attitude prevails in Fisher's *Nature of Capital and Income*,[24] and I presume in the great majority of writings not devoted to the business cycle. It is not that these writers were unaware of monetary effects of investment (even though they did not have the multiplier concept as such), but that such questions belonged to a different field, and the problem of aggregate demand was supposed to be taken care of by some variation of Say's Law.

In the business cycle literature we often find exactly the opposite situation. The whole Wicksellian tradition treated economic fluctuations as a result of monetary effects of excessive investment. It is curious that all this investment did not lead to increased output which would counteract its inflationary tendencies. Indeed, as one reads Hayek's *Prices and Production*, one gets an impression that these investment projects never bear fruit and are, moreover, abandoned after the crisis. The σ effect is entirely absent, or at least appears with such a long lag as to make it inoperative. Prosperity comes to an end because the banking system refuses to support inflation any longer.[25]

In Aftalion's hands, σ fares better.[26] His theory of the cycle is based upon what I would call a time lag between the multiplier and

[23] Marshall was very careful, however, to distinguish between the substitution of a particular piece of machinery for particular labor, and the replacement of labor by capital in general. The latter he regarded impossible, because the construction of capital creates demand for labor, essentially a sort of a multiplier effect. See *Principles of Economics*, 8th ed. (London, 1936), p. 523.

[24] Irving Fisher, *The Nature of Capital and Income* (New York, 1906).

[25] Friedrich A. Hayek, *Prices and Production* (London, 1931). I don't mean to say that Professor Hayek is not aware that capital is productive; rather that he did not make use of this fact in his theory of the business cycle. See, however, his 'The "Paradox" of Saving,' *Economica*, Vol. 11 (May, 1931), pp. 125–69.

[26] Albert Aftalion, 'The Theory of Economic Cycles Based on the Capitalistic Technique of Production,' *The Review of Economic Statistics*, Vol. 9 (Oct., 1927), pp. 165–70. This short article contains a summary of his theory.

103

the σ effects. Prosperity is started by income generated by investment in capital goods (the multiplier effect), while no increase in productive capacity has taken place as yet. As investment projects are completed, the resulting increase in productive capacity (the σ effect) pours goods on the market and brings prosperity to an end.

A similar approach is used by Michal Kalecki. His model of the business cycle makes profit expectations, and therefore investment, a function (with appropriate lags) of the relation between national income and the stock of capital. During recovery, investment and income rise, while the accumulation of capital lags behind. Presently, however, due to the structure of the model, the rise of income stops while capital continues to accumulate. This precipitates the downswing.[27]

Space does not allow us to analyze the works of a number of other writers on the subject, among whom Foster and Catchings should be given due recognition for what is so clumsy and yet has so keen an insight.[28] I am also omitting the whole Marxist literature, in which capital accumulation plays such an important role, because that would require a separate study. The few remaining pages of this section will be devoted to J. A. Hobson and Keynes.

Hobson's writings contain so many interesting ideas that it is a great pity he is not read more often.[29] Anti-Keynesians probably like him not much more than they do Keynes, while Keynesians are apt to regard the *General Theory* as the quintessence of all that was worth while in economics before 1936, and may not bother to read earlier writings. I may say that Keynes's own treatment of Hobson, in spite of his generous recognition of the latter's works, may have substantiated this impression.[30]

[27] Michal Kalecki, *Essays in the Theory of Economic Fluctuations* (New York, 1939). See particularly the last essay 'A Theory of the Business Cycle,' pp. 116–49. What Mr. Kalecki's model shows in a general sense is that accumulation of capital cannot proceed for any length of time in a trendless economy (i.e. an economy with a secularly constant income). His other results depend upon the specific assumptions he makes.
[28] William T. Foster and Waddill Catchings, *Profits* (Boston and New York, 1925). This book is the most important of their several published works. It is interesting to note that they did come to the conclusion that ' . . . as long as capital facilities are created at a sufficient rate, there need be no deficiency of consumer income. To serve that purpose, however, facilities must be increased at a constantly accelerating rate' (p. 413). This they regarded quite impossible.
[29] I am particularly referring to his *The Economics of Unemployment* (London, 1922) and *Rationalization and Unemployment* (London, 1930).
[30] See *The General Theory*, pp. 364–71.

Even though both Keynes and Hobson were students of unemployment, they actually addressed themselves to two different problems. Keynes analyzed what happens when savings (of the preceding period) are not invested. The answer was unemployment, but the statement of the problem in this form might easily give the erroneous impression that if savings were invested, full employment would be assured. Hobson, on the other hand, went a step further and stated the problem in this form: suppose savings are invested. Will the new plants be able to dispose of their products? Such a statement of the problem was not at all, as Keynes thought, a mistake.[31] It was a statement of a different, and possibly also a deeper, problem.

Hobson was fully armed with the σ effect of investment, and he saw that it could be answered only by growth. His weakness lay in a poor perception of the multiplier effect and his analysis lacked rigor in general. He gave a demonstration rather than a proof. But the problem to which he addressed himself is just as alive today as it was fifty and twenty years ago.[32]

This discussion, as I suspect almost any other, would be obviously incomplete without some mention of Keynes's treatment of the σ and of the multiplier effects. Keynes's approach is very curious; as a matter of fact, he has two: the familiar short-run analysis, and another which may be called a long-run one.[33]

Keynes's short-run system (later expressed so admirably by Oscar Lange[34]) is based on the assumption that ' . . . the existing skill and quantity of available labor, the existing quality and quantity of available equipment, the existing technique, the degree of competition, the tastes and habits of the consumer . . . ' are all given.[35] Productive capacity thus being given, employment becomes a func-

[31] Ibid. pp. 367–8.

[32] Contrary to popular impression, Hobson does not advocate a maximum reduction in the propensity to save. What he wants is to reduce it to a magnitude commensurable with requirements for capital arising from technological progress—an interesting and reasonable idea.

[33] This whole discussion is based on The General Theory and not on Keynes's earlier writings.

[34] Oscar Lange, 'The Rate of Interest and the Optimum Propensity to Consume,' Economica, n.s., Vol. 5 (Feb., 1938), pp. 12–32 [reprinted in The American Economic Association, Readings in Business Cycle Theory (Philadelphia, 1944), pp. 169–92]. This otherwise excellent paper has a basic defect in the assumption that investment is a function of consumption rather than of the rate of change of consumption.

[35] The General Theory, p. 245. See also pp. 24 and 28.

tion of national income, expressed, to be sure, not in money terms but in 'wage units.' A wage unit, the remuneration for 'an hour's employment of ordinary labor' (p. 41), is of course a perfect fiction, but some such device must be used to translate real values into monetary and vice versa, and one is about as good or as bad as another. The important point for our purposes is the assumption that the amount of equipment (i.e. capital) in existence is given.

Now, the heart of Keynesian economics is the argument that employment depends on income, which in turn is determined by the current volume of investment (and the propensity to save). But investment (in the net sense) is nothing else but the rate of change of capital. Is it legitimate then first to assume the quantity of capital as given, and then base the argument on its rate of change? If the quantity of capital changes, so does (in a typical case) productive capacity, and if the latter changes it can hardly be said that employment is determined solely by the size of national income, expressed in wage units or otherwise. Or putting it in the language of this paper, is it safe and proper to analyze the relation between investment and employment without taking into account the σ effect?

The answer depends on the nature of the problem in hand. In this particular case, Keynes could present two reasons for his disregard of the σ effect. He could assume that the latter operates with at least a one-period lag, the period being understood here as the whole time span assumed in the discussion.[36] Or he could argue that over a typical year the net addition (i.e. net investment) to the stock of capital of a society, such as England or the United States, will hardly exceed some 3 or 5 per cent; since this increment is small when compared with changes in income, it can be ignored.[37]

Both explanations are entirely reasonable provided of course that the period under consideration is not too long. A five-year lag for the σ effect would be difficult to defend, and an increase in the capital stock of some 15 or 20 per cent can hardly be disregarded. I am not aware that Keynes did present either of these explanations; but there is just so much one can do in four hundred pages.

It would be perfectly absurd to say that Keynes was not aware of

[36] This again is not quite safe unless some provision for investment projects started in preceding periods and finished during the present period is made.

[37] The second assumption is specifically made by Professor Pigou in his *Employment and Equilibrium* (London, 1941), pp. 33–4.

the productive qualities of capital. In the *long run* he laid great stress on it, possibly too great. All through the *General Theory* we find grave concern for the diminishing marginal efficiency of capital due, in the long run, to its increasing quantity.[38] There is so much of this kind of argument that it leaves the reader puzzled in the end. We are told that marginal efficiency of capital depends on its scarcity. Well and good. But scarcity relative to what? It could become less scarce relative to other factors, such as labor, so that the marginal productivity of capital in the real sense (i.e. essentially our σ) declined. But then on p. 213 we read: 'If capital becomes less scarce, the excess yield will diminish, without its having become less productive—at least in the physical sense.'

Why then does the marginal efficiency of capital fall? Evidently because capital becomes less scarce relative to income.[39] But why cannot income grow more rapidly if labor is not the limiting factor? Could it be only because of poor fiscal or monetary policy? After all, we have in investment an income-generating instrument; if investment grows more rapidly, so does income. *This* is the multiplier effect of investment on which so much of the *General Theory* is built.

I don't have the answer. Is it possible that, while Keynes disregarded the σ effect in the short-run analysis, he somehow omitted the multiplier effect from the long-run?

V

Concluding Remarks

A traveler who sat in the economic councils of the United States and of the Soviet Union would be much impressed with the emphasis placed on investment and technological progress in both countries. He would happily conclude that the differences between the economic problems of a relatively undeveloped socialist economy and a highly developed capitalist economy are really not as great as they are often made to appear. Both countries want investment and technological progress. But if he continued to listen to the debates, he would presently begin to wonder. For in the Soviet Union investment and technology are wanted in order to enlarge the country's

[38] See for instance pp. 31, 105–6, 217, 219, 220–21, 324, and 375.
[39] There is a third possibility, namely that income is redistributed against the capitalists, but Keynes makes no use of it.

productive capacity. They are wanted essentially as labor-saving devices which would allow a given task to be performed with less labor, thus releasing men for other tasks. In short, they are wanted for their σ effects.

In the United States, on the other hand, little is said about enlarging productive capacity. Technological progress is wanted as the creator of investment opportunities, and investment is wanted because it generates income and creates employment. It is wanted for its multiplier effect.

Both views are correct and each is incomplete. The multiplier is not just another capitalist invention. It can live in a socialist state just as well and it has been responsible for the inflationary pressure which has plagued the Soviet economy since the first five-year plan. And similarly, σ is just as much at home in one country as in another, and its effect—the enlarged productive capacity brought about by accumulation of capital—has undoubtedly had much to do with our peacetime unemployment.

But what is the solution? Shall we reduce α to zero and also abolish technological progress, thus escaping from unemployment into the 'nirvana' of a stationary state? This would indeed be a defeatist solution. It is largely due to technology and saving that humanity has made the remarkable advance of the last two hundred years, and now when our technological future seems so bright, there is less reason to abandon it than ever before.

It is possible that α has been or will be too high compared with the growth of our labor force, the utilization of new resources, and the development of technology. Unfortunately, we have hardly any empirical data to prove or disprove this supposition. The fact that private investment has not absorbed available savings in the past does not prove that they could not be utilized in other ways (e.g. by government), or even that had private business invested them these investments would have been unprofitable; the investing process itself might have created sufficient income to justify the investments. What is needed is a study of the magnitudes of s, of the difference between s and σ which can develop without much harm, and then of the value of α which the economy can digest at its full employment rate of growth.

Even if the resulting magnitude of α is found to be considerably below the existing one, a reduction of α is only one of two solutions, the speeding up of technological progress being the other. But it must be remembered that neither technology, nor of course saving, guarantees a rise in income. What they do is to place in our hands the *power* and the ability to achieve a growing income. And just as any power can become a blessing or a curse, depending upon the use made of it, so can saving and technological progress, depending on our economic policies, result in frustration and unemployment or in an ever-expanding economy.

V

The Problem of Capital Accumulation*

I

Capital formation has now reached a gross annual rate of some thirty-six billion dollars. A somewhat smaller amount would have been less inflationary, but aside from this inconvenience which we still hope will be temporary, there should be every reason for congratulations: the (not entirely expected) prosperity which this capital formation has given rise to as well as the resulting increase in our productive capacity should certainly be welcome. Yet looking at this remarkable amount, many an economist has wondered how much longer the economy will be able to absorb capital at this rapid rate, and what will happen when a drastic fall in capital formation takes place.

Implied by this worry is the belief that the possibilities of the so-called deepening of capital (in the sense of an increasing ratio of capital to output) are limited. Therefore the amount of capital that the economy can absorb, at a given income level and over a given period of time, is limited as well. The more rapidly it accumulates, the sooner investment opportunities are exhausted and a depression ensues.

This is the essence of a view, specifically rejected by Knight and Simons, but widely accepted in the economic literature, particularly in its Marxist, underconsumptionist, and Keynesian branches.[1] In its most definite and explicit form it is based on the assumption

* [Reprinted by permission from *The American Economic Review*, Vol. 38 (Dec., 1948), pp. 777–94. See also Ernest H. Stern's 'The Problem of Capital Accumulation,' and my rejoinder in the same *Review*, Vol. 39 (Dec., 1949), pp. 1160–72. The reader is also referred to the Foreword, pp. 6–8.]

[1] Frank H. Knight, 'Diminishing Returns from Investment,' *The Journal of Political Economy*, Vol. 52 (Mar., 1944), pp. 26–47; Henry C. Simons, 'Hansen on Fiscal Policy,' *The Journal of Political Economy*, Vol. 50 (Apr., 1942), pp. 161–96; Alvin H. Hansen, *Fiscal Policy and Business Cycles* (New York, 1941) and *Economic Policy and Full Employment* (New York, 1947); R. F. Harrod,

that there exists a fairly stable relationship between a given amount of (annual) output (or income) and the stock of capital needed to produce it. This assumption (used also in connection with the acceleration principle) may be definitely stated, as by Paul Sweezy and Harrod, or merely implied, as in the case of Hansen, but in one form or another it is behind all these apprehensions regarding the depressing effects of capital accumulation.[2] For otherwise—if we join the company of Knight and Simons—investment opportunities are practically unlimited. While neither Knight nor Simons would guarantee a permanent prosperity, for an explanation of its end they would look to factors other than capital accumulation. Whether the latter should proceed at the rate of thirty-six billions or greater need not be of particular concern unless some other assumptions or some indirect effects are brought in.[3]

The reader now has a choice. If he accepts the Knight-Simons position, he can stop worrying about capital accumulation and spare himself the trouble of reading this paper. I have no empirical information with which to settle the issue here. The other view, which I myself am inclined to take, is the more pessimistic of the two. Shouldn't we—if only out of curiosity—look into it and see where it leads?

Our journey will be perilous because we shall try, so to speak, to isolate capital accumulation from other economic factors. There will be an artificial flavor to it because (this being a paper in economics) we shall introduce several simplifying assumptions. We shall assume that we deal with a private capitalist economy in which the government plays a minor role;[4] that the relative distribution of income

---

The Trade Cycle (Oxford, 1936); Nicholas Kaldor, 'Stability and Full Employment,' The Economic Journal, Vol. 48 (Dec., 1938), pp. 642–57; Michal Kalecki, 'Full Employment by Stimulating Private Investment?,' Oxford Economic Papers, No. 7 (Mar., 1945), pp. 83–92, and 'Three Ways to Full Employment,' in The Economics of Full Employment, published by the Oxford Institute of Statistics (Oxford, 1944), pp. 39–58; Paul M. Sweezy, The Theory of Capitalist Development (New York, 1942). These are just a few examples.

[2] Not all capital formation represents accumulation. Depreciation, obsolescence, and similar charges should be subtracted.

[3] Knight recognizes that, other things remaining the same, accumulation of capital will gradually reduce its marginal rate of return. But such a process would be very gradual and hardly have much cyclical significance. Its unfavorable effects on investment could be counteracted by reducing the interest rate.

[4] This assumption will be removed when we come to questions of policy in Section III.

between labor and capital remains unchanged; that reasonably small changes in interest rate will not greatly stimulate investment (a major heretical step); that our terms—such as investment and saving—are net of depreciation and similar charges; and that saving includes undistributed corporate profits. We shall add a few more assumptions as we go along. But due to the kindness and power of persuasion of the editor of this *Review*, our journey will not be as long as it might otherwise have been.

We have thus assumed, at least for the purpose of this discussion, that there exists a fairly stable ratio between annual output (or national income) and the capital stock needed for its production, this ratio to be indicated by the letter s.[5] While, strictly speaking, we shall treat s as a given constant, it need not be so. It is certainly not the same among all firms and industries. The national average (if such exists) can be made a function of time, interest rate, or of something else. But it must have some stability, because if s can be anything, our argument falls through and we are back at the Knight-Simons position.

The assumption of a stable s is necessary but not sufficient for the purposes of the theory examined here. If, as investment opportunities disappear, the propensity to save obligingly drops as well, the fall in investment need not cause a reduction in income and employment. There is just a shift from a high investment to a high consumption economy. While such a shift requires considerable mobility of factors, and is neither simple nor easy, the speed of the post-war reconversion has shown that it can be achieved without a major breakdown. A stable propensity to save, to be indicated by α, again need not imply a permanent constancy; it could also be made a function of certain variables. All we need here is its refusal to adjust itself to changes in the volume of investment, and so assure continuous full employment.[6]

Granted a reasonable stability of s (the ratio of national income to capital stock), it follows that for any given level of income there exists some fairly determinate stock of capital needed to produce it, beyond which large-scale investment will not be undertaken in order

[5] The term 'national income' is used in this paper in a broad sense. National product or some variation of it could also be used.

[6] For a discussion of s and α see essays III and IV. No distinction is made here between the average and marginal α.

to increase output. It also follows that the faster capital accumulates, the sooner this saturation point will be reached (provided income remains the same). After it has been reached, investment will be undertaken only in response to various dynamic changes, such as the emergence of new methods of production and new products, population growth and movements, changes in tastes and habits, the appearance of new firms, etc.—which have been so well described by Hansen, Schumpeter, and others. These changes may alter the value of s, or more specifically, may lower it and thus make more capital necessary. They may also break a hole, so to speak, in the existing stock of capital by rendering a part of it useless. In any case, a relative shortage of capital is created, and so long as it persists, prosperity lasts. When the needed capital has been constructed, investment drops and depression begins.

But it is also possible that the stream of investment will raise national income (via the multiplier process) well above its original level. The gap between required and existing capital stock may then widen, at least for a while, before narrowing, and thus give rise to additional investment, via the acceleration principle. A strict distinction between these two kinds of investment is hard to make even conceptually, let alone statistically. While some business cycle theories emphasize the spontaneous type (Hansen, Schumpeter), and others the induced one (Harrod), no one would deny the importance of either. It is possible to construct a theoretical model in which investment and income continuously reinforce each other.[7] But such a model is liable to be unstable, and can hardly be relied on as a means of achieving a continuous prosperity.

This description of the end of prosperity, which has by now become fairly conventional, does not, however, answer one important question: *could* prosperity last longer? Suppose we are in a period when, owing to a rapid accumulation of capital, investment opportunities are nearly exhausted and investment is about to drop off. And suppose also that investors are *somehow* (see Section III) persuaded to undertake sufficient investment to maintain full employment for one more year (or some longer period). Will they be neces-

[7] See for instance Case D in Paul A. Samuelson's 'Interactions between the Multiplier Analysis and the Principle of Acceleration,' *The Review of Economic Statistics*, Vol. 21 (May, 1939), pp. 75–8 [reprinted in The American Economic Association, *Readings in Business Cycle Theory* (Philadelphia, 1944), pp. 261–9].

sarily disappointed? Will they find themselves burdened with excessive and useless capital and therefore refuse to repeat the experiment once more?

Two cases should be distinguished here: (1) when income has remained constant; (2) when income has risen.

1. If income has not risen, the situation is not very cheerful. It is true that our economy does not consist of one industry in which only one firm produces one kind of product. So it is possible that the newly constructed capital has somehow acquired the markets of older plants. The economy as a whole will possess excessive capital, but the resulting losses will not fall on 'our' firms, who may be perfectly contented and therefore willing to try again. It is also possible that a change in s took place and that it was labor rather than capital that the new plants displaced.[8] But if the new capital could do all this, why was there a shortage of investment opportunities in the first place? We are coming rather close to a violation of our original assumption. Therefore, while not necessarily denying that new capital might sometimes emerge unscathed even in the absence of dynamic changes, we still have to conclude that the situation described here is too optimistic to be relied upon.

2. Our second case arises when income has increased. If this rise is sufficient (to be defined presently), there is no a priori reason why our or any other investors must necessarily be disappointed, provided their investments were made in the proper fields. The income elasticity of demand for goods in general is certainly positive. Therefore there must always exist some level of income at which the new plants can be profitably used without displacing an unreasonably large number of older ones. Our next step is therefore to inquire how high this income level should be and how fast national income should increase.

The reader has undoubtedly sensed already that this rate of growth is a function of two factors: the propensity to save (α) and the ratio of output to capital (s). The higher is α, the larger must be the fraction of income invested (to maintain full employment), and the greater should be the subsequent rise in income. Similarly, the larger is s, the more output can be produced with a given amount of capital and the faster income should increase. Thus the required rate of growth of income is directly proportional to both α and s.

[8] This contradicts our original assumption that full employment is maintained.

If income is indicated by Y, the amount invested will be $Y\alpha$. Since each dollar of new capital increases possible annual output by s, the total increase in output which is required to utilize the new investment fully is $Y\alpha s$. To get a relative rate of growth (which is more meaningful), we divide the absolute rise in income by Y and get αs. The expression αs *is the required rate of growth of income* which is needed to prevent an excessive accumulation of capital.[9]

Before any use is made of this result, the following qualifications are in order:

1. The problem is presented here in the simplest possible manner. No distinction is made between average and marginal propensities to save, and s is treated as an average applicable to new investment as a whole. Also the usual lag between the disbursement of income during the construction of capital assets and the completion of these assets has been ignored. Nothing has been said about the possible effects of relative price changes (or other factors) on the magnitudes of s and α. The removal or modification of these assumptions can lead to the building of all sorts of models which can be made as fancy and as complex as the reader desires. My own feeling is that at this stage the problem of capital accumulation needs more empirical data rather than further theorizing.

2. The required rate of growth of income equals αs provided that an excessive amount of unused capital does not exist at the beginning, or at least that unused capital does not interfere with investment. If it does, a higher rate will be required until all capital is fully utilized.

3. In a large and complex economy like ours, existing capital is always replaced to some extent by newer plants (over and above depreciation), and some new investment is misdirected. This premature junking of undepreciated capital, if proceeding on an excessive scale, is socially wasteful and is likely to inhibit new investment. But a complete avoidance of this process in a dynamic society is both impossible and undesirable. To this extent and provided that new investment is not inhibited, some downward adjustment should

[9] The reader may wonder regarding the difference between the rate of growth given in essays III and IV—$\alpha\sigma$—and the αs rate stated here in the text. $\alpha\sigma$ indicates the rate of growth of income necessary for the maintenance of full employment of *labor;* αs indicates that needed for a full utilization of *capital.* The essence of the problem is that s may be larger than σ.

be made in the required rate of growth (αs), but the magnitude of this adjustment is unfortunately unknown.

II

In the preceding section it was established that if national income grows at a (relative annual) rate of αs, no excessive accumulation of capital should take place. This rate αs should of course be interpreted as a very rough approximation, or still better as a range, both because of the qualifications just stated, and in view of the uncertain nature of s itself.[10] Our next question is: *can* income grow at this rate?

We should make a very clear distinction between *can* and *will*. If income cannot grow at the required rate, it clearly will not. But if it can, there is no assurance that it will. The failure to distinguish these two aspects of the problem has been a source of considerable confusion.

Our question refers of course to real income; money income could be made to grow at almost any rate. It is doubtful whether our society would desire to solve the problem of capital accumulation by continuous inflation. Once inflation is expected by the public, it is difficult, if not impossible, to contain it within reasonable limits, such as a rise of prices of some 2 to 3 per cent per year. Nor are we at all sure that the problem of capital accumulation would be solved by inflation in the first place.[11] For these reasons, we shall reject the inflationary solution, and assume instead that a reasonably constant price level is maintained.

In a sense, the answer to our question is extremely simple. All we need is to obtain reasonably reliable estimates of α and s, compute their product, and then compare the result with the maximum rate of growth which, in our opinion, the economy can achieve.

As to the magnitude of α, many estimates are available, though it is not easy to decide which one to take. Perhaps some 10–12 per cent (including corporate saving) would not appear unreasonable

[10] We should also recognize that the propensity to save is a very rough approximation of the fraction of national income invested in income-producing assets. The presence of government complicates the situation further.

[11] This depends on the relative movements of prices of capital goods and of output taken as a whole, as well as on the strictness with which the concept of s is interpreted.

as some sort of average. We really do not know how the public will behave in a state of continuous full employment.[12] Very little information is available as yet regarding the value of s, both because of the inherent complexity and vagueness of the concept, and because very few people have bothered to estimate it. A comprehensive study of capital requirements is now being conducted by W. W. Leontief.[13] Until his results become available, we have the choice of dropping the matter completely, guessing, or taking some very rough estimates, such as the ratio between national income and national wealth. An estimate of this ratio has been made recently by William J. Fellner for the period 1879–1938.[14] It fluctuated from a high of some 39 per cent in the decade 1879–86 to a low of some 30 per cent in 1909–18 (and also 1929–38) with a possible slight downward trend. These figures do not take into account, however, large amounts of unused capital throughout a good part of the period. So an upward adjustment of an unknown magnitude has to be made, though it must be remembered that the presence of some unemployed capital is normal. If s should be in the vicinity of 35–40 per cent, and α equal to 10 or 12 per cent, the required rate of growth will be somewhere around 4 per cent and possibly higher. Over the same period of time, that is 1879–1938, the annual rate of growth of real income in the United States was something like 3.3 per cent.[15] If full employment had been continuously maintained, it would probably have been higher. But, on the other hand, a good part of this period had the advantage of rapid population growth on which we evidently cannot count in the future. At first glance therefore we could conclude that the required rate of growth is beyond our reach. Yet the crudeness of our approach, both theoretically and (most of all) statistically, is such that a definite conclusion cannot be reached. A compound interest rate of growth, even as

[12] On the subject of a long-run propensity to save see the interesting essay by James S. Duesenberry, 'Income-Consumption Relations and their Implications,' *Income, Employment and Public Policy; Essays in Honor of Alvin H. Hansen* (New York, 1948), pp. 54–81.

[13] [Since published as *Studies in the Structure of the American Economy* (New York, 1953).] I understand that the Council of Economic Advisers is also studying the problem.

[14] See his *Monetary Policies and Full Employment* (Berkeley, Calif., 1946), p. 80. His figures were subsequently revised without affecting the main conclusions significantly. I am using here the reciprocals of his ratios.

[15] See Essay II, particularly pp. 57–69.

low as 2 per cent, cannot be maintained forever, but we are interested here not in the millennium but in the prospects for the next twenty to thirty years. And over this short period a 3 per cent rate of growth is clearly not out of the question, and—who knows? —with full employment and without depression, perhaps even a higher rate.

If these rough estimates do not provide a conclusive answer, a glance at recent United States business cycle history does not help much either. If prosperity comes to an end because national income *cannot* grow sufficiently fast to prevent an excessive accumulation of capital, we should observe a severe shortage of labor and rapidly rising prices, a phenomenon apparently absent in 1907, 1929, and 1937. It is possible to argue that had those prosperities lasted another year or two, such a situation would have arisen, and that this was foreseen by the entrepreneurs who reduced their commitments in advance. But without sufficient evidence, almost anything could just as well be said. The severe shortage of labor and rising prices do not seem to clip the wings of our present prosperity at all, though the easy money and credit situation may be a contributing factor here.

If we decide that national income *can* grow at the required rate, it does not at all follow that it *will* actually do so. To confuse the two issues would show a sad lack of understanding of the nature of a capitalist society. The mere absence of physical limitations to a rise in income which is sufficiently rapid to make the investment that has caused this rise profitable does not guarantee that the required investment will be undertaken in the first place. In a capitalist society investment is influenced by a number of factors, some rational, others not. It depends to a great extent on various dynamic changes, because the most simple and obvious purpose of investment —the expansion of capacity in order to produce more goods—cannot always be relied upon, since there is no assurance that the demand of tomorrow will be greater than the demand of today.

III

Our approach to matters of policy will depend on our choice between the 'can' and the 'will' hypotheses. If we decide that, with given α and s, the required rate of growth *cannot* be achieved because of physical limitations, the prospects of maintaining full employment over a prolonged period of time become bleak indeed. If saving is not invested, we have a depression today. If it is invested, there will be an excessive accumulation of capital tomorrow, and a depression the day after. It should be recognized, however, that the presence of frequent and sharp dynamic changes reduces the importance of excessive accumulation of capital: some firms and industries expand at the expense of others. Yet it is doubtful if a prosperity exclusively so based could last for more than a few years.

Under these circumstances, the most obvious and radical remedy consists in investing less and—if this is not to result in an immediate slump—in saving less; that is, in reducing the propensity to save. This by itself would not of course guarantee stability—witness the situation today when a lower propensity to save would intensify the inflation—but it would at least eliminate one source of trouble. Measures designed to reduce the propensity to save need not be discussed here. It is important to note, however, that a 'pure' capitalist society is rather helpless in this respect and that government interference would be necessary.

The other alternative would be a reduction in s, that is, in developing those industries which require much capital and little labor per unit of output. This is, I believe, essentially a question of technology, and such industries may or may not appear, though relatively high wages and low interest rates should encourage them. The utilization of atomic power seems to be an industry of this kind. On the other hand, the increasing demand for services points in the opposite direction.[16]

If, on the other hand, we decide that the required rate of growth *can* be achieved, new possibilities open up. As before, a reduction of the propensity to save will be helpful: with any given rate of investment a lower α will result in a higher national income. But the fundamental difference between the two cases should be clearly understood: in the present case, the excessive propensity to save, of which we have heard so much lately, is not excessive any more in relation to the capital requirements and to the growth potential of the economy, but only to the volume of investment as determined by existing institutional conditions. It would be extremely regrettable,

---

[16] There is of course a third solution—to raise the maximum rate of growth to the αs level by speeding up the rate of technological progress. To the extent that this is possible it appears to me the best solution of all, except that it would contradict the case discussed in the text.

therefore, to reduce the propensity to save: if the public is *willing* to save a certain part of its income, and the required rate of growth *can* be achieved, why not concentrate our efforts to make this growth potential real?[17] This is the path that any socialist society would undoubtedly take, but must we wait for that? A depression becomes now nothing else but a vast psychological phenomenon and any effort to 'talk ourselves into prosperity' will help. The various plans for encouraging investment, such as incentive taxation, liberal loss offsets, accelerated depreciation, and scientific and industrial research, are undoubtedly familiar to the reader. There is also a somewhat different approach, proposed from time to time, which I hesitate to mention because it can be so easily misunderstood. This approach deals with a guaranteed growth of income.[18]

Theoretically speaking, the issue is this: we have found that if firms were 'somehow' induced to invest a sufficient amount, so that national income rose at the required rate, no disappointments would follow. Suppose now that it were possible for the government (presumably) to guarantee that income would actually grow at this rate for some time to come. Would not this guarantee, if taken seriously by the business public, call forth sufficient investment and thus *make* income grow at the required rate? This is full employment by magic! Yet as one reads Leo Barnes's most interesting note describing how the C.E.D., by making a few (undoubtedly unintentional) errors, managed to 'persuade industry into a prosperity,' one gets a feeling that magic sometimes works.[19] We do not know, however, how seriously these C.E.D. forecasts were actually taken; still the idea is highly suggestive.

On a more serious and practical level, this much can be said for the argument. Past depressions do exert a profound influence on business thinking, and an assurance that they will not recur would undoubtedly brighten the future and make many marginal projects worth undertaking. If, in addition, businessmen could confidently expect a growing economy, the effect would be so much stronger.

[17] This is of course a value judgment.

[18] See, for instance, John H. G. Pierson, *Full Employment and Free Enterprise* (Washington, 1947). It appears to me, however, that he lays undue stress on the level of consumption rather than on its rate of growth. See also the debate between A. R. Sweezy and E. Benoit-Smullyan, *The American Economic Review*, Vol. 34 (Dec., 1944), pp. 871–9.

[19] Leo Barnes, 'How Sound Were Private Postwar Forecasts?' *The Journal of Political Economy*, Vol. 56 (Apr., 1948), pp. 161–5.

How the absence of an assured growth affects business expectations is demonstrated by a recent publication of the American Iron and Steel Institute, *Background Memoranda—Steel Capacity*. The purpose of this memorandum is to show that the country possesses sufficient steel capacity to meet both the largest peacetime demand in our history—that of 1929—and the specific past peak demands of the most important users of steel taken together. The only growth admitted into these estimates was the growth of population! If a sufficient number of our industries make their plans along these lines, we will end up with some fifteen or more million unemployed.[20] But so long as the probability of future depressions is great, can we expect different plans to be made? And the sad joke about all this is that after the depression does come, these planners will justly congratulate themselves on their remarkable foresight!

It is realized, of course, that optimistic expectations cannot be created by a mere act of Congress. For several years at least the government would have to stabilize the economy on its own. We are painfully aware of the magnitude of this task. But only after it has been achieved and the government has shown sufficient determination to carry out its program can any reliance be placed on an assured growth of income. Here we run into paradoxes. Thus if the government acts timidly, perhaps due to fear of a deficit, and business expectations are therefore low, little will be invested and a large deficit may in fact become necessary to prevent mass unemployment. On the other hand, a bold announcement of government objectives accompanied by a determination to carry them out may call forth sufficient investment to make a deficit unnecessary. But these paradoxes, besides providing us with intellectual amusement, also show how difficult the stabilization problem really is.[21]

IV

The problem of capital accumulation has been fairly popular among economists, particularly among those with underconsump-

---

[20] This is not necessarily an argument for increasing steel capacity at present.

[21] There are grounds for believing that an economy whose investment is mainly of the induced type (i.e. depending directly on income growth) may be particularly unstable. See T. C. Schelling, 'Capital Growth and Equilibrium,' *The American Economic Review*, Vol. 37 (Dec., 1947), pp. 864–76. It should be pointed out, however, that my discussion in the text does not assume in the least the absence of spontaneous investment, though the latter may be insufficient from a full employment point of view.

tionist leanings, such as Marxists and Keynesians. In recent literature, the most interesting and explicit formulation belongs to
Paul M. Sweezy, to whom the main part of the present section will
be devoted.[22] A good theoretical exposition belongs to R. F. Harrod,
in a paper published in 1939.[23] Similar views can be found also, in
one form or another, in the writings of Hansen, Kaldor, Kalecki,
and others.[24]

The idea that smooth functioning of a capitalist society requires
continuous growth is of course not new. All of these writers have
stated, more or less explicitly, that the failure of income to grow at
some required rate (defined in one way or another) will result in an
excessive accumulation of capital, and—most probably—in a subsequent fall in investment. Looking over our past performances,
they saw the obvious fact that income did not grow for more than a
few years, if at all, at this rate. And from this they concluded that
the required rate of growth of income simply *could not* be achieved.

A clear statement of this position is given by Kaldor:

> Sooner or later, however, the point is reached where all the available labour is
> absorbed in production. Even if the installation of additional equipment goes
> on still further, current production cannot be increased much further. . . .
> It is this factor [labor shortage] that is ultimately responsible for that 'tem-
> porary exhaustion of investment opportunities' with which several economists
> explain the breakdown of the boom. . . . [25]

Similar quotations can be found in Kalecki, Harrod, and Hansen.
The latter states:

> . . . Put in another way, the amount of investment needed to maintain full
> employment has historically far exceeded the amount needed for growth and
> progress. Yet only in full-employment boom years has the amount of investment
> been adequate to provide full employment. But this amount of investment could
> not be maintained continuously without exceeding by far the requirements of
> growth and progress. This is the essential cause of depressions and unemploy-
> ment.[26]

[22] *The Theory of Capitalist Development* (New York, 1942), pp. 180–89 and
Chap. XII.
[23] 'An Essay in Dynamic Theory,' *The Economic Journal*, Vol. 49 (Mar., 1939),
pp. 14–33. See also his recent book *Towards a Dynamic Economics* (London,
1948), particularly Lecture Three.
[24] See note 1.
[25] Kaldor, op. cit. pp. 651–3. Thereupon he proceeds to give his practical
recommendations—that investment should be prevented from 'reaching beyond
a certain moderate level,' which is perfectly consistent with his theory.
[26] *Economic Policy and Full Employment* (New York, 1947), pp. 177–8.

An excessive accumulation of capital, however, takes place when income does not grow at the required rate for any reason whatsoever. Therefore the mere presence of unused capital is not a proof of the *inability* of income so to grow. As we saw in Section II, the settlement of the issue depends on an empirical verification, and the latter is neither given nor referred to by the authors mentioned.[27] This may of course be the case of keen intuitions swiftly running ahead of the slowly moving empirical wagon, and indeed they may be proved to be right in perceiving the fundamental cause of instability in a capitalist society. Yet in the absence of the requisite information, one hypothesis may be as attractive as another, and the reader will be justified in withholding his judgment.

The remaining part of this paper is concerned with Paul Sweezy's theory of underconsumption. It is based on two premises:

1. As national income grows, an increasing proportion of it is saved. To maintain full employment, increasing fractions of national income must therefore be invested.

2. In a well-developed capitalist economy, there exists a fairly constant relationship between the stock of capital and the output of consumption goods.

The first premise—the increasing proportion of income required to be invested—is derived by Sweezy from what he calls 'a fundamental feature of capitalism,' (p. 187) and is based on the increasing ratios between surplus value and income, accumulation and surplus value, and investment and accumulation. I am not aware that capitalism does possess such features, at least in the secular sense, but let us take this premise as an assumption. Besides, Sweezy treats it as a tendency which may be, or may have been, counteracted by other forces (Chapter XII).

The second premise is based on a study by Carl Snyder,[28] and is subject, I believe, to the following correction: as was argued in Section I, a case can perhaps be made for the usefulness and possible stability of the ratio between the stock of capital and the volume of its (annual) output, but what is the meaning of the ratio between the stock of capital and that part of its output which is sold to

[27] Mr. Kalecki has indeed tried to give an empirical demonstration in his essay in *Oxford Economic Papers*, mentioned in note 1. With all the respect that I have for him, I cannot agree that this demonstration proved his point.

[28] Carl Snyder, 'The Capital Supply and National Well-Being,' *The American Economic Review*, Vol. 26 (June, 1936), pp. 195–224.

consumers? Surely the whole plant and equipment of General Motors is not used for the production of passenger automobiles (more correctly—only those to be used for non-business purposes), while trucks and Diesel engines are produced in mid-air. It hardly makes any difference to the management from the point of view of utilization of capital, its profitability, investment prospects, etc., whether the capital is used to produce consumption goods, materials to be used for further production, or investment goods. Indeed, not an insignificant part of investment is made in order to produce further investment goods, and there is nothing unusual in this process.[29] I hope I do not violate the spirit of Sweezy's theory by substituting 'income' for consumption. As a matter of fact, Snyder's study to which Sweezy refers is expressed in terms of a ratio between capital and income.

To come back to the two premises. On the basis of the first premise, Sweezy tries to show that capital will grow faster (in relative terms) than income (he uses consumption), so that the ratio of capital to income will rise. This development will contradict the second premise. As a result, there will be a crisis, or—if the result had been foreseen—a long period of chronic unemployment.

To substantiate this conclusion, Sweezy presents two separate proofs—one in the text (pp. 180–86) and the other in an appendix to Chapter X (pp. 186–9). With the latter I have several quarrels, but since it is mathematical, let us relegate its examination to a similar appendix to this paper.

Let us turn to the proof given by Sweezy in his text. It does follow from the first premise that *investment* will grow at a faster relative rate than income. But from this we cannot yet conclude that *capital* will grow faster than income. In Sweezy's treatment, capital is the integral (sum) of investment. But the fact that one function (investment) grows relatively faster than another (income) does not necessarily mean that the integral of the first function (i.e. capital) must grow faster than the second function itself. The exact relationship between this integral and income will depend on the actual behavior

[29] This point was also made by Fellner, op. cit. Chap. II. This error of thinking in terms of a ratio between capital and consumption rather than that between capital and total output or income is very frequent in economic literature. It probably goes back to the idea that consumption is the final aim of production and that therefore all capital is used for the production of consumer goods. This is true only in a stationary society.

of investment and income, or more precisely on their respective rates of growth. The rate of growth is the missing link in Sweezy's argument.[30]

It can be shown that if income grows at a relative rate of r per unit of time (year), and if an α fraction of it is annually invested, the ratio of capital to income will approach as a limit the expression α/r where α and r need not necessarily be constant.[31] Now Sweezy's contention that an increasing α will result in an increasing ratio of capital to income emerges as a special case where r is constant. By itself an increasing α is neither a necessary nor a sufficient condition for producing a rising ratio of capital to income.

That this is so can be seen more or less intuitively, without going through mathematical derivations. Suppose Sweezy were right, and an increasing α by itself led toward excess accumulation of capital. Wouldn't we expect then that a constant α would automatically give the correct ratio of capital to income, while a falling α would result in a chronic shortage of capital? The last case is not at all improbable, yet we would intuitively refuse to believe that if some country's propensity to save (all this net of depreciation) was reduced, say, from 15 to 10 per cent, that country would necessarily suffer from a shortage of capital.

By committing this logical error and by insisting that a rising α is a 'fundamental feature of capitalism,' Sweezy unnecessarily weakens his own position. Even if α is constant, the problem of excess accumulation of capital is by no means solved. We saw in Section I that such a solution would require income to grow at the relative rate of αs per year, and this is by no means an easy requirement. For that matter, even a falling α will not necessarily eliminate excessive accumulation of capital.

In Sweezy's appendix the conclusion is more restricted. Here it appears that excess accumulation of capital will develop only if income does *not* grow at an accelerated absolute rate. (If it does, the answer is inconclusive.) But this is a very modest requirement indeed. Surely we can make our national income increase the first year by $1 billion, the second, by $1.1 billion, then $1.2 billion, and so on for the next thirty or even fifty years. From the point of view of practical achievement, it is not so much the mathematical

[30] It is, however, explicitly taken into account in his appendix.
[31] See Essay III.

character of the rate of growth that matters, but its actual magnitude, a question to which Sweezy pays no attention at all.

Be that as it may, Sweezy believes that his requirement—that income grow at an accelerated absolute rate—cannot be achieved in an 'old' capitalist society such as the United States. And the clarity of his exposition (p. 189 and Chapter XII) leaves no doubt about which of the two of our hypotheses he subscribes to: it is the physical limitation, and more precisely, the insufficient rate of population growth, that prevents the economy from growing at the required rate. For this reason he concluded (p. 189) that 'So far as capitalism is concerned we are undoubtedly justified in calling underconsumption a disease of old age.'

* * * *

Yet, as one meditates about the problem of capital accumulation, one still has the feeling that between the views of those economists who do not bother with the problem at all and who see a wide road to continued prosperity once a few adjustments (particularly in regard to labor unions) are made, and the opinions of those who assure us that in a capitalist society this road is closed altogether, there may exist a path which winds its way around both extremes. But it is a narrow path.

APPENDIX TO SECTION IV

We examine here the appendix to Sweezy's Chapter X, which, according to him, is based on Otto Bauer's book *Zwischen zwei Weltkriegen?*, published in 1936. Perhaps a direct quotation would be the best way to start (pp. 186–7).

If I is the net national income in value terms, w the total wage bill (= workers' consumption), l the part of surplus value consumed by capitalists, and k the part of surplus value added to constant capital (= investment), then we have the following equation:

$$(1) \qquad\qquad I = w + l + k.$$

All of these concepts, of course, represent rates of flow per unit of time . . . if K is the total stock of means of production, then $k = dK/dt$.

We assume that the national income steadily rises and that each of its three component parts also rises. Thus if we regard w and l as functions of k, it will always be true that as k increases w and l will also increase. But since it is a fundamental feature of capitalism that an increasing proportion of surplus value tends to be accumulated and an increasing proportion of accumulation tends to be invested, both w and l must grow less rapidly than k. Hence we have:

(2) $w = f(k)$ such that $0 < f'(k) < 1$ and $f''(k) < 0$

and similarly:

(3) $l = \phi(k)$ such that $0 < \phi'(k) < 1$ and $\phi''(k) < 0$.

But expressions (2) and (3) do not necessarily follow from the 'fundamental feature of capitalism' as described in the preceding paragraph. If surplus value is a non-diminishing part of national income (as shown in Sweezy's discussion), and an increasing fraction of surplus value is accumulated, and finally if an increasing proportion of accumulation is invested, then what does follow is that the ratio of investment to accumulation, to surplus value, to consumption, and to national income rises. In other words, what is given by the 'fundamental feature of capitalism' is that

$$\text{(4)} \qquad \frac{d\left(\dfrac{k}{I}\right)}{dt} > 0,$$

or that

$$\text{(5)} \qquad \frac{d\left(\dfrac{k}{m}\right)}{dt} > 0,$$

where $m = w + l = $ total consumption.[32] But it does not at all follow that $f'(k) < 1$ (or that $\phi'(k) < 1$). As a matter of fact, from what we know about the magnitude of k and w, there is a very good presumption in favor of $f'(k) > 1$. There is a confusion here between absolute and relative rates of growth. Fortunately, the assumption that $f'(k) < 1$ is not needed for his proof. But the other one—$f''(k) < 0$ is needed; yet it cannot be said that it necessarily follows from (4) in the general case. Some additional assumptions would be necessary.

Let us try to rework the problem. Our first assumption will be that the ratio of investment to income remains constant or increases,

[32] We can also say that $\dfrac{dk}{dt}\dfrac{1}{k} > \dfrac{dI}{dt}\dfrac{1}{I}$, i.e. that k will grow at a greater *relative* rate than I. Mathematically, it amounts to the same thing. The same holds true for m.

i.e. that

$$(6) \qquad \frac{d\left(\frac{k}{I}\right)}{dt} \geqq 0.$$

The second one is our familiar s, which, or rather the inverse of which, Sweezy also uses as the required ratio between capital and income. (Though he uses it as the ratio between capital and consumption.) If

$$(7) \qquad I = Ks,$$

$$(8) \qquad \frac{dI}{dt} = \frac{dK}{dt} \cdot s = ks.$$

The expression (7) is the equilibrium condition from the point of view of this problem. Differentiating (6) we get

$$(9) \qquad I\frac{dk}{dt} \geqq k\frac{dI}{dt}.$$

From (8) we obtain

$$(10) \qquad \frac{d^2I}{dt^2} = \frac{dk}{dt} \cdot s,$$

and the substitution of (8) and (10) into (9) gives us

$$(11) \qquad I\frac{d^2I}{dt^2} \geqq \left(\frac{dI}{dt}\right)^2.$$

We shall now prove that the expression (11) is equivalent to the statement that the *relative* rate of growth will be constant or will increase. For

$$(12) \qquad \frac{d\left(\frac{\frac{dI}{dt}}{I}\right)}{dt} \geqq 0$$

immediately gives

$$\frac{I\frac{d^2I}{dt^2} - \left(\frac{dI}{dt}\right)^2}{I^2} \geqq 0,$$

which is identical to (11).

We can conclude that:

1. If the ratio of investment to income is constant, the preservation of equilibrium requires that income grow at a *constant relative* rate.

2. If that ratio is, as Sweezy assumes, increasing, national income should grow at an *increasing relative* rate.

Comparing our results with Sweezy's, we find that:

1. *His* assumption that an increasing fraction of national income is invested is not necessary for *his* conclusion that income must grow at an increasing *absolute* rate. A constant, and under some conditions even a falling, fraction of income invested will give the same result.

2. Even a constant fraction of income invested yields a stronger result here than an increasing fraction does in his appendix.

VI

The Effect of Foreign Investment on the Balance of Payments*[1]

With the end of the Marshall Plan in sight, foreign investment, as distinguished from grants, may acquire increasing importance. The flow of American public and private funds overseas could bridge the still lingering dollar gap, create employment at home and—probably most important—assist in the development of less advanced countries. So envisaged, a continuous policy of this kind might be agreeable to all concerned if it did not appear to suffer from one basic defect: since loans and investments are usually subject to the payment of amortization and interest (or dividends),[2] the inflow of funds so produced is expected after a relatively short interval to exceed the outflow—a phenomenon which seems to be embarrassing to both the borrower and the lender. On the other hand, the waiving of interest and amortization, that is, the transformation of loans into grants, as a long-run policy might offend international dignity and be so upsetting to the 'sound business' sense of our Congress that the payment of amortization and interest may be the lesser of the two evils.

* [Reprinted by permission from The American Economic Review, Vol. 40 (Dec., 1950), pp. 805–26.]

[1] This study was suggested by Walter S. Salant in the fall of 1949. While writing his paper on 'The Domestic Effects of Capital Export Under the Point Four Program,' The American Economic Review, Papers and Proceedings, Vol. 40 (May, 1950), pp. 495–510, he saw the essential similarity between his problem and my earlier study of the public debt (see Essay II). At his suggestion I started working out the mathematics of foreign lending, which gradually expanded into this lengthy document. Salant's subsequent comments were most helpful. He is not to be blamed, of course, for any of my errors or conclusions. The paper gained greatly both in content and in form from suggestions made by Miss Faye M. Goldware of The Johns Hopkins University.

[2] It is true, however, that many private investments are not subject to a formal amortization schedule.

The purpose of this paper is not to argue about political implications or the propriety of interest and amortization, but to investigate the relationship between the inflow and outflow of funds which a continuous policy of foreign investment and lending will produce.[3] Perhaps the problem will disappear with time as it did for Britain a hundred years ago. But its real or imagined significance today justifies a study.

The argument is developed in three stages: a general discussion of the subject and the conclusions are in Section I; a more detailed examination of the problem with numerical examples not involving higher mathematics, in Section II; finally, the actual derivations on which the paper is based are given in the Mathematical Appendix.

I

The belief that amortization and interest payments must first approach and then exceed the flow of new investment is widely held among economists; indeed, it is one of those rare subjects on which agreement is almost complete. We all have been taught and have taught how a country passes from the young creditor stage with an export balance on goods and services to a mature creditor position and an import balance—a view which can be traced back at least to Marshall and Cairnes, and which was supported empirically by the British experience of the last century.[4] In recent discussions of the effects of investment on the balance of payments the traditional position was on the whole reaffirmed.[5] By its very nature this ques-

[3] Throughout the paper an excess of the inflow over the outflow of funds produced by foreign investment is identified with an import balance. Foreign investment and lending are used synonymously, and interest includes interest and dividends.

[4] Alfred Marshall, *Money Credit and Commerce* (London, 1923), pp. 135–7. John E. Cairnes, *Some Leading Principles of Political Economy Newly Expounded* (New York, 1874), pp. 359–63. In recent literature, the clearest statement of this view I found was in Stephen Enke and Virgil Salera, *International Economics* (New York, 1947), pp. 637–43.

[5] See, for instance, Norman S. Buchanan, *International Investment and Domestic Welfare* (New York, 1945), pp. 166–80, 206–39; also his 'International Investment: Some Post-War Problems and Issues,' *The Canadian Journal of Economics and Political Science*, Vol. 10 (May, 1944), pp. 139–49; Norman S. Buchanan and Friedrich A. Lutz, *Rebuilding the World Economy* (New York, 1947), pp. 210–30; Hal B. Lary, 'The Domestic Effects of Foreign Investments,' *The American Economic Review, Papers and Proceedings*, Vol. 36 (May, 1946), pp. 672–86; Randall Hinshaw, 'Foreign Investment and American Employment,' same source, pp. 661–71. The views expressed by Raymond F. Mikesell

tion invites formal analysis, yet the answer to it must have seemed so obvious that such inquiry has been limited, as far as I know, to a few numerical examples. The most thorough of these was worked out by Randall Hinshaw in 1946.[6] He set out to find the annual amount of new loans required to maintain an annual export surplus of one billion dollars (with and without amortization), and discovered that new loans would have to grow at some compound interest rate—a requirement he was sure could not be fulfilled. The formulation of the problem in this narrow form and the attempt to solve it solely by numerical examples hardly did it justice. Absolute magnitudes which grow at compound interest rates are always frightening, and it was probably a computation of this sort that prompted Professor Viner to declare that

. . . Debt service on amortization and interest account reaches and exceeds the annual amount of a constant gross outflow of new capital after a period surprisingly short for those like myself who are still capable of being startled by the wondrous working of compound interest. For American employment to be sustained for any length of time by American capital export there would be needed an outward gross flow of capital increasing each year at an increasing rate of increase and eventually reaching fantastic levels.[7]

These levels may be fantastic, yet our economy has been growing in precisely this manner for quite a few years, and—with sufficient wisdom and boldness in our economic policies—may continue doing so for some time to come. Fifty years ago it would have been unbelievable that the maintenance of full employment in 1950 (with due allowance for price changes) would require a gross national product of some $270 billion. Certainly startling would have seemed $80 billion of combined government expenditures (on goods and services) and gross private capital formation. Even today the $200 billion of gross private capital outlay needed (with present saving habits and government expenditures) to sustain full employ-

---

and John Parke Young in their discussion of Hinshaw's paper (pp. 710–13, 715–16) were refreshingly unorthodox. So were those of August Maffry in his 'Foreign Trade in the Post-War Economy,' *Survey of Current Business*, Vol. 24 (Nov., 1944), pp. 5–14.

[6] Op. cit. pp. 666–7. Hinshaw's tables were later reproduced by Buchanan and Lutz, op. cit. pp. 213–14. Buchanan presented several hypothetical numerical examples in his *International Investment and Domestic Welfare*, pp. 167–72, and so did Lary, op. cit.

[7] Jacob Viner, 'International Finance in the Postwar World,' *The Journal of Political Economy*, Vol. 55 (Apr., 1947), p. 106.

ment over the next five years seems staggering.[8] And a gross national product of one trillion dollars in the year 2000 is hard to take seriously, though this would merely imply no more than a repetition during the next fifty years of our past performance (an annual rate of growth of about 3 per cent).[9]

As far as the required rate of growth is concerned, foreign investment does not give rise to any problems intrinsically different from those created by domestic investment, public or private. In all of them the presence of certain conditions regarding the relative magnitude of the investment and its productivity or yield leads to a compound interest solution, and in all of them the absolute magnitudes involved, unless the assumed conditions change, become 'fantastically' high with time.[10]

It is shown in Section II that the ratio of the inflow of funds, i.e. interest and amortization, to the outflow, i.e. new investment, will gradually approach as a limit the expression

$$\frac{\text{amortization rate} + \text{interest rate}}{\text{amortization rate} + \text{rate of growth}},$$

where amortization is computed in accordance with the so-called net value method (see p. 136) and the rate of growth indicates the relative (i.e. percentage) growth of new investment.

With its rate of growth in the denominator, it follows that the faster new investment grows the smaller will be the ratio between the inflow and the outflow of funds—a conclusion strikingly similar to that reached in my study of the public debt.[11] *Whether or not an import balance* (i.e. an excess of inflow of funds over the outflow) *will at all appear depends on the relative magnitudes of the rate of growth and of the interest rate.* If the rate of growth exceeds the interest rate, this ratio will be less than one, and an import balance will never arise. If, on the other hand, the rate of growth falls below the rate of interest, an import balance will become inevitable, its timing depending on the magnitudes of the three variables

[8] *The Economic Report of the President and The Annual Economic Review by the Council of Economic Advisers* (Washington, Jan. 6, 1950), particularly pp. 6–7, 80–88. This was of course written before the Korean War.

[9] See 'The President's Report on the State of the Union,' *Congressional Record*, Vol. 96 (Jan. 4, 1950), p. 64.

[10] See essays II–V. The basic similarity of foreign and domestic investment was also pointed out by John Parke Young, op. cit., and by Walter S. Salant, op. cit.

[11] Essay II.

involved (see p. 140). In any case, the ratio between the inflow and the outflow will be gradually stabilized unless of course the variables themselves change.

That sufficiently rapid growth of new investment can indefinitely postpone the emergence of an import balance is certainly not a new discovery, and it hardly needs proof. But that such growth can continue for a prolonged period of time is not readily accepted, and concern is expressed about the state of our balance of payments when lending falls off. Domestic investment evokes a similar reaction. Even a Marxist may agree that full employment can be maintained if private investment is large enough, and his logical opposite from the N.A.M. may admit the same about 'deficit spending' by the government; yet both will argue that the respectively obnoxious methods cannot be practiced for long, and both will expect a depression when spending from one source or the other falls off. A depression may indeed arrive, but why must it be taken for granted that economic processes are finite?

If we can invest abroad for three years without injuring our economy or the borrowers', and for five years without running into trouble, why not for any number of years? If absolute figures make us feel uncomfortable, why not think in terms of some fraction of our growing (it is expected) national product? One or two per cent of the latter devoted to foreign investment each year will automatically result in an increasing stream of investment which will be ample and not at all frightening.

A paper such as this may convey the impression that an import balance is inherently undesirable; to many it appears as the main obstacle to a successful foreign investment program. There must be something very odd about our economic system if an import balance fully paid for is unwelcome, but so long as this oddity persists, remedies, or at least consolations, should be suggested. The simplest and most obvious remedy lies not in abstaining from foreign investment which the world needs so badly, but in reducing the interest rate on public lending to a minimum consistent with the preservation of international dignity; surely we don't need the interest as income. If the rate of growth of all foreign investment could exceed its yield, the problem would be solved, yet speaking realistically, for the annual growth of the national product or of new investment to exceed 3 per cent may be too much to hope for, and a yield below 3 per cent on all foreign investment in our institutional conditions is not easily achieved. A restriction of this type can hardly be imposed on private investment, but there is really no compelling reason why our government should charge as much as 3 or 4 per cent on its foreign loans.[12] A reduction of this rate to 2 per cent or less would offset the higher yields on private investment and perhaps bring about a rough equality between the rates of growth and interest.[13]

It should at least be possible to equalize the rates of growth and interest on public investment alone by the simple expedient of raising the rate of growth of new loans to the level of the interest rate charged. The inflow and outflow of government funds will then gradually balance, and a revolving fund will come into existence from which new loans can be made at an increasing (absolute) rate, and yet without any additional Congressional appropriations![14] Now assisting in the development of one project and now of another, these loans could become a major instrument of a wise foreign economic policy.

II

The relationship between the inflow and outflow of funds produced by foreign investment can be expressed in various ways, of which the difference and the ratio are the simplest and the most obvious. It seems to me that in this, as in most long-term economic problems, the difference—an absolute number—is neither significant nor meaningful, particularly in a growing economy like ours. We shall deal with the ratio—the ratio of the inflow of funds (amortization plus interest) to the outflow (new or gross investment), and indicate it by R.[15]

[12] The Export-Import Bank charges between $2\frac{3}{8}$ and 6 per cent, the majority of the loans carrying $3\frac{1}{2}$–4 per cent. The International Bank for Reconstruction and Development charges about 3–4 per cent, plus a commission of 1 per cent. On the other hand, our 1945 loan to Britain was subject to only 2 per cent. See Export-Import Bank of Washington, *Eighth Semiannual Report to Congress for the Period January–June, 1949* (Washington, 1949), pp. 22–45; the other sources are given in note 19.

[13] The possibility of defaults should also be taken into account.

[14] To take full advantage of this situation the present provision in the Export-Import Bank Act according to which its lending power is limited by an amount equal to three and one-half times its authorized capital stock would have to be revised.

[15] The strict believer in differences can compute them from the data in the Mathematical Appendix.

The following symbols are used:

A = annual amortization charge;
G = annual new or gross investment;
I = annual interest charge;

$$R = \frac{A + I}{G} = \text{ratio of the inflow of funds to the outflow;}$$

R_L = the limit of R as time approaches infinity (Case 1);
R_F = the final value of R (Cases 2 and 3);
a = annual amortization rate (Cases 1 and 2);
i = annual interest rate;
k = length of the amortization period in years (Cases 2 and 3);
r = relative annual rate of growth of G.

The problem can be finally formulated as follows: suppose G (gross or new investment) grows at a relative rate of r per year (including the case when $r = 0$ and G is constant); it is subject to amortization at the rate of a (per year), and an annual interest rate of i is charged against the outstanding debt. How will the ratio R between the inflow ($A + I$) and the outflow (G) of funds behave?[16]

We thus have three independent variables, i, r, and a,[17] and one dependent, R, though should the reader be interested in A/G (the ratio of amortization charges to gross investment), in $(G - A)/G$ (the ratio of net to gross investment), or in some other combination of A, I, and G, these can be computed from R. Of our independent variables, i is the simplest in application and in behavior and hardly requires an explanation. In our derivations it is treated as a constant, but both the formulas given in the text and the numerical examples show how a change of i affects R.

r, the relative rate of growth of G, is apt to raise more eyebrows; but it is a most useful instrument well worth its keep. Like i, r will be treated as a constant in derivations, and again both the formulas and the numerical examples will show the effects of its changes on R. For the skeptical reader, special cases with $r = 0$, that is, with G remaining constant, will be provided.[18]

[16] The case when G falls off after a few years is not considered here. That the inflow of funds will soon exceed the outflow is of course obvious.
[17] In Case 2, we can also use the length of the amortization period—$k = 1/a$.
[18] Some of the formulas hold true for a negative r, though this case has to be treated carefully to avoid nonsensical results.

a, the amortization rate, is rather troublesome because amortization can be computed in a variety of ways. It can be expressed as a constant fraction of the original value of each investment or of the debt outstanding; or the total debt service, including both interest and amortization, can be treated in one manner or another, not to mention other possibilities. We shall consider here the three simplest cases:

Case 1. Amortization is a constant fraction of the net debt outstanding—*the net value method.*

Case 2. Amortization is a constant fraction of the original value of each loan—*the original value method.*

Case 3. Amortization *and* interest on each loan are paid off in a series of equal annual installments—*the equal installment method.*[19]

The results of these three cases are, I believe, sufficiently significant to indicate the general solution of the problem.[20]

Case 1. The Net Value Method

Amortization is computed here as an *a* fraction of the *debt outstanding*. If $a = 10$ per cent, the amortization on a *single* loan of $100 will be $10 after the first year; 10 per cent of the remainder of $90 = $9 after the second year; $8.10 after the third year; and so on. If loans of $100 are made each year, the first amortization payment will be $10, the second, $.10(100 - 10 + 100) = 19; the third, $.10(190 - 19 + 100) = 27.10, etc. The loans are never really paid off, though with the passage of time, the unpaid balance of each

---

[19] In recent international lending, both the second and the third methods have been used. Thus the 1945 loan to Britain is to be amortized (beginning in 1951) according to the third method; so are the loans granted by the International Bank for Reconstruction and Development to the Finlands Bank (Aug. 1, 1949), Dominion of India (Aug. 18, 1949), and Corporacion de Fomento de la Produccion of Chile (Mar. 25, 1948). On the other hand, loans granted by the Bank to the Dominion of India (Sept. 29, 1949), the Kingdom of Belgium (Mar. 1, 1949), and to N. V. Stoomvaart Maatschappij 'Nederland' (July 15, 1948) belong to Case 2. These are of course just a few examples. My general impression is that method 3 is used more frequently than method 2. For a number of loans extended by the Bank, the amortization period is divided into parts, and within each part one or the other method is used. Some amortization schedules follow neither method. Frequently, amortization and interest payments do not begin for several years after the loan is granted. Each loan agreement is published by the Bank. For the conditions of our loan to Britain see the *Federal Reserve Bulletin*, Vol. 32 (Jan., 1946), pp. 15–19.

[20] I have not worked out the case when *a* and *i* differ among the various loans made. Some averaging method will have to be used then.

particular loan becomes very small.[21] I doubt if this method is frequently, if at all, used in practice, but it has great analytical virtues: a and i are applied here to the same magnitude, i.e. to the net debt, and this additiveness of a and i simplifies both the mathematics and the results.[22]

As the lending process goes on, R, the inflow-outflow ratio, rises from the zero point (our problem being considered in isolation from other components of the balance of payments and from any previous lending), and gradually approaches as its limit, indicated by R_L, the expression

$$(1) \qquad R_L = \frac{A + I}{G}L = \frac{a + i}{a + r}.\ ^{23}$$

The presence of i in the numerator is of course to be expected; i is the best behaved of all our variables. How r found its way into the denominator is perhaps less obvious. A and I, being functions of the outstanding debt, depend not only on the current investment but also on the sum of all preceding ones, so that if G grows rapidly, its current magnitude is large relative to that sum. Therefore R_L is correspondingly smaller.

a is our most troublesome but also our most interesting variable. In expression (1), it appears in both the numerator and the denominator. It plays a dual role: on the one hand, a larger a increases A and therefore R_L, but on the other, a larger a also decreases the outstanding debt and hence, both A and I. Its final effect on R_L will depend on the relative magnitudes of r and i.

Table I gives the numerical magnitudes of R_L for several combinations of a, r, and i. R_L ranges there from a minimum of 45 to a maximum of 220 per cent, rising with an increasing i and falling with an

[21] This process is similar to that in Keynes's multiplier, where subsequent additions to income never cease but eventually become very small.

[22] The nature of this amortization method calls for the use of continuous series which are easier to handle than the discrete.

[23] When

$$r = 0, \qquad R_L = 1 + \frac{i}{a}.$$

The following can be easily established:

$$\frac{A}{G}L = \frac{a}{a + r}, \qquad \frac{I}{G}L = \frac{i}{r}, \qquad \frac{G - A}{G}L = \frac{r}{a + r},$$

for any $r > 0$.

increasing r—a behavior which naturally follows from expression (1). But the effect of a on R_L is less clear. When $a = 10$ per cent, R_L's minimum is 63 per cent, and its maximum is 160 per cent. A lower a (5 per cent) reduces the minimum to 45 per cent, but also raises the maximum to 220 per cent. Examination of Tables I and II and of expression (1) reveals the following three possibilities:

1. If $r = i$, R_L is 100 per cent, irrespective of the magnitude of a. As times goes on, the inflow of funds will exactly equal the outflow.

TABLE I.—CASE 1: THE VALUES OF R_L FOR GIVEN MAGNITUDES OF a, r, AND i (IN PERCENTAGES)

Per Cent	$a = 10\%$					
r \ i	0	1	2	3	4	6
0	100	110	120	130	140	160
1	91	100	109	118	127	145
2	83	92	100	108	117	133
3	77	85	92	100	108	123
4	71	79	86	93	100	114
6	63	69	75	81	88	100

Per Cent	$a = 5\%$					
r \ i	0	1	2	3	4	6
0	100	120	140	160	180	220
1	83	100	117	133	150	183
2	71	86	100	114	129	157
3	63	75	88	100	113	138
4	56	67	78	89	100	122
6	45	55	64	73	82	100

2. If $r > i$, R_L is below 100 per cent, but above i/r. A smaller a moves R_L toward its minimum of i/r, while a larger a pushes it up toward its maximum of 100 per cent. If a small R_L is desirable, and it is possible to achieve an $r > i$, a should be kept as low as possible, i.e. the loans should be amortized slowly over a long period of time.

3. If $r < i$, R_L is above 100 per cent, but below i/r. The role of a is now reversed. A higher a pulls R_L down toward its minimum of 100 per cent, while a lower a raises it toward its maximum of i/r. If a small R_L is desired in the present case, a should be increased; that is, amortization should be speeded up. This conclusion contradicts the traditional recommendation; but let us withhold judgment as yet.

The case of $r < i$ has been so taken for granted in the literature that the other two possibilities have been almost completely ignored. There is no denying of course that in this case the inflow of funds will eventually exceed the outflow. To the foreign investment

TABLE II.—CASE 1: THE EFFECT OF VARYING MAGNITUDES OF a ON R_L
(IN PERCENTAGES)

a	20%	10%	5%	2%	1%	0
(1) $r > i$ $r = 4\%$ $i = 2\%$	92	86	78	67	60	50
(2) $r < i$ $r = 2\%$ $i = 6\%$	118	133	157	200	233	300

enthusiasts we may offer the following consolations: first, they need not surrender so readily the possibility of $r > i$; second, even if $r < i$, R_L (with given r, i, and a) does not increase indefinitely, but approaches a not unreasonable asymptote, as given by expression (1). And finally, all these values of R_L are limits which are not reached for quite some time. Table III gives the number of years required by R to reach 100 per cent on the extreme assumption that $r = 0$. A period of 20–30 years is by no means excluded. Perhaps by that time we shall be able to accept an import surplus with greater ease.[24]

There is something puzzling about Table III. It is based on the assumption that $r = 0$. Hence we have the case of $r < i$. A higher a should result in a lower R_L, and speaking intuitively, a high a

[24] In Cases 2 and 3, where different amortization methods are used, the final values of R are reached more rapidly.

TABLE III.—CASE 1: NUMBER OF YEARS REQUIRED FOR R TO REACH 100 PER CENT WHEN $r = 0$

Per Cent						
a \ i	0	1	2	3	4	6
20	Infinite	15	12	10	9	7
10	Infinite	24	18	15	13	10
5	Infinite	36	25	20	16	12
2	Infinite	55	35	26	20	14
1	Infinite	69	41	29	22	15
0	Impossible	100	50	33	25	17

CHART I.—THE BEHAVIOR OF R OVER TIME IN CASE 1

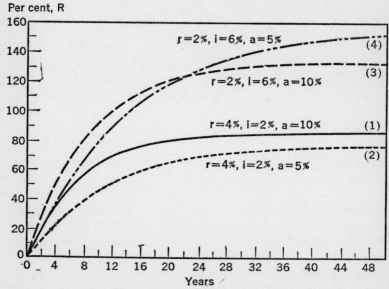

should prolong the period needed by R for reaching 100 per cent. Yet the table shows that exactly the opposite holds true.

What has been said here about the effects of a refers to R_L, and as far as it is concerned, a does play a stabilizing role in the sense that a high a invariably moves it toward 100 per cent. But to solve the puzzle of Table III we should trace the actual behavior of R over time. This is done in Table IV and Chart I.

The first two columns of Table IV where $r > i$ do not reveal anything new. But Columns 3 and 4, and their respective curves in Chart I where $r < i$, are most interesting. As expected, a higher a (Column 3 and Curve 3) gives a lower R_L. But for a rather long

TABLE IV.—CASE 1: THE BEHAVIOR OF R OVER TIME FOR GIVEN MAGNITUDES OF a, r, AND i (IN PERCENTAGES)

Years	1	2	3	4
	$r > i$		$r < i$	
	$r = 4\%$	$i = 2\%$	$r = 2\%$	$i = 6\%$
	$a = 10\%$	$a = 5\%$	$a = 10\%$	$a = 5\%$
1	11	7	15	11
2	21	13	28	21
3	29	18	40	30
4	37	24	51	38
5	43	28	60	46
10	65	46	93[a]	79
15	75	58	111	102[a]
20	81	65	121	118
25	83	70	127	130
50	86	77	133	152
At the limit	86	78	133	157

[a] In Column 3, R reaches 100 per cent after 11.6 years; in Column 4, after 14.5 years.

initial period Curve 3 is above Curve 4: during this period, a higher a increases R.[25] So when $r < i$, the traditional method of reducing R by means of a small a holds true at the beginning but brings on a punishment at the end.

All these conclusions were reached on the basis of an amortization method which, for all its analytical virtues, is not common in practice. Let us now turn to a more practical case.

Case 2. The Original Value Method

Every investment is completely amortized in a series of k annual payments, each equal to an a fraction of the *original* value of the

[25] This period during which a higher a increases R varies directly with r and inversely with a and i.

investment, so that k—the length of the amortization period—equals $1/a$. The interest, as usual, is charged against the outstanding debt. Therefore a and i are no longer additive (in the sense of Case 1), and this is one of the reasons why both the mathematics and the final results of the present case are rather clumsy.[26]

Starting from the zero point, R is moved by the lending process to its following *final value, R_F:*

$$(2) \qquad R_F = \frac{A + I}{G}_F = \frac{i}{r} + \frac{a(r - i)}{r^2}\left[1 - \frac{1}{(1 + r)^{1/a}}\right],$$

or, if the reader prefers to use k instead of $1/a$,

$$(3) \qquad R_F = \frac{A + I}{G}_F = \frac{i}{r} + \frac{(r - i)}{kr^2}\left[1 - \frac{1}{(1 + r)^k}\right].^{27}$$

However clumsy, expressions (2) and (3) have one great advantage over their counterpart (1) of Case 1. The latter expressed R_L, that is, the *limit* of R, and it held true only after a long period of time (theoretically—at infinity). Formulas (2) and (3) come into effect immediately after the expiration of the first $(k + 1)$ years, and from then on the value of R remains unchanged. The reader with an aversion to 'limits' and 'infinities' will now stand on firmer ground.

As in Case 1, a, i, and r were assumed to be constant in the derivation of (2) and (3), and again they can be allowed to vary in the interpretation of these expressions. This interpretation is by no means easy: with i present in two places, once with a plus sign and again with a minus, a appearing both in the numerator and, as an exponent, in the denominator, and r jumping all over the place, not much can be done without formal mathematics. Yet the examination

---

[26] It is assumed both in the formulas and in the tables that amortization and interest charges begin in the second year, and that interest for any given year is computed from the debt of the preceding year.

[27] For the special case $r = 0$, we have

$$R_F = 1 + \frac{(k + 1)}{2} i,$$

which is not immediately obvious from (2) or (3). Our other ratios are as follows:

$$\frac{A}{G}_F = \frac{1}{kr}\left[1 - \frac{1}{(1 + r)^k}\right]; \quad \frac{I}{G}_F = \frac{i}{r}; \quad \frac{G - A}{G}_F = 1 - \frac{1}{kr}\left[1 - \frac{1}{(1 + r)^k}\right],$$

$$\text{for } r > 0.$$

of these expressions can yield a few clues which can then be tested by numerical examples given in Tables V–VII.

Let us call i/r in (2) or (3) 'the left part,' and the remainder, 'the right part.' It is clear that the right part is positive for $r > i$, and

TABLE V.—CASE 2: THE VALUES OF R_F FOR GIVEN MAGNITUDES OF a (OR k), r, AND i (IN PERCENTAGES)

Per Cent	$k = 10$ years $a = 10\%$					
r \ i	0	1	2	3	4	6
0	100	106	111	117	122	133
1	95	100	105	111	116	126
2	90	95	100	105	110	120
3	85	90	95	100	105	115
4	81	86	91	95	100	109
6	74	78	82	87	91	100

Per Cent	$k = 20$ years $a = 5\%$					
r \ i	0	1	2	3	4	6
0	100	111	121	132	142	163
1	90	100	110	120	129	149
2	82	91	100	109	118	136
3	74	83	91	100	109	126
4	68	76	84	92	100	116
6	57	64	72	79	86	100

negative for $r < i$, and that it vanishes for $r = i$. We should again examine the three alternatives:

1. If $r = i$, R_F equals 100 per cent, irrespective of the magnitude of a (or k).

2. If $r > i$, the right side, being positive, is *added* to i/r. Therefore, i/r is the minimum of R_F, and 100 per cent is its maximum (see Appendix). As shown in Tables V and VI, a low a (or a high k), that

TABLE VI.—CASE 2: THE EFFECT OF VARYING MAGNITUDES OF a (OR k) ON R_F (IN PERCENTAGES)

k \ a	5 years 20%	10 years 10%	20 years 5%	50 years 2%	100 years 1%	No Amortization 0
(1) $r > i$ $r = 4\%$ $i = 2\%$	95	91	84	71	62	50
(2) $r < i$ $r = 2\%$ $i = 6\%$	111	120	136	174	214	300

TABLE VII.—CASE 2: THE BEHAVIOR OF R OVER TIME FOR GIVEN MAGNITUDES OF a (OR k), r, AND i (IN PERCENTAGES)

Years	1	2	3	4
	$r > i$ $r = 4\%$ $i = 2\%$		$r < i$ $r = 2\%$ $i = 6\%$	
	$k = 10$ years $a = 10\%$	$k = 20$ years $a = 5\%$	$k = 10$ years $a = 10\%$	$k = 20$ years $a = 5\%$
1	—	—	—	—
2	12	7	16	11
3	22	13	30	21
4	33	19	44	31
5	43	25	58	40
10	84	49	112[b]	80
15	91[a]	68	120[a]	111[b]
20	91	82	120	133
Final Value	91	84	120	136

[a] The final values in Columns 1 and 3 are reached in the 11th year.

[b] In Column 3, R reaches 100 per cent between the 8th and the 9th years; in Column 4, in the 13th year.

is, a long amortization period, moves R_F to its minimum, while a high a raises it to its maximum.

3. If $r < i$, the right side, now negative, is subtracted from i/r. The latter is therefore the maximum of R_F, while 100 per cent is its minimum. Rapid amortization pulls R_F down, while a small a pushes it up.

CHART II.—THE BEHAVIOR OF R OVER TIME IN CASE 2

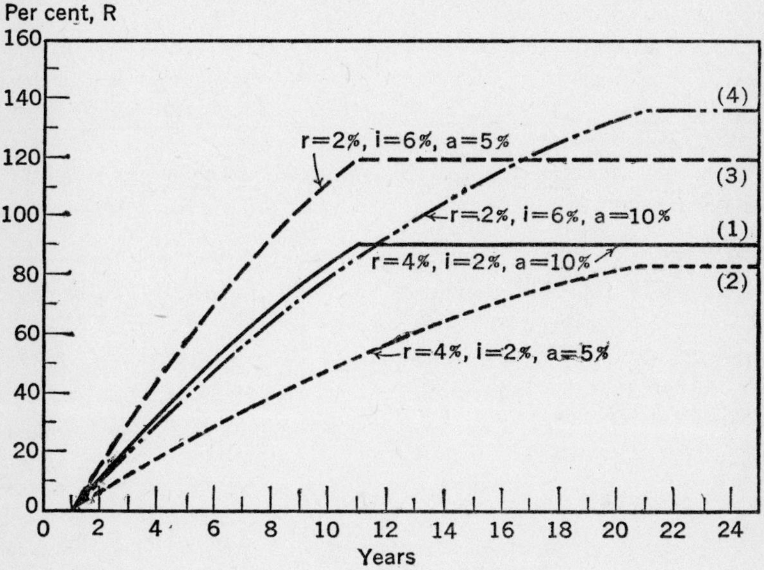

Note: The scale of this chart is twice that of Chart I.

Thus all conclusions of Case 1 are met again. Comparison of Table V with the corresponding Table I of Case 1 shows their essential similarity, and the same is true for Tables II and VI. We notice that when $r > i$, the magnitudes of R_F in Case 2 exceed those of R_L in Case 1, while for $r < i$, the situation is reversed. In Case 2, a is applied to the original value of each loan. In Case 1, on the other hand, a is applied to the net debt, which is diminished by successive amortization charges. Thus the same rate (say, 10 per cent) results in *more effective* amortization in Case 2 as compared with Case 1.

The behavior of R over time is shown in Table VII and Chart II. The similarity with Table IV and Chart I of Case 1 is striking; again Curve 4 intersects Curve 3:[28] when $r < i$, a higher a gives a lower R_F, but a higher R for an initial span of time. We should note once more, however, that R_F is reached not at infinity, but after the expiration of $(k + 1)$ years.

Case 3. The Equal Installment Method

Here the *principal and interest* of each loan are paid off in a series of k equal annual installments. While the method as such is different from that discussed in Case 2 and the appearance of the algebraic formulas given in the Appendix betrays little similarity, all limits are identical in the two cases, and the numerical results are similar to such an extent that a separate discussion of Case 3 can be dispensed with.[29]

* * * *

Because of the close similarity between the results of the three cases, we can make greater use of the formula of Case 1 than its impracticality would appear to justify. Precise numerical answers should, of course, be computed in accordance with the amortization method actually used, but the expression

$$(1) \qquad\qquad R_L = \frac{a + i}{a + r}$$

is a satisfactory working approximation of the limiting (or final) value of R for many practical purposes. Its simplicity will compensate us for the loss in rigor.

Expression (1) is an approximation to the general solution of our problem. In the general case, R_L can be larger, smaller, or equal to 100 per cent. The traditional assumption that R_L inevitably exceeds 100 per cent is only a special case of (1), when $r < i$. There may be excellent reasons for assuming that $r < i$, but it is well to remember that it is only a special case.

[28] It even intersects Curve 1. For a while a lower a can hold R down more effectively than a higher r does.

[29] This is true if we look at the problem, as we did here, from the lender's over-all point of view. To the particular borrower, the choice of amortization method may be of considerable importance.

MATHEMATICAL APPENDIX

LIST OF SYMBOLS

All flows and rates are per annum

A = amortization charge;

D = net debt outstanding;

G = gross investment or lending;

I = interest charge;

$R = \dfrac{A + I}{G}$ —ratio of inflow to outflow;

$R_L = \underset{t \to \infty}{\text{Lim}}\, R$ (Case 1);

$R_F = R_n$ for $n > k$ (Cases 2 and 3);

a = amortization rate (Cases 1 and 2);

α = service rate including amortization and interest (Case 3);

i = interest rate;

k = length of amortization period (Cases 2 and 3);

n = time in years (Cases 2 and 3);

r = relative rate of growth;

t = time in years (Case 1);

$u = 1 + r$ (Cases 2 and 3);

$v = 1 + i$ (Case 3).

In all cases, the initial value of $G = 1$. All variables are assumed to be positive, though this requirement is not always necessary.

Case 1. The Net Value Method—Continuous Series

By definition of this method,

(1.1) $$A = Da$$

and

(1.2) $$\frac{dD}{dt} = G - A.$$

Hence,

(1.3) $$\frac{dD}{dt} = G - Da.$$

With

(1.4) $$G = e^{rt},$$

the solution of the differential equation (1.3) takes the form of

$$(1.5) \qquad D = \frac{1}{(a+r)} (e^{rt} - e^{-at}).$$

Since $A + I = (a + i)D$, we next obtain

$$(1.6) \qquad R = \frac{A+I}{G} = \frac{(a+i)}{(a+r)} [1 - e^{-(a+r)t}],$$

and

$$(1.7) \qquad R_L = \operatorname*{Lim}_{t \to \infty} R = \frac{a+i}{a+r}.$$

It is obvious that

$$(1.8) \qquad \frac{i}{r} \leqq R_L \leqq 1 \qquad \text{for} \qquad r \geqq i,$$

$$(1.9) \qquad 1 \leqq R_L \leqq \frac{i}{r} \qquad \text{for} \qquad r \leqq i;$$

also that

$$\frac{\partial R_L}{\partial r} < 0, \qquad \frac{\partial R_L}{\partial i} > 0; \qquad \frac{\partial R_L}{\partial a} = \frac{r-i}{(a+r)^2},$$

which is positive for $r > i$ and negative for $r < i$.

The following properties of R can be established:

$$(1.10) \qquad \frac{\partial R}{\partial i} > 0,$$

$$(1.11) \qquad \frac{\partial R}{\partial r} < 0,$$

$$(1.12) \qquad \frac{\partial R}{\partial a} = \frac{(a+i)(a+r)t - (i-r)[e^{(a+r)t} - 1]}{(a+r)^2 e^{(a+r)t}}.$$

For $r > i$, $(\partial R/\partial a) > 0$. If $r < i$, $(\partial R/\partial a) > 0$ for small t, and $(\partial R/\partial a) < 0$ for large t. The t for which $(\partial R/\partial a) = 0$ is given by the equation

$$(1.13) \qquad \frac{e^{(a+r)t} - 1}{(a+r)t} = \frac{a+i}{i-r},$$

which can be solved to any desired degree of approximation. Its following properties can be proved:

$$\frac{\partial t}{\partial i} < 0, \qquad \frac{\partial t}{\partial r} > 0, \qquad \text{and} \qquad \frac{\partial t}{\partial a} < 0.$$

To find t required to make $R = 1$ in the case $r < i$, we set (1.6) equal to 1 and get

$$(1.14) \qquad\qquad t = \frac{1}{(a + r)} \log_e \frac{a + i}{i - r}.$$

It can be shown that in (1.14),

$$\frac{\partial t}{\partial i} < 0, \qquad \frac{\partial t}{\partial r} > 0, \qquad \text{and} \qquad \frac{\partial t}{\partial a} < 0.$$

Case 2. The Original Value Method—Discrete Series[30]

It is important to note that in this Case $a = 1/k$. It is assumed that amortization begins with the second period. The symbol n is always used in the sense $n > k$.

We first find D_n.

Periods	G	A	
1	1		—
2	u	a	$= \dfrac{a(u - 1)}{u - 1};$
3	u^2	$a(1 + u)$	$= \dfrac{a(u^2 - 1)}{u - 1};$
4	u^3	$a(1 + u + u^2)$	$= \dfrac{a(u^3 - 1)}{u - 1};$
.	.	.	
.	.	.	
.	.	.	
k	u^{k-1}	$a(1 + u + u^2 + \cdots + u^{k-2})$	$= \dfrac{a(u^{k-1} - 1)}{u - 1};$
$(k + 1)$	u^k	$a(1 + u + u^2 + \cdots + u^{k-1})$	$= \dfrac{a(u^k - 1)}{u - 1}.$

After $(k + 1)$ periods, the first investment made in period 1, and already amortized for k periods between the second and $(k + 1)$ periods inclusive, is fully written off. Its amortization is not recorded any more.

[30] [The use of continuous series could simplify the derivations without distorting the results. See the Mathematical Appendix of Essay VII.]

$$(k + 2) \qquad u^{k+1} \qquad a(u + u^2 + \cdots + u^k) \qquad = \frac{au(u^k - 1)}{u - 1}.$$

Similarly, after $(k + 2)$ periods, amortization of the second investment is not recorded any more.

$$(k + 3) \qquad u^{k+2} \qquad a(u^2 + u^3 + \cdots + u^{k+1}) \qquad = \frac{au^2(u^k - 1)}{u - 1}.$$

And in general,

$$(2.1) \qquad A_n = \frac{au^{n-k-1}(u^k - 1)}{u - 1};$$

$$(2.2) \qquad \sum_{j=1}^{k} A_j = \frac{a}{(u - 1)} [u + u^2 + u^3 + \cdots + u^{k-1} - (k - 1)]$$

$$= \frac{a}{(u - 1)} \left[\frac{u(u^{k-1} - 1)}{u - 1} - k + 1 \right];$$

$$(2.3) \qquad \sum_{j=k+1}^{n} A_j = \frac{a(u^k - 1)}{(u - 1)} (1 + u + u^2 + \cdots + u^{n-k-1})$$

$$= \frac{a(u^k - 1)(u^{n-k} - 1)}{(u - 1)^2};$$

$$(2.4) \qquad \sum_{j=1}^{n} A_j = \frac{a}{(u - 1)} \left[\frac{u(u^{k-1} - 1)}{u - 1} - k + 1 \right.$$

$$\left. + \frac{(u^k - 1)(u^{n-k} - 1)}{(u - 1)} \right]$$

$$= \frac{au^n - au^{n-k} - u + 1}{(u - 1)^2},$$

because $ak = 1$.

$$(2.5) \quad D_n = \sum_{j=1}^{n} (G_j - A_j) = \frac{u^n - 1}{u - 1} - \frac{au^n - au^{n-k} - u + 1}{(u - 1)^2}$$

$$= \frac{u^{n+1} - u^n - au^n + au^{n-k}}{(u - 1)^2}.$$

Since we assumed that amortization on any investment made in a given period does not begin until the next period, it is logical to assume that the interest charges in any period are related to the debt of the preceding period, so that

$$(2.6) \qquad\qquad I_{n+1} = D_n i.$$

For convenience, we shall compute the inflow to outflow ratio for the $(n + 1)$ period.

$$(2.7) \qquad\qquad R_{n+1} = \frac{A_{n+1} + I_{n+1}}{G_{n+1}}$$

$$= \frac{\dfrac{au^{n-k}(u^k - 1)}{u - 1} + \dfrac{i(u^{n+1} - u^n - au^n + au^{n-k})}{(u - 1)^2}}{u^n}$$

$$= \frac{i(u - 1) + a(u - 1 - i)}{(u - 1)^2} - \frac{a(u - 1 - i)}{u^k(u - 1)^2}$$

$$= \frac{i}{u - 1} + \frac{a(u - 1 - i)}{(u - 1)^2} \cdot \left(1 - \frac{1}{u^k}\right).$$

Substituting $r = u - 1$, we finally obtain

$$(2.8) \qquad\qquad R_F = \frac{i}{r} + \frac{(r - i)}{kr^2}\left[1 - \frac{1}{(1 + r)^k}\right].$$

Since (2.8) does not contain n, R_F remains constant for any $n > k$.
For the special case $r = 0$, it can be shown that

$$(2.9) \qquad\qquad R_F = 1 + \frac{(k + 1)}{2} i.$$

To establish the upper and lower limits of R_F, we first find

$$(2.10) \qquad\qquad \underset{k \to \infty}{\text{Lim}}\, R_F = \frac{i}{r};$$

next, since

$$(2.11) \quad \underset{k \to 0}{\text{Lim}}\, \frac{1}{k}\left[1 - \frac{1}{(1 + r)^k}\right] = r, \quad (\text{more exactly, } \log_e (1 + r)),$$

$$(2.12) \qquad\qquad \underset{k \to 0}{\text{Lim}}\, R_F = 1.$$

Therefore,

$$(2.13) \qquad\qquad \frac{i}{r} \leqq R_F \leqq 1, \qquad\qquad \text{for } r \geqq i,$$

$$(2.14) \qquad\qquad 1 \leqq R_F \leqq \frac{i}{r}, \qquad\qquad \text{for } r \leqq i.$$

The following properties of R_F can be established:

$$\frac{\partial R_F}{\partial i} > 0, \quad \frac{\partial R_F}{\partial r} < 0, \quad \frac{\partial R_F}{\partial k} < 0 \text{ for } r > i, \quad \text{and} \quad \frac{\partial R_F}{\partial k} > 0 \text{ for } r < i.$$

The substitution of e^{-rk} for $(1 + r)^{-k}$ simplifies some of the derivations.

These results follow closely those of Case 1.

Case 3. The Equal Installment Method—Discrete Series

The symbol n is always used in the sense of $n > k$.

According to this method, the principal and interest of each investment are paid off in a series of k equal annual installments beginning with the second year, each payment being equal to an α fraction of the original investment. These annual payments form an annuity, the present value of which should equal the original value of the investment. If the latter is G, each annual payment equals αG, and with the standard formula for the present value of an annuity, we obtain

(3.1)
$$G = \frac{\alpha G(v^k - 1)}{v^k(v - 1)},$$

where

(3.2)
$$v = 1 + i.$$

From (3.1)

(3.3)
$$\alpha = \frac{v^k(v - 1)}{v^k - 1}.$$

To avoid duplication in deriving $A + I$, we shall make use of the results obtained in Case 2, by substituting the service rate α for the amortization rate a, and hence $A + I$ for A. Such a transformation of expression (2.1) in Case 2 gives

(3.4)
$$(A + I)_n = \frac{\alpha u^{n-k-1}(u^k - 1)}{u - 1},$$

and

(3.5)
$$R_F = \frac{\alpha(u^k - 1)}{u^k(u - 1)} = \frac{\dfrac{v^k(v - 1)}{v^k - 1}}{\dfrac{u^k(u - 1)}{u^k - 1}},$$

or

$$(3.6) \qquad R_F = \frac{\dfrac{i(1 + i)^k}{(1 + i)^k - 1}}{\dfrac{r(1 + r)^k}{(1 + r)^k - 1}} = \frac{1 - \dfrac{i}{(1 + i)^k}}{1 - \dfrac{1}{(1 + r)^k}}.$$

It can be shown that for the special case $r = 0$,

$$(3.7) \qquad R_F = \frac{kv^k(v - 1)}{v^k - 1} = \frac{ik}{1 - \dfrac{1}{(1 + i)^k}}.$$

As in Case 2 we have

$$(3.8) \qquad \frac{i}{r} \leqq R_F \leqq 1, \qquad\qquad \text{for } r \geqq i,$$

$$(3.9) \qquad 1 \leqq R_F \leqq \frac{i}{r}, \qquad\qquad \text{for } r \leqq i.$$

The derivatives of R_F in respect to r, i, and k have the same signs as the corresponding ones in Case 2.

VII

Depreciation, Replacement, and Growth*[1]

Depreciation allowances in the United States have usually provided over one-half of expenditures on gross investment. The magnitude of this fraction has worried employment-minded economists like Keynes and others, and was prominently discussed in the TNEC hearings and reports.[2] The other aspect of capital depreciation— that a large part of current investment is apparently needed (and not only in the United States) just to keep the capital stock intact— becomes important there in wartime, and it is always important to those countries who do not look at investment primarily as an employment-creating device and who suffer from a shortage of savings. In Britain, depreciation charges relative to gross investment have been somewhat larger than in the United States, while the Russians have managed to get away with a mere fraction of either ratio—disparities which cannot be completely explained by differences in national temperament or by manipulations of Soviet statisticians.[3]

Much as I hate to spoil my story by announcing its plot in advance, this paper is too long and involved to be clear otherwise. It deals with growth of investment and of capital stock subject

* [Reprinted by permission from The Economic Journal, Vol. 63 (Mar., 1953), pp. 1–32.]

[1] I am very grateful to the RAND Corporation, and particularly to Joseph A. Kershaw and Norman M. Kaplan, for assistance in the preparation of this paper. A preliminary draft was presented to RAND in August 1951, and the final version in September 1952 (P-325). Thanks are also due to Edith T. Penrose for her excellent editorial assistance and to Robert I. Berg (both of The Johns Hopkins University) for his faithful help with computations.

[2] John M. Keynes, The General Theory of Employment Interest and Money (New York, 1936), pp. 98–106; Alvin H. Hansen, Fiscal Policy and Business Cycles (New York, 1941), pp. 384–8; United States Temporary National Economic Committee, Investigation of Concentration of Economic Power (Seventy-sixth Congress, Washington, 1940–41); Hearings, Part 9; Final Report of the Executive Secretary; Monographs Nos. 15 and 37.

[3] For data and sources, see pp. 158–60 and notes 10–15.

to depreciation and periodic replacement. Our first task is to inquire into the relation between annual depreciation charges and investment in a growing economy or a firm (Section I). Next, the relation between replacement on the one hand and investment and depreciation on the other is derived (Section II). It turns out that in a growing society, replacement falls far short of depreciation. Hence, investment net of depreciation cannot be identified with investment net of replacement. This suggests that existing growth models which have taken this identity for granted should be revised, and two such attempts are presented (Sections III and IV). In addition to the propensity to save and the capital coefficient (or its reciprocal) familiar to us from their past performances, a major role is played here by the life span of capital, previously neglected.

The paper is essentially an attempt to put into reasonable English the results of mathematical derivations. Its mathematical skeleton will, as usual, be hidden in an Appendix and notes; final results and numerical illustrations are given in the text, but a few sharp bones which I have not been able to conceal still protrude here and there.[4] The following assumptions are made:

1. Each capital asset has a definite life span, indicated by m (years) and is religiously retired upon the expiration of this period.

2. In accordance with prevailing American business practice, depreciation, D, is computed according to the straight-line method applied to the *original* cost of each asset. There being no scrap value, the annual depreciation rate is $1/m$.

3. The discussion proceeds as if every asset had the same life span of m years. Actually, m should be interpreted as the *average* life span of all assets, the Appendix indicating the proper averaging procedure.[5]

4. Gross investment, G, growing at a relative annual rate of r is the propelling force of the system. This rate is expressed in current prices, and will be deflated when required. The constancy of r greatly simplifies the mathematics, but not without cost.

---

[4] All our formulas and numerical illustrations are based on the so-called continuous functions from calculus, that is, investment, depreciation, and other processes take place continuously through time rather than once each period. In the text these functions are expressed in the more familiar compound interest formulas available in any college algebra text. The error involved is small enough to be disregarded.

[5] This is subject to certain qualifications to be indicated below.

Unless qualified, 'investment' is gross both of depreciation and of replacement.[6]

5. The existence of government is not explicitly recognized.

6. To make our results applicable to a new firm as well, a zero stock of capital in the initial period is assumed in Section I. This, of course, is not true of an established firm or of the economy as a whole; even the least-developed countries possess capital stocks surprisingly large relative to their outputs. In any case, the effects of this assumption do not last long.

While these assumptions simplify our task, they do, of course, restrict the usefulness of the results. A smooth and steady growth of investment is not found in a capitalist economy; a model embodying fluctuations of some form superimposed on a growth curve would be more appropriate there. Also, the treatment of the life span of assets as a given constant completely ignores the problem of replacement timing: surely assets are not retired in such an automatic fashion. There will be room for other complaints; but there is just so much one can do in one paper.

I

Like most economic problems, the present one is concerned with ratios: in Section II we will deal with ratios of replacement to investment and to depreciation; here we are concerned with the ratio of depreciation to investment, D/G. There being no capital at the start, D/G begins at zero and rises gradually to its *final* value, which, as shown on Chart I, it reaches at the expiration of m years: since assets last for m years, capital stock existing at any moment of time is the accumulation of investments over the preceding m years; the absence of investment before the zero year prevents the establishment of the final relationship between D and G until m years have expired.[7]

[6] Throughout the paper, r is assumed to be positive or zero. Since inventories are not subject to depreciation, it may be just as well to exclude them from G, though the error would not be large in any case. An attempt to assign the principal role to net rather than to gross investment did not pay for the ensuing complications.

[7] If total investment consists of two kinds, with life spans of m_1 and m_2 respectively, such that $m_2 > m_1$, the correctness of this statement, as well as of all our formulas, requires that at least m_2 years from the initial period must have elapsed. There are other conditions restricting the use of m as an average for the whole economy. See Appendix, Model 2.

The final value of D/G is given by the expression,

$$(1) \qquad D/G = \frac{1 - \dfrac{1}{(1 + r)^m}}{rm},$$

which varies inversely with both m and r.[8] The role of m is obvious: longer-lived capital reduces depreciation charges; but what r is doing here is not so clear. The more rapid the growth of investment (the higher the r), the greater is its present magnitude relative

CHART I.—THE MAGNITUDES OF D/G FOR DIFFERENT VALUES OF r AND m

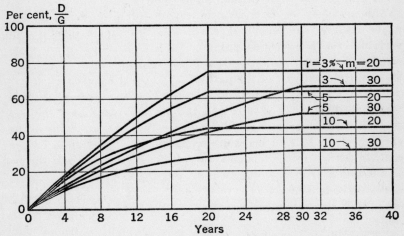

to investments of past years and hence to the existing stock of capital, the latter, as pointed out above, consisting of the accumu-

[8] Assuming that investment equalled one dollar m years ago, its growth over the last m years can be expressed as the geometric progression:

$$1, (1 + r), (1 + r)^2, \ldots \quad \ldots (1 + r)^{m-2}, (1 + r)^{m-1}.$$

Its sum over a period of m years, i.e. the present gross stock of capital, equals $\dfrac{(1 + r)^m - 1}{r}$. D, being $1/m$th of the latter, is $\dfrac{(1 + r)^m - 1}{rm}$. Dividing this by $G = (1 + r)^m$, we get the expression in the text.

If t indicates the length of time which passed from the initial period, and $t < m$,

$$D/G = \frac{1 - \dfrac{1}{(1 + r)^t}}{rm}.$$

lation of investments over the preceding m years. D, being a fraction of the capital stock, a high r reduces D/G.

It is most interesting that D/G is not only a function of r and m, but also of their product, rm, so that r and m are symmetrical in the multiplicative sense. A continuous function formula of D/G makes this obvious, but a glance at a compound interest table will convince the reader that, within a reasonable range, this is also true for expression (1): a dollar invested at 1 per cent for thirty years compounds to approximately the same amount (1.3478) as a dollar invested at 2 per cent for fifteen years (1.3459), one invested at 3 per cent for ten years (1.3439), and so on.[9]

This property of D/G—which is true for most ratios in this paper—is most convenient; it leaves us with only one independent variable—rm. The second column in Table I (p. 162) gives the magnitudes of D/G for various values of rm, and the reader can choose his own combinations of the particular values of r and m.

A reasonable approximation would place the average United States m at 30 years or so,[10] and the average real r over the last 80 years at, or slightly above, 3 per cent.[11] With rm thus being in the vicinity of 1, D/G in constant prices would approximate 60 per cent. In current prices, r comes closer to 5 per cent; this sets the rm at 1.5 and D/G around 50 per cent. Barring unforeseen changes, a 60–65 per cent average D/G in constant prices may be taken as a reasonable approximation for the United States for some time to come.[12]

---

[9] The final value of D/G in continuous form is $\dfrac{1 - e^{-rm}}{rm}$. With continuous compounding, the result of the example in the text would amount to $e^{0.3} = 1.3499$.

[10] Solomon Fabricant, *Capital Consumption and Adjustment* (New York, 1938), p. 34. Estimates obtained orally from the United States Department of Commerce also place the average American m in the vicinity of 30 years. It is possible that it has been declining over time, because of the increasing importance of equipment as compared with construction. For our purposes a rough approximation is quite satisfactory.

[11] From Simon Kuznets, *National Product since 1869* (New York, 1946), pp. 50, 115; *Survey of Current Business Supplement, National Income and Product of the United States, 1929–50* (Washington, 1951), pp. 146, 150. The rate of growth has, of course, sharply fluctuated from period to period.

[12] A comparison of these magnitudes with statistical data depends on the method of estimate and period chosen. According to George Terborgh, during the sixty years, 1869–1929, the American D/G in real terms ranged between 50

Interesting data on Soviet investment are presented in Norman Kaplan's recent study.[13] Over the period 1930–50, the Soviet D/G in current prices averaged between 12 and 25 per cent, a range that is not very meaningful because of sharp inflations. As an estimate of the real rate of growth of Soviet investment, Kaplan suggests 12 per cent; this sounds rather high, but the correct magnitude (if there is such a thing) must be extremely hard to ascertain.[14] The

---

and 70 per cent, with an upward trend due to the slight fall in the rate of growth of G. The average for the latter half of the twenties was 64 per cent (*The Bogey of Economic Maturity* (Chicago, 1945), p. 123). His investment, however, includes consumer durables as well; otherwise, D/G would be somewhat lower. From Kuznets (op. cit. p. 81), we find that over the period 1869–1908, the American D/G in real terms was only 45 per cent, evidently because of both a higher r and the relative predominance of construction over equipment, the former having a larger m. In 1909–28, D/G averaged over 60 per cent.

In current prices, Kuznets's D/G figures for 1869–1928 are practically the same as in real terms. This is rather surprising, because G in current prices grew much faster than in constant prices. More recently, D/G in the United States in current prices was as follows: in 1929, 53 per cent; 1929–41, 86.4 per cent; and since the war (1946–51), 42.2 per cent, the last figure reflecting not only a high level of investment after the war, but also the valuation of a good part of capital stock in pre-war prices. All these are the ratios of depreciation charges to the sum of new construction and producers' durable equipment (*Survey of Current Business*, op. cit. p. 151, and the Feb. 1952 issue, p. 9).

As far as the financing of investment is concerned, these ratios are overstated for two reasons: first, not all business depreciation charges are actually earned, particularly during depressions. Second, non-business investment (such as owner-occupied housing) is not subject to formal depreciation accounting, though regular mortgage payments give rise to savings considerably in excess of normal depreciation charges.

The British D/G seems to be slightly above the American, presumably owing to a lower rate of growth. In current prices the 1924 figure stood at 59 per cent (as compared with some 55 per cent for the United States); in 1929, at 61 per cent. Between 1930 and 1934 it fluctuated between 62 and 69 per cent. Since the war it has been around 50 per cent (somewhat higher if public investment is excluded). These figures should be treated as rough indications; my knowledge of British statistics is very slight. See Colin Clark, *National Income and Outlay* (London, 1937), pp. 86, 185; *National Income and Expenditure of the United Kingdom 1946 to 1950*, Command Paper 8203 (London, 1951), pp. 13, 43, 51; *Statistics of National Income and Expenditure*, Statistical Papers, Series H, No. 1 (1951, XVII, 4), prepared by the Statistical Office of the United Nations (New York, 1952), p. 46.

[13] Norman M. Kaplan, *Soviet Capital Formation and Industrialization*, a RAND Corporation Study P-277 (Santa Monica, Calif., Mar. 6, 1952), particularly pp. 1–12. [See also his 'Capital Formation and Allocation,' Abram Bergson, ed., *Soviet Economic Growth* (Evanston, Ill., 1953), pp. 37–87.]

[14] This is due not only to the peculiarities of Soviet statistics, but even more to the fact that under rapidly changing technological conditions and assort-

relative shares of equipment and construction in Soviet investment
being similar to the American, an m of 30 years may be taken
for a start; perhaps it should be lowered to take account of poorer
quality and lack of care of capital; but then obsolescence may play
a smaller role in Russia than in the United States, because it should
more often pay there to use a new machine with, rather than
instead of, an old one. Lacking knowledge about the relative magnitudes of these adjustments, we may just as well retain the above
estimate for m. The Soviet rm in real terms would reach, then, the
very high magnitude of 3.5 or so, with the corresponding D/G of
28 per cent. Even an 8 per cent rate of growth (which seems quite
conservative) would put this ratio below 40 per cent. Thus, in net
(of depreciation) investment, the Soviet advantage over the United
States and Britain must be much greater than in gross.[15]

The application of these ideas to a firm involves a very heroic
simplification; yet the results may be of some interest. As shown
on Chart I, in the first few years of a firm's existence a very small
part of investment expenditures comes from depreciation allowances; as time goes on depreciation as a source of funds plays an
increasing role, provided, of course, that the firm is able to earn it.
Finally, after the first m years are over, D/G becomes constant,
unless sharp changes in r and m take place. With stable prices, an
average American firm should eventually be able to finance nearly
two-thirds of its fixed capital requirements from depreciation; inflations such as have occurred in the past would bring this ratio
down to one-half or so.

II

We now turn to replacement (R). Since its magnitude is affected
by price changes, two separate cases will be considered.

---

ments of goods and prices, a dependable index of output is extremely difficult
to construct. On this see Alexander Gerschenkron, *A Dollar Index of Soviet
Machinery Output, 1927–28 to 1937*, a RAND Corporation Study R-197 (Santa
Monica, Calif., Apr. 6, 1951).

We should be somewhat careful in applying our formulas to the Soviet experience, because the assumption that at least m years have passed from the
initial point (and their strict interpretation would require even a longer period)
hardly fits the Soviet case.

[15] According to Kaplan, the fractions of gross national product devoted to
gross investment in Russia and in the United States (excluding the depression
years in the latter) have been quite similar, between 15 and 20 per cent. [For
a further discussion of the Soviet case see Essay IX.]

Case 1. Constant Prices

By assumption, replacement takes place exactly m years after an asset is produced, and therefore, $R = G$ made m years earlier. Let the latter equal 1. If G has remained constant, the present stock of capital, being the accumulation of investment over the past m years, is simply m. Since by definition D is $1/m$th of the capital stock, $D = 1$. Hence (after the expiration of the first m years) R and D are identical.

Growth destroys this identity. If G was at 1 m years ago, as in the preceding example, and has grown at the rate of r per year since, the present stock of capital is larger than m, and D exceeds 1. Therefore, D exceeds R.

As this excess of D over R is caused by the growth of G over the period of m years, the disparity between D and R will be greater the larger r and m are. Hence the ratio R/D varies inversely with r and m. As a matter of fact, like D/G of the preceding section, it varies inversely with their product rm.

More exactly, a stream of investment which stood at one dollar m years ago now equals $(1 + r)^m$. Hence by definition of R given above,

$$(2) \qquad R/G = \frac{1}{(1 + r)^m},$$

which does not equal D/G as given by (1). Dividing (2) by (1), we find

$$(3) \qquad R/D = \frac{rm}{(1 + r)^m - 1}.^{16}$$

Chart II and Table I show the final magnitudes of D/G, R/G, and R/D as functions of rm. Under stationary conditions they all equal 100 per cent. As rm increases, they decline, the fall in R/G being the most pronounced. Taking the United States rm (in constant prices) around 1, as before, we find that while D constitutes some 63 per cent of G, only 37 per cent of the latter is needed for replacement. Thus R/D equals only 58 per cent (37/63), the remaining 42 per cent of D being available for expansion.

[16] The corresponding continuous function formulas are: $R/G = e^{-rm}$; $R/D = \dfrac{rm}{e^{rm} - 1}$.

CHART II.—THE FINAL MAGNITUDES OF D/G, R/G, AND R/D

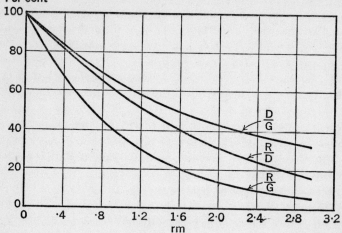

TABLE I.—THE FINAL MAGNITUDES OF D/G, R/G, AND R/D AS FUNCTIONS OF rm

rm	Percentages		
	D/G	R/G	R/D
0.1	95	91	95
0.2	91	82	90
0.3	86	74	86
0.4	82	67	81
0.5	79	61	77
1.0	63	37	58
1.5	52	22	43
2.0	43	14	31
2.5	37	8	22
3.0	32	5	16
3.5	28	3	11

The Soviet picture is even more striking. Should their real rm be as high as 3.5, only 11 per cent of their depreciation charges (as defined here) would be needed for replacement, while replacement would constitute a mere 3 per cent of investment. Even an rm of 2.5 would keep their R/G down to 8 per cent, a figure small enough to be frequently ignored. Again, their advantage over the United States and Britain in investment net of replacement is much greater than a comparison of gross investment figures would indicate.

Case 2. Changing Prices

A change in prices distorts these relationships, because the cost of R no longer equals that of G made m years earlier. Retaining r as the rate of growth of investment in current prices, we shall indicate the real rate of growth by u, and the rate of increase of prices by $i = r - u$.

Depreciation being related to the capital stock in original prices, D/G still varies inversely with r, and is entirely unaffected by the magnitude of the real rate of growth u. Whether investment grows rapidly because of real factors or merely as a result of inflation is immaterial for D/G.

The stream of investment which started from one dollar m years ago again equals $(1 + r)^m$ at present, but owing to the rise in prices at the rate of i per year, its present cost of replacement has increased to $(1 + i)^m$. Hence

$$(4) \qquad R/G = \frac{(1 + i)^m}{(1 + r)^m},$$

which, with a minor error, can be expressed as

$$(5) \qquad R/G = \frac{1}{(1 + u)^m}.$$

Dividing (4) by (1), we obtain the formidable

$$(6) \qquad R/D = \frac{rm(1 + i)^m}{(1 + r)^m - 1} = \frac{m(u + i)(1 + i)^m}{[1 + (u + i)]^m - 1}. \quad [17]$$

It can be demonstrated without too much trouble that R/D varies inversely with u (just as in (3) it did with r), and it is obvious that a rise in prices raises the cost of R and therefore the magnitude of R/D, but the relationship between m and R/D is more complex. First, an increase in m intensifies the effect of price changes on R/D;

---

[17] With continuous functions, $R/G = e^{-um}$, and $R/D = \dfrac{rme^{im}}{e^{rm} - 1} = \dfrac{(u + i)m}{e^{um} - e^{-im}}.$
The error mentioned in the text arises from the use of discrete functions. Its magnitude can be ascertained by actually performing the operation indicated. It is small enough to be disregarded.

secondly, it reduces R/D for the same reason as in Case 1. If prices fall, both effects work in the same direction, and R/D falls. If prices rise, they work in opposite directions, and an increase in m may move R/D up or down, depending on the relative magnitudes of the variables involved. (There even exists an m which maximizes R/D. This may delight amateur mathematicians, like myself, but has little economic meaning.)

We have already seen that a rise in prices reduces D/G. In other words, a smaller fraction of investment can be financed by depreciation. We now find that it also increases R/D; thus a larger part of depreciation is needed for replacement. Both aspects are inflationary and help inflation to feed on itself. Exactly the same phenomenon but in the opposite direction takes place during deflation. Thus the practice of charging depreciation on the basis of original cost of capital brings in a certain element of instability.[18]

This should not be exaggerated, however, because in depression many firms are unable to earn their depreciation charges, while allowances for price rises are made, formally or otherwise, during inflation; yet some effect on dividend and other policies remains, particularly during deflation due to the conservative basis of our accounting (embodied in mottos such as 'cost or market—whichever is lower').[19]

---

[18] Between 1929 and 1932 depreciation charges in the United States in real terms (deflated by the price index used by the Department of Commerce in computing gross private domestic investment in 1939 prices—see the *Survey of Current Business, 1951 National Income Supplement,* pp. 146, 151) increased by 16 per cent.

It should be pointed out, however, that the present depreciation practice, by understating profits during depressions and overstating them during inflations, reduces income-tax liabilities in the first instance and increases them in the second, which should have a stabilizing effect on the economy. The latter may be more important than the de-stabilizing effect discussed in the text. Also, the revaluation of assets to express depreciation charges in current prices is a most formidable task. On this see E. Cary Brown, *Effects of Taxation; Depreciation Adjustments for Price Changes* (Boston, 1952).

The application of our results to a cyclical problem should be done with care, because our formulas are based on the assumption of continuous growth over the preceding m years.

[19] These institutional factors have unfortunately been disregarded in the recent discussions of the so-called Pigou effect. I certainly dread to think of the damage that a prolonged fall in prices would do to a capitalist economy faced with unemployment. See Don Patinkin, 'Price Flexibility and Full Employment,' *The American Economic Review,* Vol. 38 (Sept., 1948), pp. 543–64.

Of the many numerical illustrations that might accompany the expressions for R/D as given by (6) (R/G can be read off Table I by substituting um for rm), only one is given here: the annual rate of inflation (the magnitude of i) required to equalize R with D. This is done in Table II.[20] With a small m, i is roughly equal to u, but as m increases, i considerably exceeds u. Taking u for the United States as before, around 3 per cent and m at 30 years, we find that the equality of R and D requires an i of some 4 per cent per year.[21] Over short periods of time, sharper price rises have taken place, but the average since 1869 or so has been about 2 per cent per

TABLE II.—THE ANNUAL RATE OF INFLATION WHICH EQUALIZES REPLACEMENT
AND DEPRECIATION FOR GIVEN m AND u

u per cent m years	Percentages				
	1	2	3	4	5
10	1.05	2.1	3.3	4.6	6.0
20	1.07	2.3	3.8	5.5	7.5
30	1.11	2.5	4.3	6.6	9.8
40	1.16	2.7	5.0	8.3	13.5

year.[22] Thus on the whole, R (as given by (6)) has been some 20 per cent below D, and barring very strong inflations (an annual rise of 4 per cent would double the price level every 17 years), a somewhat similar situation can be expected in the future.

That a change in prices can upset the relationship between R and D is well known. When prices rise, demands for larger depreciation credits for tax purposes are invariably made, the usual straight-line charges based on original costs being allegedly insufficient to finance replacement. Yet in an economy like the American, it takes

[20] It is computed from the formula $im + e^{-im} = e^{um} - um$, obtained from the expression for R/D given in note 17 by taking $R/D = 1$.

[21] With constant prices and $um = rm = 1$, R (as was shown in Case 1) falls short of D by some 40 per cent. This would suggest at first glance that a price increase of some 1 per cent per year for 30 years would be sufficient to equalize R and D, rather than the 4 per cent indicated in the text. The reason for this apparent discrepancy between common sense and mathematics lies in the fact that as prices rise, D also rises, though not to the same extent.

[22] The sources are given in note 11. All these figures are rough approximations. In the last few years, prices have risen by much more than 2 per cent per year. Whether this will be the pattern for the future remains to be seen.

quite a substantial price rise to bring about the apparently desired equality of R and D.[23] But when prices do not change, this equality is usually taken for granted.[24]

For this there are several reasons. First, there is our traditional preoccupation with stationary economics, which, of course, excludes growth. Close to this comes the deeply ingrained treatment of economic phenomena not as infinite processes but as final events which begin and end within a given period of time. An analysis of a constant stream of investment or even of a single or several separate investments are familiar examples of these types of approach. The concept of an economy growing indefinitely at some rate or rates has not yet received its deserved place in our tool-box.

But there is also a more fundamental difficulty. The demonstrated inequality between R and D depends on the definitions of these processes adopted here. If, for instance, depreciation is computed not along a straight line, but as an annuity to be invested at an interest rate equal to r so that it will accumulate to the original cost of the asset at the end of m years, the inequality between R and D disappears.[25] Conversely, the concentration of depreciation charges in the first few years of the life of an asset will increase the disparity between D and R.

The nature of replacement is more complex.[26] Even with a fixed life span of a capital asset, its removal from the books at the end of m years is an accounting entry which may or may not have

[23] While some rate of growth, such as that indicated in the text, can be assumed for the United States as a whole, there are many firms which grow more slowly, or not at all; for them any price rise may make R larger than D. The discussion in the text should not be interpreted as an argument for less liberal depreciation policy for tax purposes.

[24] The references here range all the way from an abstract article by Ragnar Frisch on 'The Interrelation between Capital Production and Consumer-Taking,' *The Journal of Political Economy*, Vol. 39 (Oct., 1931), pp. 646–54, to such diverse works as the preliminary *Estimates of the Capital Structure of American Industries, 1939*, by the Harvard Economic Project (Jan., 1950), p. 21 [since published as Wassily Leontief *et al.*, *Studies in the Structure of the American Economy* (New York, 1953), p. 189]; the TNEC *Monograph No.* 37, op. cit. pp. 69–70; and Lewis H. Kimmel, *Depreciation Policy and Postwar Expansion* (Brookings Institution, Washington, 1946), pp. 15–16. Most economists simply ignore the relationship between replacement and depreciation, which in most relevant instances implies the acceptance of their identity.

[25] I owe this observation to James S. Duesenberry.

[26] An excellent discussion of replacement timing is given by George Terborgh in *The Bogey of Economic Maturity* (Chicago, 1945), pp. 102–8.

economic significance. If the productive capacity of the asset remains more or less intact to the end, our assumption that replacement takes place in one operation is not far from reality. On the other hand, if its productive capacity declines gradually over time, its replacement by other assets (not necessarily within the same firm) is likewise a gradual process, and should the latter happen to move along a straight line, R and D become identical. If its capacity should decline particularly fast in the early years, replacement will exceed depreciation.

Thus the usually assumed identity of R and D, even in a growing economy (with constant prices), is not necessarily wrong, though I suspect that not all who accepted it had gone through this reasoning. Within a reasonable range, it should be looked upon as a more or less extreme case, the opposite extreme being our present approach. As usual, the truth lies somewhere between them.

In the United States, where assets are usually well maintained and retired more in response to technical obsolescence than because of physical deterioration, our treatment of replacement may be a better approximation of reality. In the more traditional countries the opposite may perhaps be true. Paradoxically, this may also be the case in Russia, where shortage of capital may make obsolescence relatively ineffective.

The extreme case presented here has not only made explicit the assumptions of its rival, but has also laid the groundwork for the general case as some average between them. While numerical results will depend on the averaging method chosen, I doubt if the over-all behavior of the variables will differ greatly from ours.[27]

III

So long as depreciation charges and replacement expenditures are assumed (by design or oversight) to be identical, no harm is done by excluding them from gross savings on the one hand and from gross investment on the other. This method has been followed

[27] When I first found that R differed from D (spring, 1951), I was not aware of the earlier works on the subject. Since then, I have found a reference to it in E. L. Grant and P. T. Norton, *Depreciation* (New York, 1949), pp. 292–5; a note in George O. May's 'The Relation of Depreciation Provisions to Replacement,' *The Journal of Accountancy*, Vol. 69 (May, 1940), p. 341. It is also mentioned by the Soviet economist A. I. Notkin in *Ocherki teorii sotsialisticheskogo vosproizvodstva* (Moscow, 1948), pp. 104–8, where it is traced back to Marx. (I owe this reference to Alexander Erlich.) There must be other instances as

in the existing growth models constructed by Harrod, Fellner, myself, and others.[28] But as soon as the divergence between D and R, caused both by growth and changing prices, is recognized, a revision of these models becomes necessary.

The attempts presented here follow in their main logical structure the familiar lines of their predecessors, and possess the same fundamental defect of treating all investment as a single homogeneous stream which enlarges the capacity for the production of goods in general. Capital remains the only limiting factor, all other resources being available in sufficient quantities. No explicit recognition of the government, and hence of its expenditures and taxes, is made. These limitations make our models ill suited for practical problems, but owing to the simplicity of their structure they are useful for a first examination of a new relationship in the theory of growth. In our case the innovation consists of working with gross rather than net saving, and in the substitution of replacement for depreciation in the computation of net investment.

An increase in capacity in terms of gross national product (P) is assumed to be proportional to net investment so defined (that is, net of replacement), the factor of proportionality—the capital coefficient—being indicated by $v = \dfrac{G - R}{\Delta P}$.[29] This implies that assets retain their full productive capacity until their retirement

---

well. A colleague of mine, G. H. Evans, and a former student, Robert Eisner, have also been working along these lines. But the most thorough analysis of the relation between R and D for given r and m that I know of was done by Terborgh (op. cit. pp. 108–19) in 1945. I am sure that I had read his book then, and yet I had entirely forgotten about his presentation, perhaps because of the intensely polemic nature of the book which might have concealed his positive contribution. Also, he did not go beyond numerical examples and therefore did not obtain the general relations between the variables and the symmetry between r and m. It is interesting that his replacement was defined as a simple arithmetic mean between our R and D—a simplified general case.

[28] For a bibliography on this mushrooming subject, see William Fellner, 'The Capital–Output Ratio in Dynamic Economics,' *Money, Trade and Economic Growth; in Honor of John Henry Williams* (New York, 1951), p. 106, and note 5 in Essay I.

[29] The reader may wonder about the difference between the concepts of s and σ used in essays III and IV and this new v. v is the gross capital coefficient, while s is the reciprocal of the net. σ is adjusted for the possible reduction in the productive capacity of other parts of the economy as a result of a given investment program.

at the end of m years. By contrast, the old growth models work with output, saving, and investment net of depreciation and define their capital coefficients as $\dfrac{G - D}{\Delta(P - D)}$, so that productive capacity of an asset is always proportional to its net-of-depreciation value. Each approach has its own virtues, but since the other has been explored in considerable detail, it may be interesting to find where our new trail will lead. And in following it, we will be able to assign a new and important role to m, and to present a few other novelties as well.[30]

Dealing with an economy rather than with a firm, we can dispense here with the initial m years when no replacement is required. This is not a great loss, but to make use of the results of the first two sections, it is necessary to assume that the rate of growth r (or u) has been maintained for at least m preceding years—a rather uncomfortable position from which to study rapid industrialization of undeveloped countries. Moreover, r (with constant prices—otherwise u) acquires a new meaning: up to now it has simply been the rate of growth of investment; now it also becomes that rate of growth (of investment and of national product) which is made possible by (or imperative for) the full utilization of the stock of capital. In other words, the actual and potential rates of growth are assumed to be identical, which is not very realistic for a capitalist economy. Both of these assumptions could be dropped, but not without mathematical complications.

As in other models, the rate of growth is expressed in terms of the capital coefficient and the propensity to save. The former has already been defined; for the latter there are several possibilities. The simplest definition of the propensity to save is to express it as a given fraction—β—of the gross national product, without any special provision being made for depreciation (or replacement). Our first model will be so constructed, and its simplicity is gratifying, but it is more applicable to a centrally directed economy, where a part of total output is set aside for investment, rather than to a society like the United States. For the latter, a second model will be presented in which total savings consist of two components: net savings of individuals and corporations, plus depreciation

[30] The models presented here are by no means the only ones that can be constructed on the basis of the difference between D and R.

charges. For depreciation, we have the formulas of Section I, while net savings will be expressed as a fraction—α—of the net national product $(P - D)$.[31]

Our task is as follows: express the rate of growth of gross product and of investment in terms of m, v and β or α. Since $\beta = G/P$ is assumed to be constant (and a constant α yields a constant β), the relative rates of growth of P and G are the same.

THE β MODEL

Case 1. Constant Prices (v and m Mutually Independent)

By definition of v, $\Delta P = \dfrac{G - R}{v}$. Divide both sides by P and substitute $P = G/\beta$ into the right-hand side:

$$(7) \qquad \frac{\Delta P}{P} = \frac{G - R}{vP} = \frac{\beta}{v}\left(\frac{G - R}{G}\right) = \frac{\beta}{v}\left(1 - \frac{R}{G}\right).$$

From expression (2), Section II, $\dfrac{R}{G} = \dfrac{1}{(1 + r)^m}$. Substituting this into (7) and observing that the left-hand side equals the relative rate of growth of P, that is, r, we finally get

$$(8) \qquad r = \frac{\beta}{v}\left[1 - \frac{1}{(1 + r)^m}\right].^{31a}$$

This is one of our simpler expressions, yet it cannot (to my knowledge) be solved explicitly for r. Taking advantage of the

---

[31] Two implicit assumptions should be pointed out: first, there is no gestation period of capital assets; second, both (the net and the gross) propensities to save exclude that part of saving which goes into inventory accumulation because our investment is limited to fixed capital. This, however, is a minor item.

There are other ways of defining the propensity to save. For instance, it could be made a function of the rate of growth of income, as suggested by James S. Duesenberry in his *Income, Saving and the Theory of Consumer Behavior* (Cambridge, Mass., 1949). This would not involve circular reasoning, but merely give us a system of simultaneous equations.

[31a] [Actually (8) is only a solution of a special case of (7) based on the assumption that the rate of growth r has been maintained for at least m preceding years (see p. 169). The general solution of equation (7) involves other roots besides (8), including a number of complex ones. I expect to show in a subsequent paper that none of the latter exceeds unity in absolute value. They may be of considerable interest, however, in a cyclical problem. Cf. Hans Neisser, 'Depreciation, Replacement and Regular Growth,' *The Economic Journal*, Vol. 65 (Mar., 1955), pp. 159–61.]

fact that the right-hand side of (8) is a function of rm, numerical solutions can be easily obtained for given ratios of $\frac{\beta}{v}$ by setting up an rm column, computing the values of r, and then dividing them into the corresponding values of rm to find the magnitudes of m. Such a calculation is presented in Table III.

TABLE III.—THE RELATIONSHIP BETWEEN m AND r FOR GIVEN $\frac{\beta}{v}$

rm	$\frac{\beta}{v} = 5\%$		$\frac{\beta}{v} = 7.5\%$		$\frac{\beta}{v} = 10\%$	
	$r\%$	m years	$r\%$	m years	$r\%$	m years
0.1	0.5	21.0	0.7	14.0	1.0	10.5
0.2	1.0	22.1	1.4	14.7	1.8	11.0
0.3	1.3	23.1	1.9	15.4	2.6	11.6
0.4	1.6	24.3	2.5	16.2	3.3	12.1
0.5	2.0	25.4	3.0	16.9	3.9	12.7
0.6	2.3	26.6	3.4	17.7	4.5	13.3
0.7	2.5	27.8	3.8	18.5	5.0	13.9
0.8	2.8	29.1	4.1	19.4	5.5	14.5
0.9	3.0	30.3	4.5	20.2	5.9	15.2
1.0	3.2	31.6	4.7	21.1	6.3	15.8
1.5	3.9	38.6	5.8	25.7	7.8	19.3
2.0	4.3	46.3	6.5	30.8	8.6	23.1
2.5	4.6	54.5	6.9	36.3	9.2	27.2
3.0	4.8	63.1	7.1	42.1	9.5	31.6
3.5	4.8	72.2	7.3	48.1	9.7	36.1
Lim $m \to \infty$	5.0		7.5		10.0	

Its striking characteristic is the extreme sensitivity of r to m. A $\frac{\beta}{v}$ of 5 per cent (with $\beta = 15$ per cent, for instance, and $v = 3$) is not at all uncommon; the American figure is not much higher, and it is certainly lower in most non-communist undeveloped countries, yet an m of 20 years results in a microscopic growth of less than $\frac{1}{2}$ of 1 per cent; an r of 2 per cent is not reached until m exceeds 25 years. As rapid deterioration of industrial equipment due to improper care is quite common in these countries, even a β of 20 per cent may not give them any significant growth, unless a more intensive utilization of capital (that is, a reduction in v) can be achieved. The fact that the absence of replacement in the first few years (e.g. of an industrialization program) will conceal the true state of affairs makes the situation particularly dangerous.

The last case of Table III, where $\frac{\beta}{v}$ equals 10 per cent, was constructed with Russia in mind. If we should take Kaplan's estimate of the Soviet β in the vicinity of 18 per cent (excluding inventories), which appears surprisingly low, and an m of 30 years, a 10 per cent rate of growth is possible, provided their v is below 2.[32] A rate of growth of 12 per cent suggested by Kaplan would require v to drop to approximately 1.5. Compared with American coefficients, this would indicate either a much more intensive utilization of capital or the improbability of such rapid growth.[33]

Case 2. Constant Prices (v a Function of m)

The conclusion of Case 1 that larger m is always conducive to growth suggests that the best path to economic development lies in the building of pyramids. So it would be (in the framework of this model) if a larger m were not accompanied by a higher v, that is, if longer-lived capital were not more expensive relative to output. There is no doubt that beyond a certain range greater

[32] When rm is large, R/G as given in Table III is so small that r almost equals β/v.

[33] Kaplan, op. cit.

In the United States the over-all capital coefficient defined as the ratio of gross fixed capital to gross national product (both in constant prices) has been around 3, evidently with a downward trend (it was near 4 in 1900). During World War II it went down to something like 2.5 (including military assets), and has apparently stayed around this figure since. So a Soviet capital coefficient of 2 does not appear impossible. It should be made clear, of course, that these are extremely rough estimates and that we should not accept or reject any estimated rate of growth for Russia *merely* because it does or does not imply a 'reasonable' capital coefficient. [See also Essay IX, particularly pp. 235–40.]

For sources, see the following studies of the National Bureau of Economic Research: R. W. Goldsmith, 'A Perpetual Inventory of National Wealth,' Conference on Research in Income and Wealth, *Studies in Income and Wealth*, Vol. 14 (New York, 1951), pp. 18–19; J. E. Reeve *et al.*, 'Government Component in the National Wealth,' same publication, Vol. 12 (New York, 1950), p. 502; Simon Kuznets, *Annual Estimates of National Product 1869–1949* (mimeographed), Capital Requirements Study (Mar., 1951).

Goldsmith's net of depreciation estimates were divided by 0.6 to obtain the corresponding gross magnitudes.

capital longevity becomes very expensive (in terms of v) and even completely useless due to obsolescence. It is quite reasonable to assume then that v should vary directly with m, at least over a certain range, but the exact form of the function is not easy to ascertain.

An attempt to derive a regression of v on m from Leontief's capital coefficient data covering a number of manufacturing industries, plus several categories of mining, public utilities, transportation, and housing failed completely.[34] But if each of these broad

CHART III.—THE v-m CURVE

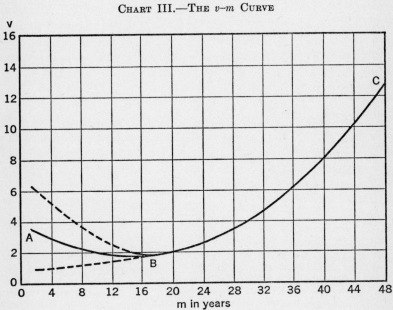

classes (such as manufacturing or transportation) is treated as a single industry, a pattern begins to emerge: industries heavily dependent on construction, such as transportation, public utilities, and housing, have considerably higher magnitudes of v and m than is the case with manufacturing. What we really need, however, is

[34] Harvard Economic Research Project, *Estimates of the Capital Structure of American Industries, 1939* (Jan., 1950) [see note 24]. Capital coefficients given there are ratios of capital to output. For our purposes, ratios of capital to value added would be more meaningful, but even this adjustment failed to give any results.

not so much a cross-sectional study by industries, but the magnitudes of m and v of different varieties of assets fulfilling similar functions (stone or wooden houses, roads with deep or shallow foundations, high quality or ordinary tools, etc.) because practical choices are usually made between these. In the absence of such a study we shall assume that v as a function of m is expressed by the hypothetical v–m curve ABC on Chart III.[35] It must have a positive slope in the relevant range (BC), because otherwise we'll be back

CHART IV.—THE r–m CURVES

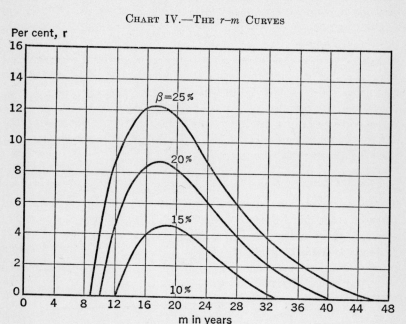

at the pyramids. But a negative slope for very low magnitudes of m is possible; sometimes short-lived assets may be extremely inefficient. It is obvious, however, that it would not pay to stay on the AB part of the curve, and it can be omitted from consideration in the present case.[36]

BC has an *increasing* slope, because, among other reasons,

[35] The formula of the curve is $v = 4 - 0.3m + 0.01m^2$. Though I have tried to make it reasonable, it should not be taken too seriously.

[36] A short range of the curve to the left of B becomes relevant in Case 2 of the α model.

obsolescence limits the effective life span of assets. This attribute of the curve, however, is not so important as the positive character of the slope itself.

Now that a large m has become expensive in terms of v, growth is not necessarily speeded up by increasing m, as it was in Case 1. The relationship between m and r has become more complex, and there exists an optimum m which maximizes r. Chart IV shows the family of r–m curves for given values of β. Their exact shape and position depend, of course, on those of the v–m curve ABC on the basis of which they are drawn, but their general form appears quite reasonable.

A β of 10 per cent gives no growth whatsoever, the maximum value of r being exactly zero for $m = 20$ years. As β increases, the r–m curve moves upward, but it is interesting that even with a relatively high β, r remains vulnerable to a low m: even a high propensity to save offers only a limited protection against the dissipation of savings on replacements when no depreciation (or replacement) reserves are set up.[37]

Case 3. Changing Prices

It is assumed here (as we did in Case 2 of Section II) that all prices change in the same proportion. Since neither v nor β are affected, there being no depreciation charges, the whole system is perfectly neutral to price changes and the results of Cases 1 and 2 remain unchanged, except that u—the real rate of growth—should be used instead of r.

IV

THE α MODEL

This is the 'capitalist' model in which investment is financed from two sources: net savings which constitute an α fraction of net (of depreciation) national product, and depreciation allowances.

[37] It is curious that the optimum m (corresponding to the maximum r) falls with increasing β. Thus a β of 15 per cent sets the optimum m near 18 years, while with a β of 25 per cent the corresponding m falls to 16.5 years. This relation between β and m depends on the secondary characteristics of the v–m curve: that its slope be increasing, constant, or slightly decreasing. If it should decrease sharply instead, the conclusion is reversed and a rising β will increase the optimum m.

The essence of this model lies not in a variable fraction invested of total product (our old β), because a constant α yields a constant β as well (after the first m years), but in allowing β to emerge from the model in such a manner as to assure a given α.[38]

The financing of investment from these two sources creates mathematical complications which are hardly explainable in non-technical language. For that matter, some of them are hard to explain in any language.

Case 1. Constant Prices (v *and* m *Mutually Independent*)

The simplest expression of r as a function of m, v, and α that I have been able to derive takes this form:

$$(9) \qquad r = \left(\frac{\alpha}{v} + \frac{1-\alpha}{m}\right)\left[1 - \frac{1}{(1-r)^m}\right],$$

which again cannot be solved explicitly for r. But by a short transformation it is possible to compute from it numerical illustrations given in Table IV.[39]

Its most interesting aspect is the fact that r is almost completely independent of m, contrasting sharply with the results of Table III in the β model. When gross savings contain a 'sound' provision for depreciation in addition to net savings, however modest the latter may be, growth is never in danger. Even with an α of 5 per cent and a v of 3, an r of about 2.5 per cent is virtually assured. For the United States in peacetime this may be quite a source of embarrassment, because failure to grow at the required rate creates unemployment, but for countries who know how to use their savings—certainly a blessing. An export of some of the accounting conservatism out of the United States and into less developed countries might benefit all concerned. Depreciation accounting really sets up hidden reserves, and a glance at the β column shows what a large sacrifice of possible consumption may be involved even when α does not exceed some 5–10 per cent.

r is practically independent of m because the model does not have to pay, so to speak, for replacement: the latter is automatically provided for by depreciation charges which are more than ade-

[38] See expression (5.2) in the Appendix.

[39] Both sides of (9) are multiplied by m, and the latter is expressed as a function of rm, v, and α. Then the method of Table III is used.

quate. As a matter of fact, a closer examination of Table IV reveals that there even exists an m (and by no means a large one) which maximizes r. It leads to the amusing conclusion that in a society represented by this model, output will grow slightly faster if capital

TABLE IV.—THE BEHAVIOR OF r AS A FUNCTION OF m, v, AND α

rm	$\alpha = 5\%$						$\alpha = 10\%$					
	$v = 3$			$v = 2$			$v = 3$			$v = 2$		
	$r\%$	m years	$\beta\%$	$r\%$	m years	$\beta\%$	$r\%$	m years	$\beta\%$	$r\%$	m years	$\beta\%$
0.1	1.7	6.0	52.3	2.5	4.0	52.3	2.2	4.5	69.8	3.3	3.0	69.8
0.2	2.2	9.2	36.0	3.3	6.1	36.0	3.3	6.1	54.3	4.9	4.1	54.3
0.3	2.4	12.4	27.9	3.6	8.3	27.9	3.9	7.7	45.0	5.8	5.1	45.0
0.4	2.5	15.8	23.1	3.8	10.5	23.1	4.3	9.4	38.7	6.4	6.3	38.7
0.5	2.6	19.2	19.8	3.9	12.8	19.8	4.5	11.1	34.3	6.7	7.4	34.3
0.6	2.6	22.8	17.5	4.0	15.2	17.5	4.7	12.9	30.9	7.0	8.6	30.9
0.7	2.6	26.4	15.8	4.0	17.6	15.8	4.8	14.7	28.3	7.1	9.8	28.3
0.8	2.7	30.2	14.5	4.0	20.1	14.5	4.8	16.6	26.3	7.2	11.1	26.3
0.9	2.6	34.0	13.4	4.0	22.7	13.4	4.9	18.5	24.6	7.3	12.3	24.6
1.0	2.6	37.9	12.5	4.0	25.3	12.5	4.9	20.5	23.2	7.3	13.6	23.2
1.1	2.6	41.9	11.8	3.9	28.0	11.8	4.9	22.5	22.0	7.3	15.0	22.0
1.2	2.6	46.0	11.2	3.9	30.7	11.2	4.9	24.5	21.0	7.3	16.3	21.0
1.3	2.6	50.2	10.7	3.9	33.5	10.7	4.9	26.6	20.1	7.3	17.7	20.1
1.4	2.6	54.5	10.2	3.9	36.3	10.2	4.9	28.8	19.4	7.3	19.2	19.4
1.5	2.5	58.9	9.8	3.8	39.2	9.8	4.8	30.9	18.7	7.3	20.6	18.7
1.6	2.5	63.3	9.5	3.8	42.2	9.5	4.8	33.1	18.1	7.2	22.1	18.1
1.7	2.5	67.8	9.2	3.8	45.2	9.2	4.8	35.4	17.6	7.2	23.6	17.6
1.8	2.5	72.4	8.9	3.7	48.3	8.9	4.8	37.7	17.2	7.2	25.1	17.2
1.9	2.5	77.0	8.7	3.7	51.4	8.7	4.7	40.0	16.7	7.1	26.7	16.7
2.0	2.4	81.8	8.5	3.7	54.5	8.5	4.7	42.4	16.4	7.1	28.3	16.4

Note: The underlined figures are the maximum magnitudes of r.

stock is not too durable, and this is not because durable capital is expensive, as was assumed in Case 2 of the β model, but only due to accounting peculiarities.

Case 2. Constant Prices (v a Function of m)

As soon as v becomes a function of m, that is, when greater capital longevity must be paid for, the insensitivity of r to m

disappears and the $r-m$ curve acquires a pronounced maximum. The exact position of the optimum m which maximizes r depends on the magnitude of α and on the form of the $v-m$ function, but on the whole there is little doubt that under reasonable conditions, it will be in the vicinity of the lowest point of the $v-m$ curve: since for any value of m depreciation charges are automatically provided for from the outside, so to speak, a higher m offers no particular advantage. On the other hand, a low m reduces v (until its minimum is reached), which is the only cost from the point of view of the model. Hence the movement toward that m which minimizes v.[40]

Case 3. Changing Prices (v and m Mutually Independent)

In its logical structure, this case is similar to Case 3 of the β model, but the heavy reliance of total savings on depreciation charges makes the real rate of growth highly sensitive to price changes, and thus leads to conclusions quite different from those of the other case. The formula expressing u as a function of α, v and i (or r) is more complex than ever and is tucked away into a footnote.[41] At this late hour, we shall forego the quest for a maximum u and only try to determine the rate of growth of prices (the magnitude of i) which could eliminate growth altogether.

The Appendix (with the usual apologies to the reader) shows that a necessary but not a sufficient condition for $u \leqq o$ is $\alpha \leqq \dfrac{v}{m}$ (which can also be expressed as $m \leqq \dfrac{v}{\alpha}$, or $v \geqq \alpha m$, depending on the most convenient point of view). Should m be near 30 years,

---

[40] It is interesting that as α increases, the optimum value of m which maximizes r is pushed somewhat to the left of that m which gives the lowest point on the $v-m$ curve. I have not analyzed this in any detail, but I believe that it is due to the same causes which created the maximum r in Case 1: that a slightly lower m than would be expected on purely rational grounds yields a higher r because the lower m gives rise to larger depreciation charges.

[41] This formula is

$$\frac{u}{1 - \dfrac{1}{(1+u)^m}} = \frac{\alpha}{v} \cdot \frac{1}{\left\{ 1 - \dfrac{\left[1 - \dfrac{1}{(1+r)^m} \right](1-\alpha)}{rm} \right\}}.$$

It cannot be solved explicitly for u; the right side can be readily computed for given α, v, r, and m, and the magnitudes of u are obtained by equating the left side to the right by a process of successive approximations.

and v not below 3, this condition will be satisfied if $\alpha \leqq 10$ per cent, which is highly probable for many countries.

This, however, is not a sufficient condition, the actual outcome depending also on the degree of inflation. Table V gives the annual rate of growth of prices required to reduce u to zero.[42] For $\alpha = 10$ per cent with $v = 2$ or 3, or $\alpha = 5$ per cent with $v = 2$, the rise in prices must be very rapid indeed. But with $\alpha = 5$ per cent and $v = 3$, which is more reasonable, particularly for non-communist

TABLE V.—ANNUAL RATE OF INFLATION (i) REQUIRED TO ELIMINATE REAL GROWTH ($u = 0$)

m	$\alpha = 5\%$		$\alpha = 10\%$	
	$v = 3$	$v = 2$	$v = 3$	$v = 2$
	Per cent		Per cent	
5	1.4	3.3	3.1	7.5
10	2.7	4.9	6.3	13.2
15	3.3	6.0	8.8	23.3
20	3.8	7.3	12.3	∞
25	4.3	9.1	21.4	impossible
30	4.9	12.4	∞	"
35	5.6	21.7	impossible	"
40	6.6	∞	"	"
45	8.2	impossible	"	"
50	11.4	"	"	"
55	20.6	"	"	"
60	∞	"	"	"

undeveloped countries, the elimination of growth (and even retrogression) becomes a distinct possibility, particularly if careless treatment of capital should reduce m. A strong inflation destroys depreciation charges in real terms to such an extent that a moderate net propensity to save is insufficient to finance replacement, let alone to provide for the expansion of the capital stock.

Comparing the results of the two models, we find that in the β

[42] It is based on the formula

$$\frac{rm}{1 - \dfrac{1}{(1 + r)^m}} = \frac{1 - \alpha}{1 - \dfrac{\alpha m}{v}},$$

which is obtained from that presented in note 41 by taking $u = 0$.

model the real rate of growth is highly sensitive to m, but is immune to inflation, while in the α model, it is very vulnerable to inflation but does not depend as much on m.

* * * *

Any person who has had the patience to get through these twenty-six pages (not to mention the next fourteen pages of the Appendix) must be so well aware of the limitations of the paper that there is no need to belabor them further. The large number of constants (which show amazing variability in real life) and of the simplifying assumptions (many of which do not exist) may have well given the reader a feeling of an analytical strait-jacket. Many of these defects can be remedied, but not before there is a greater assurance that the effort is worth while.

I hope very much that the paper has not given the impression that the subject of replacement and depreciation must necessarily be tied to models such as presented here. It is a large and important subject which has been considerably neglected in economics. If we reflect on the fact that some 50 per cent of investment expenditures in the United States are made for replacement purposes and that over the period 1929–40 and 1947–51 depreciation charges (as defined by the United States Department of Commerce) exceeded personal savings by a ratio of almost 3 to 1, the potentialities for public policy in this field will become quite impressive. The next step is to investigate the proper form which this policy should take.

MATHEMATICAL APPENDIX

LIST OF SYMBOLS

In order of their appearance and with the model of their first appearance indicated.

Model 1. t = time in years;
  m = life span of capital assets in years;
  G = annual gross investment;
  r = relative annual rate of growth of G in current prices;
  K = gross (of depreciation) stock of capital;
  D = annual depreciation charges;
  R = annual replacement expenditures.

Model 2. b = a constant;
   a = depreciation rate = $1/m$;
   z = a symbol used for abbreviation;
   y = a symbol used for abbreviation.

Model 3. i = relative annual rate of growth of prices;
   u = relative *real* annual rate of growth of G ($u = r - i$);
   T = a symbol used for abbreviation.

Model 4. β = gross propensity to save = G/P;
   v = capital coefficient;
   P = annual gross national product;
   H = a symbol used for abbreviation;
   x = a symbol used for abbreviation;
   L = a symbol used for abbreviation;
   N = investment net of replacement per year ($N = G - R$);

$\bar{N}, \bar{G}, \bar{P}$ = the corresponding concepts in real terms.

Model 5. α = net (of depreciation) propensity to save;
   W = a symbol used for abbreviation.

Throughout the paper it is assumed that $G = e^{rt}$, and that $r \geqq 0$. No revaluation of capital assets takes place. Maximum conditions are established by equating the first derivative to zero, the nature of the problem making further proof unnecessary. In several cases complicated derivations of relatively unimportant propositions have been omitted.

MODEL 1. ONE KIND OF INVESTMENT. CONSTANT PRICES

Case 1. $t < m$

From

(1.1)
$$G = e^{rt},$$

(1.2)
$$K = \int_0^t e^{rt}dt = \frac{e^{rt} - 1}{r};$$

(1.3)
$$D = \frac{K}{m} = \frac{e^{rt} - 1}{rm};$$

(1.4)
$$\frac{D}{G} = \frac{1 - e^{-rt}}{rm}.$$

Case 2. $t \geqq m$

By definition,

(1.5)
$$R_t = G_{t-m} = e^{r(t-m)};$$

(1.6)
$$K = \int_{t-m}^{t} Gdt = \frac{e^{rt}(1 - e^{-rm})}{r};$$

(1.7)
$$D = \frac{K}{m} = \frac{e^{rt}(1 - e^{-rm})}{rm};$$

(1.8)
$$\frac{D}{G} = \frac{1 - e^{-rm}}{rm};$$

(1.9)
$$\frac{R}{G} = e^{-rm};$$

(1.10)
$$\frac{R}{D} = \frac{rm}{e^{rm} - 1}.$$

It can be readily shown that the derivatives of $\dfrac{D}{G}$, $\dfrac{R}{G}$, and $\dfrac{R}{D}$ with respect to r, m, and rm are negative, and (by differentiating the numerator and denominator when necessary) that

(1.11)
$$\operatorname*{Lim}_{rm \to 0} \left(\frac{D}{G}\right) = \operatorname*{Lim}_{rm \to 0} \left(\frac{R}{G}\right) = \operatorname*{Lim}_{rm \to 0} \left(\frac{R}{D}\right) = 1;$$

(1.12)
$$\operatorname*{Lim}_{rm \to \infty} \left(\frac{D}{G}\right) = \operatorname*{Lim}_{rm \to \infty} \left(\frac{R}{G}\right) = \operatorname*{Lim}_{rm \to \infty} \left(\frac{R}{D}\right) = 0.$$

For D to be equal to R, the depreciation rate should be

(1.13)
$$\frac{R}{K} = \frac{r}{e^{rm} - 1},$$

which is the reciprocal of an amount of annuity for m years invested at the rate of r (see text, p. 166).

Model 2. Two Kinds of Investment. Constant Prices

Symbols with subscripts refer to specific investments; symbols without subscripts indicate averages for both investments. Assume $m_2 > m_1$.

Let

(2.1)
$$G = e^{rt} = b_1 e^{rt} + b_2 e^{rt}.$$

Case 1. $t < m_1 < m_2$

It is obvious from (1.2) that $K_1 = \dfrac{b_1(e^{rt} - 1)}{r}$, $K_2 = \dfrac{b_2(e^{rt} - 1)}{r}$,

and $K = \dfrac{e^{rt} - 1}{r}$. Hence,

$$(2.2) \qquad a = \frac{D}{K} = \frac{a_1K_1 + a_2K_2}{K} = a_1b_1 + a_2b_2.$$

Thus a and $m = 1/a$ are constant.

Case 2. $m_1 \leqq t < m_2$

By assumption, $R_2 = 0$.
From (1.6), (1.2), and (2.2),

$$(2.3) \quad a = \frac{a_1K_1 + a_2K_2}{K} = \frac{a_1b_1e^{rt}(1 - e^{-rm_1}) + a_2b_2(e^{rt} - 1)}{b_1e^{rt}(1 - e^{-rm_1}) + b_2(e^{rt} - 1)}.$$

Here a is not a constant, and we cannot take m as its reciprocal because by the nature of the problem m is supposed to be constant, though if needed, it could be re-defined.

$$(2.4) \qquad \frac{D}{G} = \frac{a_1b_1(1 - e^{-rm_1}) + a_2b_2(1 - e^{-rt})}{r};$$

$$(2.5) \qquad \frac{R}{G} = \frac{b_1e^{r(t-m_1)}}{e^{rt}} = b_1e^{-rm_1},$$

because $R_2 = 0$. $\dfrac{R}{D}$ can be derived but it is too complicated to be of theoretical value.

Consider the special case when the second investment represents an accumulation of inventories, so that $a_2 = 0$. Then,

$$(2.6) \qquad a = \frac{a_1b_1(1 - e^{-rm_1})}{b_1(1 - e^{-rm_1}) + b_2(1 - e^{-rt})};$$

$$(2.7) \qquad \lim_{t \to \infty} a = \frac{a_1}{1 + \dfrac{b_2}{b_1}\left(\dfrac{1}{1 - e^{-rm_1}}\right)}.$$

Over the period 1929–50 in the United States, investment in inventories comprised about 5 per cent of investment in construc-

tion and producers' durables (all in constant prices).[43] Taking therefore $\frac{b_2}{b_1} = 0.05$, and assuming $rm = 1$, we find that

$$(2.8) \qquad\qquad \lim_{t \to \infty} a = 0.93a_1.$$

It therefore makes little difference whether G does or does not include
investment in inventories.

Case 3. $t \geqq m_2 > m_1$

Following the results of Cases 1 and 2, we can establish that

$$(2.9) \qquad a = \frac{a_1 b_1 (1 - e^{-rm_1}) + a_2 b_2 (1 - e^{-rm_2})}{b_1 (1 - e^{-rm_1}) + b_2 (1 - e^{-rm_2})};$$

$$(2.10) \qquad \frac{D}{G} = \frac{a_1 b_1 (1 - e^{-rm_1}) + a_2 b_2 (1 - e^{-rm_2})}{r};$$

$$(2.11) \qquad \frac{R}{G} = b_1 e^{-rm_1} + b_2 e^{-rm_2};$$

$$(2.12) \qquad \frac{R}{D} = \frac{r(b_1 e^{-rm_1} + b_2 e^{-rm_2})}{a_1 b_1 (1 - e^{-rm_1}) + a_2 b_2 (1 - e^{-rm_2})}.$$

We shall now prove that $m = \frac{1}{a}$ as given by (2.9) can be used as
the average life span of both investments so as to obtain the expres-
sions for $\frac{D}{G}$ and $\frac{R}{G}$ given by (1.8) and (1.9) respectively. $\left(\frac{R}{D} \text{ can be}\right.$
omitted because it is the ratio of $\frac{R}{G}$ to $\frac{D}{G} \cdot \right)$ In other words, we want
to show that

$$(2.13) \qquad \frac{D}{G} = \frac{a_1 b_1 (1 - e^{-rm_1}) + a_2 b_2 (1 - e^{-rm_2})}{r} = \frac{1 - e^{-rm}}{rm},$$

and

$$(2.14) \qquad \frac{R}{G} = b_1 e^{-rm_1} + b_2 e^{-rm_2} = e^{-rm}.$$

Introduce the notation

$$(2.15) \qquad\qquad b_1 e^{-rm_1} + b_2 e^{-rm_2} = z;$$
$$(2.16) \qquad a_1 b_1 (1 - e^{-rm_1}) + a_2 b_2 (1 - e^{-rm_2}) = y.$$

---

[43] *Survey of Current Business Supplement, National Income and Product of the
United States, 1929–50* (Washington, 1951), p. 146.

m as given by (the reciprocal of) (2.9) can be expressed as

$$(2.17) \quad m = \frac{b_1(1 - e^{-rm_1}) + b_2(1 - e^{-rm_2})}{a_1b_1(1 - e^{-rm_1}) + a_2b_2(1 - e^{-rm_2})}$$

$$= \frac{1 - (b_1e^{-rm_1} + b_2e^{-rm_2})}{a_1b_1(1 - e^{-rm_1}) + a_2b_2(1 - e^{-rm_2})},$$

because $b_1 + b_2 = 1$. Hence,

$$(2.18) \qquad\qquad m = \frac{1 - z}{y},$$

and

$$(2.19) \qquad\qquad y = \frac{1 - z}{m}.$$

From (2.13), (2.14), (2.15), and (2.16),

$$(2.20) \qquad\qquad \frac{D}{G} = \frac{y}{r} = \frac{1 - e^{-rm}}{rm};$$

$$(2.21) \qquad\qquad \frac{R}{G} = z = e^{-rm}.$$

Therefore,

$$(2.22) \qquad\qquad y = \frac{1 - z}{m},$$

which is identical to (2.19). Hence, the expressions (2.13) and (2.14) are correct, and m as given by (2.17) can be used as the average life span of both investments.

These results can be generalized to include any number of investments. The remaining part of the Appendix (as well as the text of the paper) deals only with m. Strictly speaking, it is assumed not only that t is at least as large as the average m, but that t at least equals the largest m.

MODEL 3. CHANGING PRICES

Case 1. $t < m$

Since $R = 0$, the results of Case 1 of Model 1 remain unchanged.

Case 2. $t \geqq m$

All results of Case 2 of Model 1 not involving R remain unchanged.

$$(3.1) \qquad\qquad R_t = G_{t-m}e^{im} = e^{r(t-m)+im};$$

(3.2) $\dfrac{R}{G} = e^{-m(r-i)} = e^{-um};$

(3.3) $\dfrac{R}{D} = \dfrac{rme^{im}}{e^{rm} - 1} = \dfrac{rm}{e^{(r-i)m} - e^{-im}} = \dfrac{(u+i)m}{e^{um} - e^{-im}}.$

It is obvious that $\dfrac{\partial\left(\dfrac{R}{D}\right)}{\partial i} > 0$ and almost obvious that $\dfrac{\partial\left(\dfrac{R}{D}\right)}{\partial u} < 0$, because a change in u, with i fixed, means exactly the same change in r, and we know that the derivative of (1.10) in respect to r is negative. The relationship between $\dfrac{R}{D}$ and m is more complex.

(3.4) $\dfrac{\partial\left(\dfrac{R}{D}\right)}{\partial m} = \dfrac{(e^{rm} - 1)(re^{im} + rime^{im}) - r^2me^{im+rm}}{(e^{rm} - 1)^2};$

(3.5) $\dfrac{\partial\left(\dfrac{R}{D}\right)}{\partial m} = \dfrac{re^{im}}{(e^{rm} - 1)^2} \cdot [(e^{rm} - 1)(im + 1) - rme^{rm}].$

Since the first part of the right side of (3.5) is always positive, we can concentrate on the expression in the brackets. Let

(3.6) $T = (e^{rm} - 1)(im + 1) - rme^{rm}.$

The value of i for which $T < 0$ is

(3.7) $i < \dfrac{re^{rm}}{e^{rm} - 1} - \dfrac{1}{m}.$

Divide both sides by r:

(3.8) $\dfrac{i}{r} < \dfrac{e^{rm}}{e^{rm} - 1} - \dfrac{1}{rm}.$

It can be shown that the magnitude of the right side of (3.8) is between $\frac{1}{2}$ and 1. Therefore, a sufficient but not necessary condition for $\dfrac{\partial\left(\dfrac{R}{D}\right)}{\partial m} < 0$ is $i < \dfrac{r}{2}.$

The maximum condition for $\dfrac{\partial\left(\dfrac{R}{D}\right)}{\partial m}$ is obtained from (3.6) by setting

$$(3.9) \qquad T = (e^{rm} - 1)(im + 1) - rme^{rm} = 0.$$

It cannot be solved explicitly for m, but it can be shown that m is subject to the following conditions:

$$\frac{\partial m}{\partial i} > 0, \frac{\partial m}{\partial r} < 0.$$

The proof is omitted because the subject is not sufficiently important.

To find the i which sets $\frac{R}{D} = 1$, start from (3.3):

$$(3.10) \qquad \frac{R}{D} = \frac{(u + i)m}{e^{um} - e^{-im}} = 1,$$

which reduces to

$$(3.11) \qquad im + e^{-im} = e^{um} - um.$$

This cannot be solved explicitly for i, but Table II gives its numerical magnitudes.

MODEL 4. THE β MODEL

Conditions are explained in the text. Note that $t \geqq m$. Strictly speaking, a single m is assumed.

Case 1. Constant Prices (v *Independent of* m)

As shown in the text,

$$(4.1) \qquad r = \frac{\beta}{v} (1 - e^{-rm}).$$

It is clear that

$$(4.2) \qquad \frac{\partial r}{\partial \beta} > 0, \frac{\partial r}{\partial v} < 0, \frac{\partial r}{\partial m} > 0.$$

(4.1) cannot be solved explicitly for r, but numerical magnitudes can be derived by the method described on pp. 170–71; they are given in Table III.

Case 2. Constant Prices (v = f(m))

From (4.1) we have

$$r = \frac{\beta}{v} (1 - e^{-rm}).$$

Define

(4.3) $$v' = \frac{dv}{dm}, \ v'' = \frac{d^2v}{dm^2}.$$

We want to find the m which maximizes r. From (4.1),

(4.4) $$\frac{\partial r}{\partial m} = \frac{r(\beta e^{-rm} - v')}{v\left(1 - \frac{\beta m e^{-rm}}{v}\right)}.$$

Consider the part of the denominator in the parentheses. Let

(4.5) $$H = 1 - \frac{\beta m e^{-rm}}{v}.$$

From (4.1)

(4.6) $$\frac{\beta}{v} = \frac{r}{1 - e^{-rm}};$$

substitute (4.6) into (4.5):

(4.7) $$H = \frac{e^{rm} - 1 - rm}{e^{rm} - 1}.$$

A Maclaurin's expansion shows that the numerator of H, and therefore H itself, is positive (for $rm > 0$). Hence the denominator of (4.4) is positive and the sign of (4.4) depends only on its numerator. The maximum condition is now given by

(4.8) $$v' = \beta e^{-rm},$$

which cannot be solved explicitly for m in terms of β. But by treating (4.1) and (4.8) as a system of simultaneous equations, it is possible to establish that

(4.9) $$\frac{dm}{d\beta} = \frac{e^{-rm}(v - m\beta)}{(v'' + r\beta e^{-rm})(v - m\beta e^{-rm})}.$$

The derivation of (4.9) is quite involved and not sufficiently important to justify the use of several pages.

Consider the part of the numerator of (4.9) in parentheses. Let

(4.10) $$L = v - m\beta = v\left(1 - \frac{\beta m}{v}\right).$$

But by (4.1),

$$(4.11) \qquad \frac{\beta}{v} = \frac{r}{1 - e^{-rm}};$$

therefore

$$(4.12) \qquad L = v\left(1 - \frac{rm}{1 - e^{-rm}}\right) = v\left(\frac{1 - e^{-rm} - rm}{1 - e^{-rm}}\right).$$

Let $rm = x$. Consider the part of the numerator of (4.12) in **parentheses**. Prove that

$$(4.13) \qquad 1 - e^{-x} - x < 0.$$

We shall make use here and elsewhere in the paper of the following proposition for $x > 0$:

$$(4.14) \qquad F(x) > 0, \text{ if } F(0) = 0 \text{ and } F'(x) > 0.$$

If the sign of $F'(x)$ cannot be established directly, but

$$(4.15) \qquad F'(0) = 0 \text{ and } F''(x) > 0,$$

then $\qquad F'(x) > 0$ and therefore $F(x) > 0$.

Sometimes it may be necessary to take several derivatives before the sign of $F(x)$ can be determined. The same proposition, but of course reversed, can be used to establish that $F(x) < 0$.

Applying this method to (4.13), we have:

$$(4.16) \qquad F'(x) = e^{-x} - 1 < 0.$$

Therefore (4.13) and the numerator of (4.9) are negative.

The expression in the second parentheses of the denominator of (4.9) is positive because (4.5) is positive. Therefore,

$$(4.17) \qquad \frac{dm}{d\beta} < 0,$$

if

$$(4.18) \qquad v'' > -r\beta e^{-rm}.$$

Case 3. Changing Prices

See the statement in the text. The formal proof is omitted.

Model 5. The α Model

Conditions are explained in the text. Note that $t \geqq m$. Strictly speaking, a single m is assumed.

Case 1. Constant Prices (v *Independent of* m)

From the nature of this model,

(5.1) $\qquad G = \alpha(P - D) + D = \alpha P + D(1 - \alpha).$

Divide both sides by G, and substitute $\dfrac{P}{G} = \dfrac{1}{\beta}$, and $\dfrac{D}{G} = \dfrac{1 - e^{-rm}}{rm}$ from (1.8):

(5.2) $\qquad \dfrac{\alpha}{\beta} + \dfrac{(1 - e^{-rm})(1 - \alpha)}{rm} = 1.$

From (4.1), $\beta = \dfrac{rv}{1 - e^{-rm}}$. Inserting it into (5.2), we finally get

(5.3) $\qquad r = \left(\dfrac{\alpha}{v} + \dfrac{1 - \alpha}{m}\right)(1 - e^{-rm}).$

We shall try to find the value of m which, for given α and v, maximizes r.

(5.4) $\quad \dfrac{\partial r}{\partial m} = \left(\dfrac{\alpha}{v} + \dfrac{1 - \alpha}{m}\right)\left(m\dfrac{\partial r}{\partial m} + r\right)e^{-rm} + (1 - e^{-rm})\left(-\dfrac{1 - \alpha}{m^2}\right).$

From (5.3),

(5.5) $\qquad \dfrac{\alpha}{v} + \dfrac{1 - \alpha}{m} = \dfrac{r}{1 - e^{-rm}}.$

Substituting (5.5) into (5.4), we get, after a series of transformations,

(5.6) $\qquad \dfrac{\partial r}{\partial m} = \dfrac{r^2 m^2 e^{rm} - (e^{rm} - 1)^2(1 - \alpha)}{m^2 e^{rm}(e^{rm} - 1 - rm)}.$

The denominator of (5.6) is positive because (4.7) is positive. Hence the sign of (5.6) depends on that of the numerator only.

The maximum value of r with respect to m is given by

(5.7) $\qquad r^2 m^2 e^{rm} - (e^{rm} - 1)^2(1 - \alpha) = 0,$

or

(5.8) $\qquad \dfrac{r^2 m^2 e^{rm}}{(e^{rm} - 1)^2} = 1 - \alpha.$

The explicit solution of (5.8) for m is impossible. The sign of $\dfrac{\partial m}{\partial \alpha}$ from (5.8) can be established after a long series of manipulations which are not sufficiently important to be given here. They show that

$$(5.9) \qquad \frac{\partial m}{\partial \alpha} < 0 \text{ for } rm \leqq 3.1,$$

which is quite sufficient for our purposes.

Case 2. Constant Prices $(v = f(m))$

v' and v'' are defined as in (4.3).

From (5.3)

$$(5.10) \qquad r = \left(\frac{\alpha}{v} + \frac{1 - \alpha}{m}\right)(1 - e^{-rm}),$$

where $v = f(m)$. As in the preceding case, we want to find the value of m which maximizes r. Differentiating (5.10) in respect to m and substituting (5.5) in the appropriate place, we emerge with

$$(5.11) \qquad \frac{\partial r}{\partial m} = \frac{r^2 e^{rm} - (e^{rm} - 1)^2 \left(\dfrac{\alpha v'}{v^2} + \dfrac{1 - \alpha}{m^2}\right)}{e^{rm}(e^{rm} - 1 - rm)}.$$

Since the denominator of (5.11) is positive because (4.7) is positive, the sign of (5.11) depends on that of the numerator only. Equating the numerator to zero to get the maximum condition and solving it for v', we obtain

$$(5.12) \qquad v' = \frac{v^2}{\alpha m^2}\left[\frac{r^2 m^2 e^{rm}}{(e^{rm} - 1)^2} - (1 - \alpha)\right].$$

The expression in the brackets can be zero, positive or negative, so that the optimum m can be at the lowest point B on the v–m curve on Chart III, or to its right or left. Numerical examples show that for reasonable magnitudes of the variables, v' is apt to be close to zero, and therefore—the optimum m not far from B.

Attempts to derive $\dfrac{dm}{d\alpha}$ from (5.12) have not given satisfactory results. I don't believe that any additional effort is justified.

Case 3. Changing Prices

By definition,

$$(5.13) \quad N = \alpha(P - D) + D - R = \alpha P + D(1 - \alpha) - R;$$

also

$$(5.14) \qquad P = \frac{G}{\beta} = \frac{e^{rt}}{\beta}.$$

From (1.7) and (3.1),

$$(5.15) \qquad D = \frac{e^{rt}(1 - e^{-rm})}{rm},$$

and

$$(5.16) \qquad R = e^{r(t-m)+im}.$$

Substitute (5.14), (5.15), and (5.16) into (5.13):

$$(5.17) \qquad N = e^{rt}\left[\frac{\alpha}{\beta} + \frac{(1 - e^{-rm})(1 - \alpha)}{rm} - e^{-um}\right].$$

The deflation of (5.17) gives

$$(5.18) \qquad \bar{N} = e^{ut}\left[\frac{\alpha}{\beta} + \frac{(1 - e^{-rm})(1 - \alpha)}{rm} - e^{-um}\right].$$

By definition,

$$(5.19) \qquad u = \frac{\bar{N}}{\bar{P}v};$$

replacing $\bar{N}$ by (5.18), and expressing β in terms of u, we derive after several simplifications

$$(5.20) \qquad \frac{u}{1 - e^{-um}} = \frac{\alpha}{v} \cdot \frac{1}{1 - \dfrac{(1 - e^{-rm})(1 - \alpha)}{rm}}.$$

Like so many of our results, this expression cannot be solved explicitly for u. We shall only investigate here the conditions which give $u \lessgtr 0$. First we prove that (5.20) varies directly with u.

$$(5.21) \qquad \frac{\partial\left(\dfrac{u}{1 - e^{-um}}\right)}{\partial u} = \frac{1 - e^{-um} - ume^{-um}}{(1 - e^{-um})^2}.$$

The denominator of (5.21) is of course positive. Prove that the numerator is also positive. Let $um = x$ and

$$(5.22) \qquad W(x) = 1 - e^{-x} - xe^{-x}.$$

We use the procedure suggested in (4.14) and (4.15). Clearly, $W(O) = 0$.

$$(5.23) \qquad W'(x) = e^{-x} + xe^{-x} - e^{-x} = xe^{-x}.$$

Thus, $W'(O) = 0$, $W(x) > 0$ for $x > 0$, and $W'(x) < 0$ for $x < 0$. In other words, the slope of $W(x)$ is positive in the first quadrant and negative in the second, while $W(O) = 0$. Therefore, for any x, $W(x) > 0$, and

$$(5.24) \qquad \frac{\partial \left(\dfrac{u}{1 - e^{-um}} \right)}{\partial u} > 0.$$

Now, by differentiating the numerator and denominator of the left side of (5.20) we find that

$$(5.25) \qquad \lim_{u \to 0} \left(\frac{u}{1 - e^{-um}} \right) = \frac{1}{m}.$$

On the right side of (5.20) the expression $\dfrac{1 - e^{-rm}}{rm} = \dfrac{D}{G}$ by (1.8) varies inversely with r, and it is easy to see that the whole right side of (5.20) varies inversely with r as well. Therefore, an increase in r reduces (5.20) and by (5.24) reduces u. This shows that $\dfrac{\partial u}{\partial r} < 0$ and of course $\dfrac{\partial u}{\partial i} < 0$; in other words, inflation reduces the real rate of growth. (I tried to get these two derivatives by direct differentiation but the mathematics became rather involved.)

To find the asymptote approached by the right side of (5.20) as r increases we take

$$(5.26) \qquad \lim_{r \to \infty} \frac{\alpha}{v} \cdot \frac{1}{1 - \dfrac{(1 - e^{-rm})(1 - \alpha)}{rm}} = \frac{\alpha}{v},$$

because

$$(5.27) \qquad \lim_{r \to \infty} \frac{1 - e^{-rm}}{rm} = 0,$$

by (1.12). Hence the necessary but not sufficient condition for $u \leqq 0$ is by (5.25) and (5.26)

$$(5.28) \qquad \frac{1}{m} \leqq \frac{\alpha}{v},$$

or

$$(5.29) \qquad \alpha \leqq \frac{v}{m}.$$

No degree of inflation can reduce u to zero if $\alpha > \dfrac{v}{m}$.

To find the exact value of i which gives $u = 0$, and therefore $r = i$, we obtain from (5.20) and (5.25),

$$(5.30) \qquad \frac{\alpha}{v} \cdot \frac{1}{1 - \dfrac{(1 - e^{-rm})(1 - \alpha)}{rm}} = \frac{1}{m},$$

which can be reduced to

$$(5.31) \qquad \frac{1 - e^{-rm}}{rm} = \frac{1 - \dfrac{\alpha m}{v}}{1 - \alpha}.$$

Numerical magnitudes of $r = i$ from (5.31) are given in Table V.

VIII

The Case for Accelerated Depreciation[*]

This paper takes for granted (1) that economic growth is necessary and desirable; (2) that it should include the development of new firms; and (3) that tax policy should be oriented toward these ends.[1] Its purpose is to discuss a method which would relieve a growing firm, and particularly a new firm, from part of its income tax liability. A direct exemption (of a new firm) is hardly practicable because a firm newly organized in the legal sense need not be new in any other sense; nor does it appear feasible to make the tax rate a function of the firm's rate of growth.[2] An indirect approach must then be sought, and accelerated depreciation for income tax purposes may provide one solution.

This method of tax relief, in one form or another, has been used both in the United States and abroad,[3] but its significance for a new and a growing firm has not, to my knowledge, been properly brought out. In a large measure this omission is due to our old but persistent habit of thinking in static terms; in the present case—in terms of a single investment. So viewed, accelerated depreciation merely results in a postponement of tax payments, an interest-free loan

* [Reprinted by permission from *The Quarterly Journal of Economics*, Vol. 67 (Nov., 1953), pp. 493–519. See also the discussion by Robert Eisner, George O. May, and myself in the same *Journal*, Vol. 69 (May, 1955), pp. 285–304.]

This essay was written under a Fulbright grant at the University of Oxford Institute of Statistics. Thanks are due to F. A. Burchardt, the Director, for his generous offer of the facilities of the Institute, and for many other things. Comments made by P. H. Ady, E. J. M. Buckatzsch, D. G. Holland, A. W. Romanis, P. P. Streeten, and G. D. N. Worswick made me rewrite many a paragraph. I am very grateful to them. The responsibility for any remaining errors and for all conclusions is, of course, mine.

1 This implies neither the exclusion of other measures to promote growth, nor the confinement of tax policy to this aim only.

2 That is, I am not aware of the existence of a practical plan of this nature.

3 For a description of the various methods see J. Frank Gaston, *Effects of Depreciation Policy*, National Industrial Conference Board Studies in Business Economics, No. 22 (New York, 1950), pp. 41–52.

which must sooner or later be repaid.[4] Even so, to a new firm such a postponement may be of the utmost importance. If we turn next to a stream of investment it will soon become obvious that this loan need never be repaid unless the investment stream declines, and further, that a growing stream—the most realistic American case—will result in a permanent reduction in the effective tax rate. But with a few notable recent exceptions, most proponents of accelerated depreciation, perhaps in their anxiety to assure the government that no permanent loss of revenue is involved, do not consider the dynamic case and therefore miss the most interesting and promising aspects of the plan which they advocate.[5]

I

Throughout this paper, growth is expressed exclusively in terms of investment in fixed capital. A growing firm means a firm with a growing stream of investment. Obviously, this is the only aspect of growth to which accelerated depreciation can be relevant.

Ideally, we should want to know the effects of accelerated depreciation on investment decisions. Existing investment theory, however, is so inadequate that it has to be built anew for practically every purpose.[6] Having no desire to attempt this here, we shall set

[4] With progressive taxes, a constant income stream, and no carry-over of depreciation credits, accelerated depreciation will even increase total tax payments over the life of a given asset, so that this 'loan' will not be entirely interest-free.

[5] See for instance Gaston, op. cit. pp. 22–6; Committee for Economic Development, *Taxes and the Budget: A Program for Prosperity in a Free Economy* (New York, 1947), p. 53. The disregard of the dynamic case is also true of such scholarly writers as Harold M. Groves, *Postwar Taxation and Economic Progress* (New York, 1946), p. 160; William Vickrey, *Agenda for Progressive Taxation* (New York, 1947), p. 111; E. Cary Brown, 'Business-Income Taxation and Investment Incentives,' in *Income, Employment and Public Policy; Essays in Honor of Alvin H. Hansen* (New York, 1948), p. 315; while Randolph E. Paul, *Taxation for Prosperity* (New York, 1947), p. 380, evidently cannot make up his mind. The best analysis of accelerated depreciation under conditions of growth that has come to my attention is by Richard Goode, *The Corporation Income Tax* (New York, 1951), p. 216; see also S. P. Dobrovolsky, 'Depreciation Policies and Investment Decisions,' *The American Economic Review*, Vol. 41 (Dec., 1951), pp. 909–10; and more recently, Robert Eisner, 'Accelerated Amortization, Growth, and Net Profits,' *The Quarterly Journal of Economics*, Vol. 66 (Nov., 1952), pp. 533–44. This last paper was published after my own research was completed.

[6] See, however, George Terborgh's *Dynamic Equipment Policy* (New York, 1949).

ourselves a more modest assignment—to investigate the behavior of the ratio between accelerated and normal depreciation allowances under different sets of conditions—in the hope that a high ratio will be conducive to investment and to development of new firms. This modesty obviates the need of specifying the exact nature of the income tax, and allows us to disregard the saving of interest which accelerated depreciation affords and which has been treated in detail elsewhere. But certain assumptions must be made. Here they are:[7]

1. The firm begins with no fixed capital.

2. Its gross investment (G) increases at an annual relative rate of r, where r is usually positive, but can also be made zero or negative. G consists of fixed capital only and is gross of depreciation or replacement.

3. Fixed assets remain on the books for m years and are immediately removed thereafter. A strict interpretation of m would make it identical for all assets, but broadly speaking it can be treated as an average for the firm as a whole.[8]

4. Unless otherwise indicated, normal depreciation is computed according to the straight line method, the annual charge thus being $1/m$ and applied to the original cost of each asset. There is no scrap value.

5. All magnitudes are expressed in money terms.

It is fully understood that no firm invests in the smooth and steady manner assumed here. But actual investment patterns are of infinite variety, and little will be gained by trying to imitate them here. Even the treatment of our simple functions requires a Mathematical Appendix, and as the number of variables rises, it becomes increasingly difficult to express mathematical results by means of charts or numerical tables.[9] In any case, our numerical illustrations should not be taken too literally in a world of investment fluctuations. On the other hand, the method used here can be readily

---

[7] A similar model, containing most of these assumptions, was constructed to find the interrelationship between depreciation, replacement, and growth. See Essay VII.

[8] The exact conditions are given on pp. 182–5 of Essay VII. If a firm (and particularly a new one) has assets of widely varying longevities, and if precise results are desired, it would be better to treat it as if consisting of separate departments each containing assets with a particular length of life.

[9] All formulas and numerical illustrations are based on continuous exponential functions. In the notes, the latter are replaced by discrete compound interest series. The errors involved are sufficiently small to be ignored.

applied to other investment patterns which may be of interest to the reader.[10]

All symbols are explained when first introduced in the text, and a complete list is given in the Appendix.

To spare some readers a disappointment, it should be made clear that I am not concerned here with the now popular subject of the alleged deficiency of normal depreciation charges in inflationary periods to finance replacement and do not present accelerated depreciation as a solution of this real or imaginary problem.[11]

II

Before turning to accelerated depreciation, let us examine how our firm fares in its absence, or more specifically, what fraction of its investment can be financed from internal funds, that is, from normal

CHART I.—THE BEHAVIOR OF D/G OVER TIME FOR DIFFERENT VALUES OF r AND m

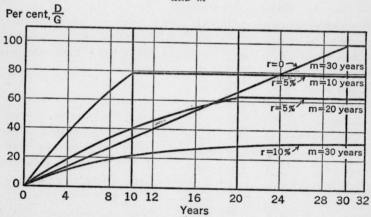

Per cent, $\dfrac{D}{G}$

depreciation charges and retained profits. Take depreciation charges (D) first. Since their relation to investment (G) has been discussed elsewhere, we can be brief here.[12] It is shown on Chart I that the

[10] It may be particularly worth while to experiment with a cyclical model, even as simple as a sine curve superimposed on a rising (or falling) trend.

[11] On this see E. Cary Brown, *Effects of Taxation; Depreciation Adjustments for Price Changes* (Boston, 1952), and Essay VII.

[12] Essay VII, pp. 156–60. Since we are interested here only in financial matters, the life span of assets, the size of the capital stock, and other terms should be understood purely in the accounting sense. It makes no difference here if assets are used long after they have been completely depreciated on the books.

annual ratio of normal depreciation charges to investment (D/G) begins at zero (there being no capital and hence no depreciation at the start) and gradually rises to its final value which it reaches at the end of m years. Since capital assets are assumed to stay on the books for m years, capital stock existing at any given moment is the accumulation of investments made in the preceding m years; hence the final relationship between capital stock and depreciation charges on the one hand and investment on the other is not established until this period has expired.[13]

This final value of D/G is an inverse function of both r and m, or more precisely of their product rm, and Table I gives its numerical

TABLE I.—THE FINAL MAGNITUDES OF D/G OR D'/G AS FUNCTIONS OF rm OR rm'

rm or rm'	$\dfrac{D}{G}$ or $\dfrac{D'}{G}$ per cent	rm or rm'	$\dfrac{D}{G}$ or $\dfrac{D'}{G}$ per cent
0.1	95	0.9	66
0.2	91	1.0	63
0.3	86		
0.4	82	1.5	52
0.5	79	2.0	43
0.6	75	2.5	37
0.7	72	3.0	32
0.8	69	3.5	28

Note: For the meaning of D' and m' see pp. 202 and 216.

magnitudes for certain values of rm. Disregarding here, as elsewhere in the paper, the question of fluctuations, and taking the average rate of growth of investment in money terms in the United States as a whole at some 4–5 per cent (the rate in real terms being closer to 3 per cent), and an average m of some 25–30 years,[14] we find that with an rm of 1–1.5 the average American firm should eventually be

[13] At the end of m years, $\dfrac{D}{G} = \dfrac{1 - \dfrac{1}{(1 + r)^m}}{rm}$. The method of deriving this formula, as well as all others in the paper, is explained in note 9.

[14] From Simon Kuznets, *National Product since 1869* (New York, 1946), pp. 50, 115; *Survey of Current Business Supplement, National Income and Product of the United States, 1929–50* (Washington, 1951), pp. 146, 150; Solomon Fabricant, *Capital Consumption and Adjustment* (New York, 1938), p. 34.

able to finance some 50–60 per cent of its investment (in fixed capital) from depreciation charges. For a firm growing at 10 per cent per year (rm of 2.5–3.0) this fraction is reduced to 35 per cent. On the other hand, a stationary firm ($rm = 0$) can eventually break even, while a declining one will have an excess of funds.[15]

Retained profits form the second principal source of internal funds. To approximate the traditional usage, the relation between retained profits and investment will be expressed here in terms of the rate of retained profits (p) on the stock of capital net of depreciation. This is not identical with the rate of retained profits on net worth, but any attempt to come closer to the latter would lead us astray, and the vagaries of business financing (shares, bonds, etc.) might make the result completely meaningless.

The annual ratio of total internal funds (retained profits plus depreciation charges) to investment expenditures behaves very similarly to D/G: it also rises gradually and becomes stabilized at the end of m years.[16] Table II gives some idea of the numerical magnitudes involved. If the rate of retained profits (p) and the rate of growth of investment (r) happen to be equal, the whole investment program of a growing firm can be financed internally year after year. A $p > r$ will create an excess of funds, while a $p < r$ will maintain the need for external financing. The equalization of p and r at some 4–5 per cent on the average, over a period of years, is not an impossible task for an ordinary, well-established American firm; for that matter, a p only half as large as r will allow the financing of some three-quarters of investment from internal sources.[17]

All this after the expiration of the first m years. By that time an old, moderately growing firm can take care of most of its financial

---

[15] Throughout the paper it is assumed that these depreciation charges are actually earned. If they are not, the firm has no taxable income and needs no tax relief.

[16] It is then expressed by the formula $\dfrac{p}{r} + \dfrac{(r - p)\left[1 - \dfrac{1}{(1 + r)^m}\right]}{r^2 m}$. See Appendix, p. 219.

[17] Internal financing by American corporations was strongly emphasized in the Hearings and Reports of the United States Temporary National Economic Committee, *Investigation of Concentration of Economic Power* (Seventy-sixth Congress, Washington, 1940–41), and data taken from the records of fifty-eight corporations which were almost financially self-sufficient were prominently displayed. (See particularly *Monograph No. 37*, pp. 50–58.) Those were well-

requirements and hardly needs any tax relief, such as could be provided by accelerated depreciation. But this independence comes about rather slowly, and is usually absent in the first few years of a firm's existence (unless it is very fortunate). Thus with an r of 5 per cent and an m of 30 years, D/G after five years is still below

TABLE II.—THE RATIO OF DEPRECIATION CHARGES AND RETAINED PROFITS
TO GROSS INVESTMENT AT THE END OF m YEARS (IN PERCENTAGES)
$m = 20$ years

p per cent	1	2	3	4	5	6
r per cent						
1	*100*	109	119	128	137	147
2	91	*100*	109	118	126	135
3	83	92	*100*	108	117	125
4	77	84	92	*100*	108	116
5	71	78	85	93	*100*	107
6	65	72	79	86	93	*100*

$m = 30$ years

p per cent	1	2	3	4	5	6
r per cent						
1	*100*	114	127	141	154	168
2	88	*100*	112	125	137	150
3	77	89	*100*	111	123	134
4	69	79	90	*100*	110	121
5	61	71	81	90	*100*	110
6	55	64	73	82	91	*100*

15 per cent; it will reach 35 per cent only after 15 years, and a 5 per cent rate of growth for a new firm is quite modest. A rapidly growing firm, unless its rate of retained earnings (p) is very high, will always be in need of outside funds.

---

established, large, and rather prosperous companies, and it would have been most surprising had they still needed large outside funds. But to treat them as a representative sample of American industry was unjustified.

During inflation, r rises, but so usually does p, and it is hard to tell on a priori grounds what the net outcome will be. All these variables are of course expressed in money terms.

III

Accelerated depreciation of fixed assets for income tax purposes can be and has been devised in a variety of ways;[18] the three simplest methods are considered here.

1. The American System, with straight line depreciation over a short period of time (equal to m' years).
2. The British System, with an initial allowance and a declining balance method of depreciation.
3. The Hybrid System.

As explained previously, we shall be mostly concerned with the ratio of accelerated (D') to normal depreciation (D) for given r and m. This implies that neither the rate of growth of investment nor the length of the economic life of assets is affected by the presence of accelerated depreciation. It is hoped that the latter will stimulate investments both for expansion and for replacement purposes, and thus raise r and lower m, but to assume this here would be illegitimate, and to attempt an investigation would carry us beyond the scope of this article.[19]

In order to avoid confusion in wage, dividend, and other policies, it is suggested that in addition to its regular books where normal depreciation is recorded, each firm should keep a special set of books for income tax purposes.

THE AMERICAN SYSTEM

It was shown above that the final relations between the dependent variables (such as depreciation and investment) are not reached until the expiration of m years. This is according to the firm's regular set of books. Since for income tax purposes all assets are written off over a shorter period of time indicated by m' (years), on the 'tax books' these relations are established after the end of the first m' years. Hence we have to deal with three separate periods: (1) $t < m' < m$; (2) $m' \leq t < m$; and (3) $m' < m \leq t$, where t

---

[18] See Gaston, op. cit.

[19] I am not referring here to the frequently reported and misguided method of making replacement decisions on the basis of the depreciated book value of capital assets, in which case accelerated depreciation should speed up replacements, but to the perfectly rational case when the tax saving afforded by accelerated depreciation may make earlier replacements possible and worth while.

indicates the number of years elapsed since the establishment of the firm.

The First Period: the first m' years $(t < m' < m)$

No assets have been completely written off as yet on either set of books and the ratio of accelerated to normal depreciation (D'/D) simply equals m/m' irrespective of r. With an m of 30 years and an m' of 5 (as the latter has been set on American defense plants), D' will be six times as large as D. The deduction of such heavy depreciation charges from gross profits will make it rather unlikely that any firm will have a taxable income in the first m' years of its existence, and if it has, its profits relative to its investment must be so large as not to warrant special concern. Many new firms will hardly have gross profits sufficiently large to take full advantage of accelerated depreciation in the first few years, and unless a long carry-over of depreciation credits is permitted, which is highly desirable, these credits will be partially lost to them.

The Second Period: the interval between m' and m years $(m' \leqq t < m)$

Starting from its high plateau in the First Period, D'/D gradually declines and reaches its final value at the end of m years, as shown by the *solid* curves on Chart II.[20] The rate of growth, which played no role in the preceding period, now comes into its own and keeps the D'/D of a rapidly growing firm consistently above that of a slowly expanding or a stationary one. But on the whole, under reasonable conditions, the decline of D'/D is not very rapid in any case. Even with $r = 0$, D'/D (for $m = 30$ and $m' = 5$ years) is still above 2 at the end of 15 years, and it does not reach 1.5 until 20 years have passed.

The Third Period: after the end of m years $(m' < m \leqq t)$

Table III presents the final magnitudes of D'/D for given r, m, and m'.[21] With $r = 0$, the equality between D' and D is finally

---

[20] Strictly speaking this is true if no asset has a life span (for depreciation purposes) in excess of m. See note 8.

[21] Its formula is $\dfrac{m}{m'} \cdot \dfrac{\left[1 - \dfrac{1}{(1 + r)^{m'}} \right]}{\left[1 - \dfrac{1}{(1 + r)^{m}} \right]}$.

restored, but even in this case the firm need not repay the benefits from accelerated depreciation which it had received in the first m years. Only for a declining firm does this method merely result in an interest-free loan which must eventually be repaid. A growing firm enjoys a permanent dispensation. Thus with $r = 5$ per cent, and m and m' of 30 and 5 years respectively, D' becomes stabilized at 70 per cent above D. A 10 per cent rate of growth would raise it to almost 150 per cent above D, that is, 2.5 times the normal depreciation charge.[22]

TABLE III.—THE FINAL MAGNITUDES OF THE SIMPLE RATIOS D'/D AS FUNCTIONS OF r, m, AND m' UNDER THE AMERICAN SYSTEM (IN PERCENTAGES)

r	$m = 30$ years m'				$m' = 5$ years m		
	1	2	5	10	10	30	50
−0.10	17	17	20	27	76	20	4
−0.05	44	45	49	56	88	49	25
−0.03	63	64	67	72	93	67	47
−0.01	86	87	88	90	98	88	79
0	100	100	100	100	100	100	100
0.01	115	115	113	110	103	113	124
0.03	149	147	141	131	108	141	179
0.05	188	184	171	152	112	171	241
0.10	300	286	248	200	125	248	396

A study of the behavior of D'/D over time may fail to convey the full importance of accelerated depreciation, particularly if the whole accelerated credit cannot be utilized every year (owing to temporary insufficiency of gross profits), but its unutilized portion can be carried forward for a long period of time. Then the relation between some form of cumulative D' and that of D may be more significant than their simple ratio studied so far. The exact form which this cumulative ratio should take depends on the availability and distribution of gross profits over time and on the length of the carry-

[22] The effect of accelerated depreciation can also be seen from a study of the behavior of D'/G. The latter also begins at zero, but rises very rapidly and reaches its final value after m' years. Its final magnitudes can be read from Table I by substituting m' for m.

over period. We shall examine here only the most favorable case when these two conditions are such that no part of accelerated credit is ever lost, and define the *cumulative ratio* between D' and D as the ratio between their respective sums from the date of the firm's establishment to the given point of time. The behavior of this cumulative ratio is shown by the dotted lines on Chart II; the formulas are given in the Appendix.

CHART II.—THE BEHAVIOR OF THE SIMPLE AND CUMULATIVE RATIOS
D'/D OVER TIME UNDER THE AMERICAN SYSTEM
$m = 30$ years
$m' = 5$ years

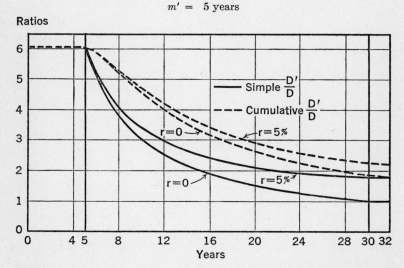

During the first m' years, the cumulative ratio also equals m/m'. Then it declines, but more slowly than the simple D'/D and, after a long period of time, gradually approaches the latter as a limit. Similarly to the simple D'/D, the rate of decline of the cumulative ratio over time (after the end of the first m' years) is also inversely related to r.

On the whole, the American system of accelerated depreciation gives an impression of being rather generous. The decline of the simple D'/D, and particularly of the cumulative ratio, is very gradual and a large advantage accrues for a long time even to a nongrowing firm. Perhaps m' should be extended, say, to 10 years, but this would weaken the psychological impact of accelerated depreciation on investment decisions without greatly reducing the final magnitude of D'/D. Thus the change from a 5 to a 10 year period (with m of 30 years) would bring the final value of D'/D from 171 to 152 per cent; yet the permission to write off a 30 year asset in 10 years, which would raise a 3.3 per cent normal annual depreciation rate to 10 per cent, somehow does not appear very striking. Moreover, an m' of 10 years would be almost useless for many kinds of machinery and equipment whose normal amortization period is not much longer. For that matter, even an m' of 5 years may be of little value in such a case.

A good argument can be made for discarding a constant m' and making it instead a certain function of m, such as one-third or one-fourth. Then all assets, irrespective of their longevity, would, in a sense, be treated equally. A fixed m' has the advantage of eliminating the frequent disputes between taxpayers and the government regarding the proper depreciation rates; these disputes would remain if m' became a function of m, but no new problems would be added. The method certainly deserves serious study.[23]

A variable m' will not eliminate a certain degree of inflexibility in the American system because large depreciation credits are given not only when the investment is made, but in the subsequent $(m' - 1)$ years as well. A very short m' results, I believe, in unnecessary generosity, while a longer m' may completely fail to affect investment decisions and thus make accelerated depreciation almost useless. Empirical studies usually indicate an overwhelming importance attached to the results obtained in the first few years after an investment is made.[24] If so, D'/D should be very high in the first year or two, but fall off rapidly thereafter. This is accomplished under the British system.

THE BRITISH SYSTEM

Normal depreciation on machinery and plant is usually computed in Britain according to the declining balance method, where a given annual amortization rate (a) is applied to the stock of capital net of depreciation. Thus the annual depreciation allowances decline with

[23] Perhaps m' should vary among industries depending upon their social or military importance, though this may involve political difficulties.

[24] This conclusion is suggested by the very short pay-off periods so frequently required when an investment is made. See, for instance, Terborgh, op. cit., and P. W. S. Andrews and Elizabeth Brunner, *Capital Development in Steel* (Oxford, 1951).

time, and a final allowance equal to the depreciated value of the asset (less the scrap value) is given when the asset is retired.[25] This final allowance, which at the end of an asset's normal life amounts to only a few per cent of its original cost, is disregarded here, and it is in fact assumed that the annual allowances on a given asset never cease. The error involved is, however, insignificant, and both this simplified and the correct method are treated in the Appendix.

Accelerated depreciation takes the form of an initial allowance (i) such as 20 or 40 per cent on machinery and plant and 10 per cent on industrial buildings, which is given in the first year in addition to the normal charge (a). Thereafter, only the latter is computed by taking an a fraction of the stock of capital net of total depreciation as explained above.[26]

Chart III shows the behavior of the simple (solid curves) and cumulative (dotted curves) ratios between D' and D.[27] In the first year all are very high, though the initial magnitudes of the cumula-

[25] See *The Income Tax Act, 1952 and Finance Acts, etc.*, H.M.S.O. (London, 1952), pp. 197–226. The rate of annual allowance (a) is computed in two stages: first it is set so as to reduce the depreciated value of an asset after the end of its normal life to 10 per cent of the original cost. For a 30 year asset this would give a rate of some 7.5 per cent per year, obtained by solving the equation $(1 - x)^{30} = 0.1$ for x (or with continuous functions, the equation $e^{-30x} = 0.1$). Then a, the effective rate, is taken at five-fourths of x. As a result, the depreciated value of the asset at the end of its normal life is reduced to some 5 per cent.

A 30 year asset is amortized at some 10 per cent per year applied to its depreciated value. As compared with the normal American system, where the corresponding rate is 3.3 per cent per year applied to the original cost, the British method contains an element of acceleration even without any special provisions to that effect. One should not take it for granted, however, that the assumed normal life of a given asset is necessarily the same in the two countries.

Straight line depreciation of plant and equipment is allowed in Britain as an alternative method. On industrial buildings this seems to be the prevailing practice.

[26] All initial allowances were suspended on investments made during the period from Apr. 6, 1952 to Apr. 14, 1953. They were reintroduced on the latter day as follows: 20 per cent on machinery and plant, 10 per cent on industrial buildings, and 40 per cent on mining works. See the *Financial Statement (1953–54)*, H.M.S.O. (London, Apr. 14, 1953), p. 15. Prior to Apr. 6, 1952, the initial allowance on machinery and plant had been 40 per cent. It is very interesting that the former Labor Chancellor of the Exchequer, Mr. Hugh Gaitskell, commenting on the 1953 Finance Act, urged the full restoration of the 40 per cent. See House of Commons, *Parliamentary Debates (Hansard)*, Fifth Series, Vol. 514 (Apr. 15, 1953), p. 227.

[27] The a of 10 per cent used in the chart implies an m of approximately 30 years, as shown in note 25. A 30 year normal life may be too long for plant and machinery, but it has the advantage of conforming to the other illustrations given in the paper.

tive ratios are a mathematical freak arising out of the use of continuous functions, and should not be taken seriously. All curves, both the simple and the cumulative, decline very rapidly even when the initial allowance is as high as 40 per cent.

Owing to our assumption that depreciation charges on a given asset never cease, D'/D does not become abruptly constant after the end of m years, but approaches asymptotically its limiting value,

CHART III.—THE BEHAVIOR OF THE SIMPLE AND CUMULATIVE
RATIOS D'/D OVER TIME UNDER THE BRITISH SYSTEM
$r = $ 5 per cent
$a = $ 10 per cent

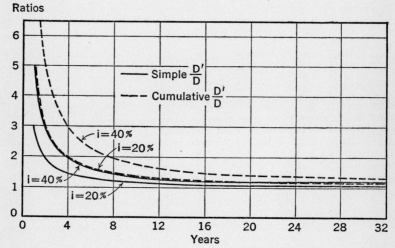

which is a direct function of r and of the ratio i/a.[28] Its numerical magnitudes given in Table IV show the same general pattern as those of Table III, but a closer comparison reveals that the British ratios are much smaller than the roughly corresponding American ones. Thus taking $r = 5$ per cent and $m = 30$ years for both systems (which gives an a of approximately 10 per cent in the British case) and an m' of 5 years for the American case, we get a D'/D of 171

---

[28] The limiting value of D'/D is given by the formula $1 + \dfrac{ri}{a}$. Its numerical difference from its respective final value which D'/D would reach at the end of m years in the absence of the simplifying assumption made above is very small. See the Appendix.

per cent, which is much larger than the 125 per cent obtained even with an initial allowance of 50 per cent (so that $i/a = 5$) under the British method.

Thus under the British system it is possible to give quite a large initial allowance in the first year without any special future commitments (beyond the carry-over provision) and without showing too great a generosity over the long pull. The initial allowance, as a device for accelerating depreciation, appears to be simpler and more flexible than the American method, and possibly more effective in its impact on investment decisions as well. But since the declining

TABLE IV.—THE LIMITING VALUES OF THE SIMPLE RATIOS D'/D AS FUNCTIONS OF r AND i/a UNDER THE BRITISH SYSTEM (IN PERCENTAGES)

r \ i/a	1	3	5	10	15
0	100	100	100	100	100
0.01	101	103	105	110	115
0.03	103	109	115	130	145
0.05	105	115	125	150	175
0.10	110	130	150	200	250

balance method is not common in the United States, an arrangement can be made by which the initial allowance is taken at once, and the remaining cost of the asset written off in m equal installments. This gives us the Hybrid system.

THE HYBRID SYSTEM

The movements of the simple and of the cumulative ratios between D' and D are presented on Chart IV. The curves look very similar to their British equivalents of Chart III (note, however, the difference in scale), except for the very high initial values. These are caused by the low rate of normal depreciation (3.3 per cent for an m of 30 years) allowed here as compared with that (10 per cent) under the British system. All curves decline very rapidly, and the simple D'/D ratios reach their final values at the end of m years.[29]

These final values are direct functions of the initial allowance

[29] The formula of the final value is $1 - i + \dfrac{irm}{1 - \dfrac{1}{(1+r)^m}}$.

(i) and of the product rm, and their numerical magnitudes are given in Table V. They are not strongly affected by increases in i, and on the whole they are considerably smaller than what can be roughly taken as the corresponding magnitudes of Table III: again taking $r = 5$ per cent and $m = 30$ years, we find that an i as high as 50 per cent gives a smaller final D'/D—147 per cent—than the 171 per cent obtained with an m' of 5 years under the American system. And an initial allowance of 50 per cent is certainly very

CHART IV.—THE BEHAVIOR OF THE SIMPLE AND CUMULATIVE RATIOS
D'/D OVER TIME UNDER THE HYBRID SYSTEM
$r = 5$ per cent
$m = 30$ years

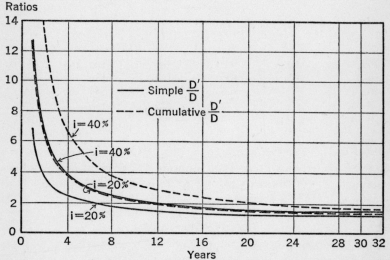

liberal. If accelerated depreciation as an investment stimulant is of any use at all, an initial allowance of 40 or 50 per cent should be quite effective and, one would think, more effective than is the 5 year amortization allowed on American defense plants; yet in the long run it yields a smaller tax concession than does the other method.[30] Of course, all these calculations should not be taken too literally because they are so far removed from reality; but the

[30] It is true, however, that in the first few years both the simple and the cumulative ratios of D' to D, and hence the resulting loss of tax revenue, are much higher in the Hybrid than what may be taken as the equivalent case under the American method.

general tendencies indicated here are not, I believe, devoid of significance.

*   *   *   *

The emphasis placed here on a new firm may obscure the position of one already in existence and possessing a stock of capital prior to the enactment of accelerated depreciation. Assuming that the latter is not made retroactive—and I cannot see any reason why it should be—we can think of all subsequent investment as if it were undertaken, so to speak, by a special department, which for our purposes

TABLE V.—THE FINAL MAGNITUDES OF THE SIMPLE RATIOS D'/D AS FUNCTIONS OF rm AND i UNDER THE HYBRID SYSTEM (IN PERCENTAGES)

rm \ i per cent	10	20	30	40	50
0.1	101	101	102	102	103
0.2	101	102	103	104	105
0.3	102	103	105	106	108
0.4	102	104	106	109	111
0.5	103	105	108	111	114
1.0	106	112	118	123	129
1.5	109	119	128	137	147
2.0	113	126	139	153	166
2.5	117	135	152	169	186
3.0	122	143	165	186	208

can be treated like a new firm. Owing to the existence of the old stock of capital, the (simple) D'/D ratio for the firm as a whole will not start from a high point or plateau as was shown on our charts; it will begin near one and then gradually *rise* to its final (or limiting) value, although, depending on the magnitude and longevity of the old stock of capital relative to those of new investment, D'/D may exhibit a more complex behavior during the first m years. But the fact that D'/D starts from a low point does not imply that the existing firm does not derive the same *absolute* advantage from accelerated depreciation as a new firm does, though its *relative* advantage is smaller.[31]

[31] I did not include the depreciation on the old stock of capital in the numerical examples and the formulas in order to avoid the use of two additional variables. The necessary adjustment of the formulas can, however, easily be made by adding this depreciation both to D' and D before taking their ratio.

IV

That accelerated depreciation affords considerable tax relief to a new and growing firm[32] can, I believe, safely be accepted, but how effective this relief will be in encouraging the organization and survival of new firms and in promoting growth in general is not easy to predict. Much will depend on the awareness of businessmen that the risk of investing in fixed capital is considerably reduced because no income tax need be paid until a substantial part of the cost has been recovered; also on their understanding that such investment offers a perfectly legitimate method of tax avoidance, and on their readiness to consider these facts in their investment decisions. Here (as was argued previously) a substantial initial allowance may have a stronger effect than a short amortization period, though one should not be dogmatic about it. Like any conventional form of tax relief, accelerated depreciation is useless to a firm without taxable income.[33] It is certainly not a method for encouraging the feeble; on the contrary, a growing firm is likely to gain at the expense of a stationary or a declining one.

This partial transfer of the tax burden will be intensified if the government tries to recoup any revenue losses suffered from accelerated depreciation (and they can be quite large in the first few years) by raising the general level of the corporate income tax. There is no particular reason why this tax should bring in a given amount of revenue, but those who insist on it either from a passion for balancing budgets or from concern for its effects on income distribution[34] need not treat the existing tax rate as fixed. Given the choice between a lower tax rate with normal depreciation or a higher rate with accelerated depreciation, I would, except in severe infla-

[32] At the time of its enactment it is beneficial to any firm investing in fixed capital.

[33] Except in so far as a carry-over of depreciation credits makes them useful in the future when taxable income appears. To help a firm without taxable income we would have to use the very unconventional method of making losses not only deductable from profits of the same or of another year, but actually reimbursable by the Treasury to the extent of the tax rate. This is not as fantastic as it sounds because diversified firms with income from several different sources usually enjoy this privilege more or less automatically. Combined with complete freedom of depreciation allowances this reimbursement of losses would make the Treasury the industry's true partner who provides a part of the fixed capital and shares in the profits and losses to the extent of the tax rate.

[34] See Eisner, op. cit.

tion, certainly recommend the latter. Should deflationary tendencies appear, an enactment of accelerated depreciation may indeed be preferable to a reduction of the corporate income tax rates.[35]

Once enacted and left to itself, however, accelerated depreciation is very likely to intensify economic fluctuations: it will encourage investment when profits are high and tax relief important, while in the absence of profits during depressions it will become ineffective, or even worse, because it may make worth while the postponement of investment until profits appear and the larger allowances can be taken advantage of. Moreover, the heavy amortization of investments during the boom will leave little depreciation to charge during the slump and thus understate taxable profits in the first instance and overstate them in the second, with parallel and highly undesirable movements of tax liabilities.[36]

A measure designed to encourage growth should not, however, be rejected on these grounds alone, because growth is the best remedy against depressions. But the defects of accelerated depreciation just described are real and must be dealt with. The most obvious remedy would consist in setting the initial allowance (if this method is chosen) at a certain rate in the usual course of events, and reducing or even suspending it completely during inflation.[37] This should cause the postponement of at least some investments during the boom, until the initial allowance comes into effect again, which is exactly the aim of anti-cyclical fiscal policy.[38] But it should not be delayed until a serious slump has developed. I doubt whether in a period like 1932–33 an initial allowance of even 100 per cent would have induced much investment.

An additional observation is particularly relevant to the American scene. Since the setting of normal depreciation rates by the Bureau of Internal Revenue is not considered an unconstitutional delegation

[35] This does not imply, however, that the existing tax structure (excess profits taxes, for instance) or existing tax rates *must* remain unchanged. That the introduction of accelerated depreciation may be more effective in stimulating investment than a reduction in corporate tax rates was also suggested by Goode, op. cit.

[36] An extended carry-over and carry-back of depreciation credits will mitigate this effect, but not eliminate it completely. See the text below.

[37] This was the reason for suspending initial allowances in Britain during the period between Apr. 6, 1952 and Apr. 14, 1953. See note 26.

[38] It is also possible to vary the rate at which initial allowances are given not only in time, depending on economic conditions, but also among industries.

of legislative powers to the Executive, we may hope (little as I know about this subject) that the extension of these powers to the enactment, suspension, and variation of the rates of initial allowance will be accepted by the courts as well. The Executive will then possess an additional fiscal instrument, easier to handle and perhaps no less effective than many changes in tax rates which must go through the cumbersome Congressional process. But it is just an instrument, one of many, and it is certainly not offered as a panacea.[39]

It is frequently suggested that in underdeveloped areas foreign investments in a socially desirable field should be exempt from taxation for the first few years. Accelerated depreciation can achieve this result without any special provision. If allowed on a sufficiently liberal scale, it will automatically relieve a firm from paying any income taxes until it has recovered a substantial part of its investment in fixed capital, unless the firm is very prosperous from the very beginning, in which case it can hardly ask for special help. This treatment need not be restricted to foreign capital only, and its general use may play an important role in economic development of less advanced countries.

A number of other questions which accelerated depreciation would raise should be mentioned. A good case can be made for limiting it to firms below a certain size: there is no need to encourage the growth of industrial giants. But a size limit is difficult to establish in practice. A 'giant' is a relative concept which differs from one industry to another. Still, the point deserves further thought.

In the practical application of accelerated depreciation one would wish to see a happy combination of orderliness with freedom. It is hardly desirable to grant firms complete discretion in the timing of depreciation charges. This could easily result in a 100 per cent initial allowance, which would be unnecessarily generous, and in addition bring in an extra element of uncertainty—about future tax rates— to business decisions; it would also allow business to thwart fiscal measures by increasing depreciation charges as tax rates are raised. The initial allowance (assuming that this method is chosen) should

[39] The flexibility of this instrument should not be exaggerated. Some investment projects require several years of construction and, if started when the initial allowance was in force, should remain entitled to it until their completion.

The results of this paper derived on the basis of steady growth should be applied to cyclical problems with care. A study of the effects of the liberal depreciation policy pursued in Sweden would be very desirable in this connection.

be available in the first year of the acquisition of the asset or not at all. But it should not be made compulsory, even though the choice would involve some speculation about future tax rates.[40] Capital already in the possession of a firm requires no initial allowance, and to prevent wholesale abuses from reorganizations, only assets constructed after its enactment need be covered by it. When an asset is sold above its depreciated book value, the difference should be taxed.

If the initial allowance is to be taken in the first year or not at all, the length of the carry-over period of depreciation credits becomes very important, particularly for a new firm which may, for several years, have no income from which to deduct this allowance. As in the treatment of actual losses, it pays here to be liberal and make the carry-over period as long as is practicably possible. A carry-back period may also be considered, although it will be of little help to a new firm.

There must be many administrative problems which the enactment of accelerated depreciation in one form or another would create, such, for instance, as the treatment of second-hand equipment which is frequently so important to a new firm. I am not taking them up here simply because I know little about practical tax matters. The fact that this method has existed in a number of countries, including the United States, shows that these problems can be solved.

* * * *

In these days of heavy taxation, concern is often expressed (particularly in Great Britain, but elsewhere as well) that the financing of risky ventures, connected with innovations, for instance, which in times past was performed by wealthy individuals out of their personal savings, is no longer possible, and that such ventures can now be undertaken only by well-established large firms or by the government. In the belief that this latter is undesirable, a reduction of the tax rates in the upper income brackets is advocated. Yet a brief reflection will show that out of a given amount of tax reduction only a relatively small fraction is likely to be spent in this particular manner, which makes this method of financing of risky (or other)

[40] The voluntary nature of the initial allowance is particularly important to unincorporated firms subject to a progressive income tax because the latter discriminates against fluctuating incomes.

ventures rather expensive from the social point of view. Perhaps it would be more promising to retain the existing tax rates (unless there are special reasons for their reduction), and to approach the problem by redefining taxable income so as to allow a liberal treatment (in one form or another) of amounts actually spent on, or lost in, socially important investments. Accelerated depreciation is but one example of this type of approach.

MATHEMATICAL APPENDIX

LIST OF SYMBOLS

In order of their appearance and with the case of their first appearance indicated.

The American
    System

G = annual gross investment;

r = relative annual rate of growth of G;

t = number of years elapsed from the establishment of the firm;

m' = length of the period of accelerated depreciation;

m = same, of normal depreciation;

K = stock of capital gross of depreciation and subject to normal depreciation only;

K' = same, subject to accelerated depreciation;

D = normal annual depreciation charge;

D' = same, accelerated;

C = stock of capital net of normal depreciation;

p = average annual rate of retained profits on C.

The British
    System

I = amount of initial allowance;

i = rate of I;

A = amount of annual allowance;

a = annual rate of A;

C' = stock of capital net of accelerated depreciation;

F = amount of final allowance.

The Hybrid
    System

K'' = stock of capital net of initial allowance only.

It is assumed in all models that $G = e^{rt}$. Since some of these results were obtained elsewhere[41] their derivation here is condensed.

THE AMERICAN SYSTEM

Period 1: $t < m' < m$

$$(1.1) \qquad K = K' = \int_0^t G dt = \frac{e^{rt} - 1}{r}.$$

Hence,

$$(1.2) \qquad D = \frac{e^{rt} - 1}{rm};$$

$$(1.3) \qquad D' = \frac{e^{rt} - 1}{rm'};$$

$$(1.4) \qquad \frac{D'}{D} = \frac{m}{m'};$$

$$(1.5) \qquad \frac{D}{G} = \frac{1 - e^{-rt}}{rm}.$$

Also,

$$(1.6) \qquad \int_0^t D dt = \frac{e^{rt} - 1 - rt}{r^2 m};$$

$$(1.7) \qquad \int_0^t D' dt = \frac{e^{rt} - 1 - rt}{r^2 m'};$$

and therefore

$$(1.8) \qquad \frac{\int_0^t D' dt}{\int_0^t D dt} = \frac{m}{m'}.$$

Period 2: $m' \leqq t < m$

As before,

$$(1.9) \qquad D = \frac{K}{m} = \frac{e^{rt} - 1}{rm},$$

but since K' on the 'tax books' is the accumulation of investments for the preceding m' years, and the first m' years have already expired,

$$(1.10) \qquad K' = \int_{t-m'}^t e^{rt} dt = \frac{e^{rt}(1 - e^{-rm'})}{r},$$

[41] See the Mathematical Appendix to Essay VII.

and

(1.11) $$D' = \frac{e^{rt}(1 - e^{-rm'})}{rm'};$$

therefore,

(1.12) $$\frac{D'}{D} = \frac{(1 - e^{-rm'})}{(1 - e^{-rt})} \cdot \frac{m}{m'}.$$

It can be shown that

(1.13) $$\frac{\partial \left(\frac{D'}{D}\right)}{\partial r} > 0, \qquad \frac{\partial \left(\frac{D'}{D}\right)}{\partial m} > 0, \qquad \frac{\partial \left(\frac{D'}{D}\right)}{\partial m'} < 0,$$

all as expected; also that

(1.14) $$\operatorname*{Lim}_{r \to 0} \frac{D'}{D} = \frac{m}{t}.$$

$\frac{D}{G}$ remains unchanged from (1.5) and

(1.15) $$\frac{D'}{G} = \frac{1 - e^{-rm'}}{rm'}.$$

By simple integration we derive

(1.16) $$\frac{\int_0^t D' dt}{\int_0^t D dt} = \frac{[e^{rt}(1 - e^{-rm'}) - rm']}{[e^{rt} - rt - 1]} \cdot \frac{m}{m'};$$

it can be shown that

(1.17) $$\operatorname*{Lim}_{r \to 0} (1.16) = \frac{m(2t - m')}{t^2}.$$

Period 3: $m' < m \leqq t$

D' remains unchanged from (1.11), while the application of the reasoning used in (1.10) gives

(1.18) $$D = \frac{K}{m} = \frac{e^{rt}(1 - e^{-rm})}{rm},$$

and hence

(1.19) $$\frac{D'}{D} = \frac{m(1 - e^{-rm'})}{m'(1 - e^{-rm})} = \frac{m}{1 - e^{-rm}} \cdot \frac{1 - e^{-rm'}}{m'}$$
$$= \frac{rm}{1 - e^{-rm}} \cdot \frac{1 - e^{-rm'}}{rm'},$$

the last variation of (1.19) being perhaps best suited for computations.

It can be shown that

$$(1.20) \qquad \underset{r \to 0}{\text{Lim}} \, \frac{D'}{D} = 1;$$

also that the results of (1.13) hold true in Period 3 as well. (1.15) remains unchanged, while

$$(1.21) \qquad \frac{D}{G} = \frac{1 - e^{-rm}}{rm}.$$

We can also derive

$$(1.22) \qquad \frac{\int_0^t D' dt}{\int_0^t D dt} = \frac{[e^{rt}(1 - e^{-rm'}) - rm']}{[e^{rt}(1 - e^{-rm}) - rm]} \cdot \frac{m}{m'},$$

and show that

$$(1.23) \qquad \underset{t \to \infty}{\text{Lim}} \, (1.22) = \frac{(1 - e^{-rm'})}{(1 - e^{-rm})} \cdot \frac{m}{m'} = \frac{D'}{D},$$

as given by (1.19), and that

$$(1.24) \qquad \underset{r \to 0}{\text{Lim}} \, (1.22) = \frac{2t - m'}{2t - m}.$$

C, the stock of capital net of normal depreciation, is the accumulation of investments over the past m years from $(t_{\prime} - m)$ to $t_{\prime}$, each investment weighted by its undepreciated fraction $\dfrac{t - (t_{\prime} - m)}{m}$, where $t_{\prime}$ indicates a given instant of time. Therefore,

$$(1.25) \quad C = \frac{1}{m} \int_{t_{\prime} - m}^{t_{\prime}} e^{rt}[t - (t_{\prime} - m)]dt = \frac{e^{rt_{\prime}}(rm - 1 + e^{-rm})}{r^2 m}.$$

(The subscript of $t_{\prime}$ can now be omitted.)

From (1.25) and (1.18), the ratio of total gross savings (retained earnings plus depreciation charges) to investment is

$$(1.26) \qquad \frac{Cp + D}{G} = \frac{(r - p)(1 - e^{-rm})}{r^2 m} + \frac{p}{r}.$$

By examining the $\underset{\substack{m \to 0 \\ m \to \infty}}{\text{Lim}}$ (1.26) and by noticing that $\dfrac{(r - p)(1 - e^{-rm})}{r^2 m}$

is *added* to $\dfrac{p}{r}$ when $r > p$, and is *subtracted* when $r < p$, we can prove that at the limit

(1.27) $r = p,$ $\dfrac{Cp + D}{G} = 1;$

(1.28) $r < p,$ $1 \leqq \dfrac{Cp + D}{G} \leqq \dfrac{p}{r};$

(1.29) $r > p,$ $\dfrac{p}{r} \leqq \dfrac{Cp + D}{G} \leqq 1.$

THE BRITISH SYSTEM

The Simplified Case without the Final Allowance

By definition,

(2.1) $I = iG = ie^{rt};$
(2.2) $A = C'a.$

Therefore,

(2.3) $\dfrac{dC'}{dt} = G - I - A = (1 - i)e^{rt} - C'a.$

The solution of this differential equation gives

(2.4) $C' = \dfrac{(1 - i)(e^{rt} - e^{-at})}{a + r},$

and by (2.1) and (2.2),

(2.5) $D' = A + I = \dfrac{a(1 - i)(e^{rt} - e^{-at})}{a + r} + ie^{rt}.$

D is obtained from (2.5) by taking $i = 0;$

(2.6) $D = Ca = a\dfrac{(e^{rt} - e^{-at})}{a + r}.$

(2.7) $\dfrac{D'}{D} = 1 - i + \dfrac{i(a + r)}{a[1 - e^{-(a+r)t}]};$

(2.8) $\underset{t \to \infty}{\text{Lim}} \dfrac{D'}{D} = 1 + \dfrac{ri}{a}.$

(2.9) $\dfrac{D}{G} = \dfrac{a[1 - e^{-(a+r)t}]}{a + r};$

(2.10) $\dfrac{D'}{G} = \dfrac{a(1 - i)[1 - e^{-(a+r)t}]}{a + r} + i.$

From (2.5) and (2.6) we obtain

$$(2.11) \qquad \frac{\int_0^t D'dt}{\int_0^t Ddt} = 1 - i + \frac{i(a+r)}{a - \dfrac{r(1-e^{-at})}{e^{rt}-1}},$$

and

$$(2.12) \qquad \lim_{t\to\infty}(2.11) = 1 + \frac{ri}{a} = \lim_{t\to\infty}\frac{D'}{D}, \text{ as given by (2.8).}$$

The Correct Case with the Final Allowance

Period 1: $t < m$

Since no assets have been retired, no final allowance has been given and the results of the Simplified Case still hold true.

Period 2: $t \geqq m$

The final allowance equals that part of investment made m years earlier which has not been amortized by the initial and annual allowances, that is

$$(2.13) \qquad F = (1-i)e^{-am}G_{t-m} = (1-i)e^{rt-m(a+r)}.$$

Equation (2.3) now takes the form of

$$(2.14) \quad \frac{dC'}{dt} = G - I - A - F = (1-i)e^{rt} - aC'$$
$$- (1-i)e^{rt-m(a+r)},$$

which gives the solution

$$(2.15) \qquad C' = \frac{(1-i)[1 - e^{-m(a+r)}]e^{rt}}{a+r}.$$

Following the method of the Simplified Case we finally obtain

$$(2.16) \qquad \frac{D'}{D} = 1 - i + \frac{i(a+r)}{a + re^{-m(a+r)}}.$$

As was shown in the text, the British rates of annual allowance are so arranged that e^{-ma} equals about 0.05. Therefore the expression $re^{-m(a+r)}$ is so small relative to a that it can be disregarded. This immediately reduces (2.16) to (2.8).

The Hybrid System

Period 1: $t < m$

It is convenient to think of the initial allowance as simply placing an ith part of investment into, so to speak, a special compartment. Therefore,

$$(3.1) \qquad K'' = (1 - i)K,$$

and

$$(3.2) \qquad A = aK'' = aK(1 - i) = (1 - i)D;$$

$$(3.3) \qquad D' = A + I = (1 - i)D + iG.$$

$$(3.4) \qquad \frac{D'}{D} = 1 - i + \frac{iG}{D} = 1 - i + \frac{irm}{1 - e^{-rt}},$$

and by (1.5)

$$(3.5) \qquad \frac{D'}{G} = \frac{(1 - i)(1 - e^{-rt})}{rm} + i.$$

$$(3.6) \qquad \frac{\int_0^t D'dt}{\int_0^t Ddt} = \frac{(1 - i + irm)(e^{rt} - 1) - (1 - i)rt}{e^{rt} - 1 - rt}.$$

Period 2: $t \geqq m$

From (3.3) and (1.21),

$$(3.7) \qquad \frac{D'}{D} = 1 - i + \frac{irm}{1 - e^{-rm}};$$

$$(3.8) \qquad \lim_{r \to 0} \frac{D'}{D} = 1.$$

The respective derivatives have the same signs as in (1.13).

$$(3.9) \qquad \frac{D'}{G} = \frac{(1 - i)(1 - e^{-rm})}{rm} + i.$$

$$(3,10) \qquad \frac{\int_0^t D'dt}{\int_0^t Ddt} = \frac{e^{rt}[(1 - e^{-rm})(1 - i) + irm] - rm}{e^{rt}(1 - e^{-rm}) - rm}.$$

$$(3.11) \qquad \lim_{t \to \infty} (3.10) = 1 - i + \frac{irm}{1 - e^{-rm}} = \frac{D'}{D}.$$

IX

A Soviet Model of Growth*

I

This essay is based on a remarkable article 'On the Theory of National Income Growth' published in 1928 by the Soviet economist G. A. Fel'dman in the organ of the Soviet State Planning Commission, *The Planned Economy* (*Planovoe Khoziaĭstvo*).[1]

In those days, *The Planned Economy* was a lively journal. A monthly, with over three hundred pages per issue, it was not unfriendly to theory, and its empirical studies, international surveys, and statistical appendixes were rich in content and full of interest. The proposed transformation of a backward peasant economy into a great industrial power in a period then believed to be amazingly short, and in a manner unique in history, must have provided a great intellectual stimulus which was not yet destroyed by the pressure of party orthodoxy. Naturally, not all articles were good, and some suffered from scholasticism and dogmatism, but the general level was high and the pages still uncluttered with the repetitious propaganda clichés of later years. One could not of course

* A good part of this essay was written at the Baker Library, Dartmouth College, in the summer of 1955. Thanks are due to the College authorities and the Library staff for their kindness and help; and to G. Diran Bodenhorn for his patience and suggestions. The comments received on a preliminary version of the paper from Abram Bergson, Alexander Erlich, Gregory Grossman, Oleg Hoeffding, Holland Hunter, Naum Jasny, Norman M. Kaplan, and Paul M. Sweezy were most helpful. None of them is of course responsible for any views expressed here. Bernard Okun, of The Johns Hopkins University, assisted me with computations, and my colleague Edith T. Penrose once again improved both the content and the style. I am very grateful to all of them.

[1] G. A. Fel'dman, 'K teorii tempov narodnogo dokhoda,' *Planovoe Khoziaĭstvo*, Nov., 1928, No. 11, pp. 146–70, to be referred to as Fel'dman, Ia; Dec., 1928, No. 12, pp. 151–78—Fel'dman, Ib. I am grateful to Gregory Grossman for telling me about this article.

The Library of Congress system is used for the transliteration of all Russian words.

advocate a return to capitalism, but compared with the Stalin era to come, expression was still relatively free. Criticism of the status quo and of economic policies then in use was frequent and sharp; so were the polemics, but more frequently than not they were based on logic rather than authority. Even Marx and Engels were quoted sparingly; Lenin appeared only now and then, and Stalin almost had to compete for space with—Henry Ford, the great symbol of mass production! In an argument, opponents might call each other naïve, ignorant, inattentive, and even outright stupid; they might rudely question each other's socialist faith, but not yet accuse each other of being saboteurs or enemies of the people. To a student of growth and development, the Soviet economic literature of the nineteen-twenties is of great interest; it certainly does not deserve the scant attention received from us in recent years.[2]

Besides the first five-year plan (undoubtedly familiar to the reader), the Soviet State Planning Commission was working then on a so-called General Plan extending over a period of some ten to twenty years.[3] Fel'dman was instructed to prepare a theoretical model as a basis for this plan, and his report was embodied (or possibly summarized) in the article mentioned above. It was followed by two other articles which did not add much to the original one.[4] Being concerned with the theory of long-range planning, Fel'dman could disregard the immediate and pressing practical

[2] The most substantial recent work on the subject is that of Alexander Erlich, *The Soviet Industrialization Controversy*, submitted to the Graduate Faculty of Political and Social Science of the New School for Social Research in Partial Fulfillment of the Requirements for the Degree of Doctor of Philosophy, Jan., 1953. The major part of this dissertation is still (as of summer, 1956) unpublished. See, however, his 'Preobrazhenski and the Economics of Soviet Industrialization,' *The Quarterly Journal of Economics*, Vol. 64 (Feb., 1950), pp. 57–88, and also 'Stalin's Views on Economic Development,' Ernest J. Simmons, ed., *Continuity and Change in Russian and Soviet Thought* (Cambridge, Mass., 1955), pp. 81–99.

[3] See N. A. Kovalevskiĭ, 'Metodologiia plana rekonstruktsii,' *Planovoe Khoziaĭstvo*, Apr., 1928, No. 4, pp. 7–45, and 'Metodologiia general'nogo plana,' *Diskussiia* v klube planovykh rabotnikov im. G. M. Krzhizhanovskogo, *Planovoe Khoziaĭstvo*, June, 1928, No. 6, pp. 134–207. See also Section V of this paper.

[4] G. A. Fel'dman, 'O limitakh industrializatsii,' *Planovoe Khoziaĭstvo*, Feb., 1929, No. 2, pp. 184–96, to be referred to as Fel'dman, II; and 'Analitischeskiĭ metod postroeniia perspektivnykh planov,' same journal, Dec., 1929, No. 12, pp. 95–127, to be referred to as Fel'dman, III.

problems of his day; this explains the academic and abstract nature of his article, and is also responsible both for its high quality and for its striking naïveté.

At first I intended to translate his original article in full. But it is long (fifty-three printed pages), involved, and repetitious. He does not go beyond elementary calculus, and yet his derivations are hard to follow. There is too much detail. However significant his achievement is from a historical point of view, his results are essentially similar and reducible to those since developed in the West. We shall share his start—the most interesting part of his model—bypass his derivations, and reconstruct his model in the simpler manner used in the other essays; and proceed then to some of the implications of this model for economic development.

II

As a good Marxist, Fel'dman starts with Marx's celebrated division of the total output of an economy (W) into Category 1— Producer goods (raw materials and capital), and Category 2— Consumer goods, the production of each category expressed as the sum of C (constant capital = depreciation plus raw materials broadly defined), V (variable capital = payrolls), and S (surplus value):

$$+ \frac{\begin{array}{c} C_1 + V_1 + S_1 = W_1 \\ C_2 + V_2 + S_2 = W_2 \end{array}}{C \ + V \ + S \ = W.}$$

With certain changes, this scheme would approximate our allocation of output by factor costs (depreciation, wages and salaries, and property income).[5] Fel'dman, however, was not concerned with

---

[5] The major adjustment would consist in eliminating inter-firm purchases within each category from both sides of each equation. On the comparison between Marxist and Keynesian schemes see Shigeto Tsuru, 'On Reproduction Schemes,' Appendix A of Paul M. Sweezy's *The Theory of Capitalist Development* (New York, 1942), pp. 365–74; also Tsuru's essay on 'Keynes versus Marx: The Methodology of Aggregates,' in Kenneth K. Kurihara, ed., *Post Keynesian Economics* (New Brunswick, N. J., 1954), pp. 320–44.

The Marxian scheme would cause no special difficulties if the Marxists did not try simultaneously to incorporate into it the corresponding allocation of output by expenditures (consumption and investment), a procedure which leads to unnecessary complications even in skillful hands. This is particularly true of problems involving capital accumulation. See Chapter XXI of Vol. II of the *Capital;* also Sweezy and Tsuru, op. cit.; and Evgeniĭ Preobrazhenskiĭ,

factor costs; his Marxism was sufficiently flexible to allow him to dismiss this question entirely, and concentrate all his attention on the distribution of currently produced capital goods (a part of the output of Category 1) between the two categories. But first he had to modify Marx's scheme once more by redefining the categories.

Since in Marx's scheme C_2 consists not only of depreciation, but also of raw materials (in the broad sense), presumably all made good by or obtained from Category 1,[6] Category 2 should contain only the final stage of production of consumer goods, that is, retail trade, utilities, services, and the like. A more liberal interpretation would add the last stage of manufacturing, but this is a vague notion: now the consumer buys bread and now flour. In any case, as a starting point for a model of economic development, which to Fel'dman (and to others) meant the expansion of capital goods industries, what use could Marx's scheme be if the bakery was placed in Category 2, while the flour mill remained in Category 1? Surely Category 2 should contain not only the bakery, but also the flour mill, the grain elevator, some transportation, the farm, and so on. Fel'dman's real aim was to place all activities merely sustaining output at the present level in Category 2, while all capacity-increasing ones were located in Category 1. This is an attractive proposal, and not only to a Marxist,[7] but how is it to be carried out in practice? In many countries, a part of expenditures on food, education, public health, and so forth, serves to increase productive capacity. (And wouldn't we also have to allow for depreciation or replacement of human beings?) No wonder that economists usually settle for a less satisfying but more practical division of total output into consumption and investment along more or less traditional

---

Zakat kapitalizma (Moscow-Leningrad, 1931), as examples. Additional difficulties (connected with stocks and flows) arise in computations of the organic composition of capital and of the rate of profit, but we are not concerned with them here. On this see Joan Robinson, *An Essay on Marxian Economics* (London, 1942), Chap. 2.

[6] In this connection, C_2 really includes replacement rather than depreciation. I wonder if those who use Marx's scheme are aware that in a growing economy replacement and depreciation are not identical. See Essay VII.

[7] A similar suggestion was made by Simon Kuznets in 'International Differences in Capital Formation and Financing,' *Capital Formation and Economic Growth*, A Conference of the Universities-National Bureau Committee for Economic Research (Princeton, N. J., 1955), pp. 19–106.

lines, and Fel'dman is forced to follow this course as well. So in his final version, Category 1 produces all capital goods for both categories, while all consumer goods, including the corresponding raw materials, are produced in Category 2, the output of each category consisting of its respective final products only.[8]

As a result, the economy is literally split from top to bottom into these two categories. Theoretically, the scheme is still attractive, but it is impossible to give it any but the roughest empirical meaning simply because an economy is not organized in this manner. Many industries produce raw materials, semi-finished goods, and services used by both categories—metals, chemicals, coal, petroleum, transportation, power, and even textiles, to name only a few. Perhaps Fel'dman could claim that in the Russia of his day practically all metals were used in Category 1 only, but what could he say about the rest? Nor would it help to divide an industry (like coal or transportation) between the two categories, because the respective proportions would by their very nature lack stability. Of course any division of an economy by industries, or even of output between consumption and investment, is difficult and arbitrary, but it is clear that Fel'dman's method creates special difficulties.[9]

The empirical content of his model worried Fel'dman less than its deviation from the standard Marxist scheme. The latter he justified at some length by the difference between his problem and that of Marx (Ib, pp. 173–6; III, pp. 96–102). As to the former, he was rather inconsistent, now expecting his scheme to be applied with absolute exactness (Ia, p. 152), then admitting that this could

[8] Similar schemes were suggested by Fritz Burchardt, 'Die Schemata des stationären Kreislaufs bei Böhm-Bawerk und Marx,' *Weltwirtschaftliches Archiv*, Vol. 34 (II part, 1931), pp. 525–64 and Vol. 35 (I part, 1932), pp. 116–76; by Ragnar Nurkse, 'The Schematic Representation of the Structure of Production,' *The Review of Economic Studies*, Vol. 2 (1934–35), pp. 232–44; and by Adolph Lowe, 'A Structural Model of Production,' *Social Research*, Vol. 19 (June, 1952), pp. 135–76, and 'Structural Analysis of Real Capital Formation,' *Capital Formation and Economic Growth*, A Conference of the Universities-National Bureau Committee for Economic Research (Princeton, N. J., 1955), pp. 581–634.

[9] This difficulty was recognized by the Soviet economist B. Ignatov in his paper 'Balans narodnogo khoziaĭstva,' *Planovoe Khoziaĭstvo*, June, 1932, No. 2, pp. 112–36. He tried to solve it by assigning individual industries to the two categories in accordance with the nature of the major part of each industry's production.

not be done 'at the moment, on the basis of materials on hand' (Ib, p. 169), and finally suggesting that the categories need not be separated physically, but only in an accounting sense (III, p. 105). At the end of his third article (III, pp. 119–25), he did make an attempt to divide the capital invested in each industry into two parts, one to be used for current production, and the other for increasing the latter, as if agriculture were to produce its own tractors, an exercise which leaves me rather puzzled regarding Fel'dman's understanding of the empirical meaning of his own model.[10]

Should Fel'dman's model be abandoned altogether? This, I believe, would be too extreme a step. Pigou's wage-goods industries, Hayek's stages of production, Marx's standard scheme, Hicks's induced versus autonomous investment, to name only a few, all give rise to models with an elusive empirical content and yet not devoid of interest.[11] It seems to me worth while to explore a growth model constructed on a Marxist foundation,[12] even if modified, and to show its relation to a corresponding Keynesian one. For all its empirical shortcomings, Fel'dman's model is not inapplicable, in very broad terms of course, to the Soviet experience, and it may be of use in unraveling a few puzzles in Soviet economic development and in achieving a better understanding of Soviet economic thinking. It also raises some questions regarding economic development in general.[13]

[10] He computed the expected increments in output of the several industries from Apr. 1, 1927 to Apr. 1, 1928 and then multiplied each increment by its respective capital coefficient (actually divided each increment by its capital productivity) to obtain the amount of capital devoted to the increase in output (III, pp. 124–5). It is interesting that a report of the Committee on the General Plan based on Fel'dman's model did not use Fel'dman's division of the economy into these two categories. See below, Section V.

[11] A. C. Pigou, *The Theory of Employment* (London, 1933); Friedrich A. Hayek, *Prices and Production*, second ed. (London, 1935); J. R. Hicks, *A Contribution to the Theory of the Trade Cycle* (Oxford, 1950). I should add here that the empirical content of my own models is certainly not beyond reproach.

[12] This was suggested by Paul M. Sweezy, 'In Answer to Criticisms on *The Theory of Capitalist Development*,' *The Economic Review*, Vol. 1 (Apr., 1950), pp. 135–9. (A publication of Hitotsubashi University, Tokyo.) This article was reprinted in Sweezy's collection of essays, *The Present as History* (New York, 1953), pp. 352–62.

[13] There is one more difficulty. Investment, all of which is produced by Category 1, presumably contains increments to inventories held by both categories. But this contradicts the assumption that Category 2 produces all its raw mate-

III

Like other growth models, Fel'dman's is based on a number of simplifying assumptions, such as: constant prices (with a five-page justification, Ia, pp. 146–50); capital as the only limiting factor; absence of lags; a closed economy (except for a short section in Ib, pp. 165–9); production independent of consumption;[14] absence of government expenditures as a separate category distinct from consumption and investment; absence of bottlenecks; and several others which will come to the surface as we go along. But one important attribute of the model should be indicated now.

The division of the economy between the two categories is complete, in the sense that no existing capital can be transferred from one to another (there being no other limitations on production). Thus the rate of investment is rigidly determined by the capital coefficient and the stock of capital in Category 1. Similarly, the output of consumer goods is determined by the stock of capital and the capital coefficient of Category 2.[15] Hence the division of total output between consumption and investment at any given moment depends on the relative productive capacities of the two categories, and not on the propensity to save, though the latter can reassert itself by causing an underutilization of the capital stock in one category or another, a waste ruled out in the model. The division of total investment (that is, of output of Category 1) between the two categories is, however, completely flexible. Indeed, the fraction of total investment allocated to Category 1 is the key variable of the model.

---

rials and finished goods, including such quantities as are added to its inventories. Fel'dman was not aware of this problem. It could be solved by allowing the capital in Category 2 to produce a part of itself. I have not made this adjustment because it is of little importance in comparison with the basic defect of the model.

[14] Kovalevskiĭ did recognize the dependence of labor productivity on consumption. See Section V and the reference in note 51.

[15] If the productive capacity of Category 1 is so small that it is merely sufficient for replacement of wearing-out capital assets in both categories (a possible situation in an undeveloped country), then in Fel'dman's model growth can be achieved only by a temporary failure to replace wearing-out assets in Category 2. Whether total output of the economy will show growth during this process will depend on the valuation weights assigned to the outputs of the two categories.

We shall now put Fel'dman's work aside, and derive his major results in an easier way.[16] Two separate cases will be considered: 1, Permanent Assets, and 2, Assets Subject to Wear.

Case 1. Permanent Assets[17]

List of Symbols

In order of their appearance.

γ = fraction of total investment allocated to Category 1;

I = annual rate of net investment (output of Category 1);

I_1 and I_2 indicate annual rates of net investment allocated to the respective categories, so that $I_1 + I_2 = I$;

t = time measured in years;

V = marginal capital coefficient for the whole economy;

V_1 and V_2 indicate the marginal capital coefficients of the respective categories (not to be confused with Marx's V, p. 225);

C = annual rate of output of consumer goods (not to be confused with Marx's C, p. 225);

Y = annual net rate of output of the whole economy (national income);

α = average propensity to save (ratio of total investment to national income);

α' = marginal propensity to save (ratio of the increment in total investment to the increment in national income);

I_0, C_0, and Y_0 indicate the respective initial magnitudes of these variables (when $t = 0$).

By definition of γ,

(1.1) $$I_1 = \gamma I,$$

and since only I_1 increases the capacity of Category 1,

(1.2) $$\frac{dI}{dt} = \frac{I_1}{V_1}.$$

---

[16] A similar model was constructed by P. C. Mahalanobis, 'Some Observations on the Process of Growth of National Income,' *Sankhyā, The Indian Journal of Statistics*, Vol. 12 (Sept., 1953), pp. 307–12. Mr. Mahalanobis was evidently not aware of Fel'dman's work.

[17] The permanency of assets is assumed merely to avoid questions related to depreciation and replacement, which are considered in Case 2. Alternatively,

Substituting (1.1) into (1.2), we obtain

(1.3)
$$\frac{dI}{dt} = \frac{\gamma I}{V_1},$$

the solution of which is

(1.4)
$$I = I_0 e^{\frac{\gamma}{V_1}t}.$$

To simplify all derivations, we set $I_0 = 1$; then

(1.5)
$$I = e^{\frac{\gamma}{V_1}t};$$

in other words, total investment will grow at a constant exponential rate of $\frac{\gamma}{V_1}$.

Again by definition of γ,

(1.6)
$$I_2 = (1 - \gamma)I = (1 - \gamma)e^{\frac{\gamma}{V_1}t}.$$

I_2 being the only source of increased capacity in Category 2,

(1.7)
$$\frac{dC}{dt} = \frac{I_2}{V_2} = \frac{(1 - \gamma)}{V_2} e^{\frac{\gamma}{V_1}t},$$

and

(1.8)
$$C = C_0 + \left(\frac{1 - \gamma}{\gamma}\right) \frac{V_1}{V_2} (e^{\frac{\gamma}{V_1}t} - 1),$$

(1.9)
$$\frac{dY}{dt} = \frac{dC}{dt} + \frac{dI}{dt} = \frac{e^{\frac{\gamma}{V_1}t}}{V_1 V_2} [V_1 - \gamma(V_1 - V_2)],$$

(1.10)
$$Y = I + C = Y_0 + \left[\left(\frac{1 - \gamma}{\gamma}\right) \frac{V_1}{V_2} + 1\right] (e^{\frac{\gamma}{V_1}t} - 1).$$

Thus C and Y each represent a sum of a constant and an exponential in t. Their rates of growth will therefore differ from $\frac{\gamma}{V_1}$. As time goes on, the exponential will dominate the scene and the rates of growth of C and Y will gradually approach $\frac{\gamma}{V_1}$. But this may take quite a long time, unless of course it so happens that

---

this assumption can be removed, and all variables interpreted net of depreciation which is made good continuously. This approach was used in essays III and IV of this volume.

$C_0 = \dfrac{(1 - \gamma)}{\gamma} \dfrac{V_1}{V_2}$, in which case the constants will vanish and C

and Y will grow at the rate of $\dfrac{\gamma}{V_1}$ from the very beginning—not an

interesting case from the point of view of this model. Table I shows the behavior of the rates of growth of I, Y, and C over time under given conditions. It is based on the simplifying assumption that $V_1 = V_2$, which will be discussed shortly.

TABLE I.—A COMPARISON OF THE RELATIVE RATES OF GROWTH OF
I, Y AND C OVER TIME FOR GIVEN α_0, γ AND V*
$(V_1 = V_2 = 3)$

t	$\alpha_0 = .1;$ $\gamma = .3$			$\alpha_0 = .2;$ $\gamma = .5$		
	Percentage Rates of Growth of			Percentage Rates of Growth of		
	I	Y	C	I	Y	C
0	10.0	3.3	2.6	16.7	6.7	4.2
1	10.0	3.6	2.8	16.7	7.3	4.7
2	10.0	3.8	3.0	16.7	8.0	5.3
3	10.0	4.0	3.2	16.7	8.7	5.9
4	10.0	4.3	3.4	16.7	9.4	6.6
5	10.0	4.5	3.7	16.7	10.1	7.2
10	10.0	5.8	4.9	16.7	13.0	10.6
20	10.0	7.9	7.2	16.7	15.8	15.1
30	10.0	9.1	8.8	16.7	16.5	16.3
50	10.0	9.9	9.8	16.7	16.7	16.7

* Based on the expressions

$$\frac{\frac{dy}{dt}}{Y} = \frac{\frac{\gamma}{V}}{(\gamma Y_0 - 1)e^{-\frac{\gamma}{V}t} + 1},$$

and

$$\frac{\frac{dC}{dt}}{C} = \frac{\frac{\gamma}{V}}{\left(\frac{\gamma C_0}{1 - \gamma} - 1\right) e^{-\frac{\gamma}{V}t} + 1},$$

derived from (1.7)–(1.10). In all examples $I_0 = 1$.

The reader familiar with my other essays (particularly III and IV) may wonder now why the rate of growth of investment here differs from the one derived there. The latter was equal to $\frac{\alpha}{V}$ where α indicated both the marginal and the average propensities to save and V was the over-all capital coefficient. To compare the earlier models with Fel'dman's it is necessary to rework their results *without* the assumption that the average propensity to save, α, equals the marginal one, α'. We shall continue to treat α' as a constant, but since $\alpha \neq \alpha'$, α has now become a variable. It can be easily shown that the rate of growth of investment will now be $\frac{\alpha'}{V}$, while that of income will remain $\frac{\alpha}{V}$.[18] The expression $\frac{\alpha'}{V}$ is of course the ratio of the marginal propensity to save to the over-all capital coefficient. In Fel'dman's model, however, we have obtained $\frac{\gamma}{V_1}$ as the rate of growth of investment, where γ is the fraction of investment allocated to Category 1, and V_1 is the capital coefficient of this category only.

Let us find α' of the present model. From (1.5) and (1.9) we obtain

$$(1.11) \qquad \alpha' = \frac{\gamma V_2}{V_1 - \gamma(V_1 - V_2)} = \frac{\gamma}{\dfrac{V_1}{V_2} - \gamma \left(\dfrac{V_1}{V_2} - 1 \right)}.$$

---

[18] *The first proposition:* Let $I = b + \alpha'Y$, and hence $\frac{dY}{dt} = \frac{\frac{dI}{dt}}{\alpha'}$. By definition of V, $\frac{dY}{dt} = \frac{I}{V}$. Substituting this into the previous expression, we obtain $\frac{dI}{dt} = \frac{\alpha'I}{V}$ and $\frac{\frac{dI}{dt}}{I} = \frac{\alpha'}{V}$.

The second proposition: The results just obtained give us $\frac{\frac{dY}{dt}}{Y} = \frac{\frac{dI}{dt}}{\alpha'Y} = \frac{\alpha'I}{V\alpha'Y} = \frac{I}{YV} = \frac{\alpha}{V}$, since $\alpha = \frac{I}{Y}$.

In essays III and IV, the rate of growth was expressed as $\alpha\sigma$. Since capital in Fel'dman's model is the only limiting factor and it is fully used, we can disregard the difference between σ and s; s being the reciprocal of V, that rate of growth of income can be written as $\frac{\alpha}{V}$.

In the special case when $V_1 = V_2$ we obtain the not-quite-expected result that

(1.12) $\alpha' = \gamma,$

that is, Fel'dman's fraction of investment allocated to Category 1 and Keynes's marginal propensity to save become identical.[19] If $V_1 > V_2$ then of course $\gamma > \alpha'$. Table II shows the magnitudes of the ratio $\frac{\gamma}{\alpha'}$ for given α' and $\frac{V_1}{V_2}$. It is interesting that for reasonably small magnitudes of α', $\frac{\gamma}{\alpha'}$ is close to $\frac{V_1}{V_2}$. As α' increases, $\frac{\gamma}{\alpha'}$ moves

TABLE II.—THE MAGNITUDES OF $\frac{\gamma}{\alpha'}$ FOR GIVEN VALUES OF α' AND $\frac{V_1}{V_2}$*

$\frac{V_1}{V_2}$ / α'	.50	.75	1.00	1.50	2.00
.05	.51	.76	1.00	1.46	1.90
.10	.53	.77	1.00	1.43	1.82
.20	.56	.79	1.00	1.36	1.67
.50	.67	.86	1.00	1.20	1.33
.75	.80	.92	1.00	1.09	1.14
1.00	1.00	1.00	1.00	1.00	1.00

* Based on the expression $\dfrac{\gamma}{\alpha'} = \dfrac{\frac{V_1}{V_2}}{1 + \alpha'\left(\frac{V_1}{V_2} - 1\right)}$ derived from (1.14).

toward unity from below or above depending upon whether V_1 is smaller or larger than V_2.

That Fel'dman's γ and Keynes's α' should be so closely related, and even identical when $V_1 = V_2$, may be surprising, but it is

[19] The case where $V_1 = V_2$ may appear rather unrealistic because we usually think of Category 1 as heavy industry with high capital coefficients. And yet according to Leontief, the highest capital coefficient (in 1939)—7.1—was in home renting, a branch of Category 2, while the lowest but one—.076—was in construction, which belongs to Category 1. Other high coefficients were found in petroleum and natural gas, communications, steam railroads, transportation, electric public utilities, etc.—industries belonging to both categories. It should be noted, however, that these coefficients represent the ratios of the stock of capital to productive capacity, and not to value added. Wassily Leontief *et al.*, *Studies in the Structure of the American Economy* (New York, 1953), pp. 191, 220–21.

merely a reflection of the fact that if a certain fraction of the increment in national income (α') is to be devoted to investment, a corresponding fraction of investment (γ) must be allocated to capital goods industries to make the production of this increment in investment possible.[20] In other words, in a growing economy some capital is used to make more capital. The explicit recognition of this fact is, I believe, one of the virtues of Fel'dman's model, though ironically enough its author kept insisting that the final purpose of all production is consumption. In a growing economy this is simply not true.

The relationship between V_1 and V_2 on the one hand and V (the over-all coefficient for the whole economy) on the other is also simple. The rate of growth of investment being independent of the manner in which it is expressed,

$$(1.13) \qquad \frac{\gamma}{V_1} = \frac{\alpha'}{V}.$$

Solving (1.11) for γ in terms of α', we have

$$(1.14) \qquad \gamma = \frac{\alpha' V_1}{V_2 + \alpha'(V_1 - V_2)},$$

and inserting (1.14) into (1.13), we obtain

$$(1.15) \qquad V = \alpha' V_1 + (1 - \alpha') V_2,$$

that is, V is a weighted average of V_1 and V_2.

Thus development decisions made in terms of α or α' imply corresponding decisions regarding the magnitude of γ, and vice versa.

The average propensity to save (ratio of investment to income) α plays a minor role in Fel'dman's model. It can be computed and it is relevant to many policy decisions (the level of taxation, for

[20] Perhaps a simple numerical example will help us understand the relation between α' and γ. Let us take $\alpha' = 10$ per cent, and let $V_1 = V_2$. Then if the ratio between C and I is to be maintained at 9 to 1, the new investment must be allocated between the consumer and capital goods industries in the same ratio. On the other hand, if $V_1 = 4$, $V_2 = 2$, the corresponding division of investment will be approximately in the ratio of 1.8 to 8.2.

This relation between α' and γ (though not in these terms) was also pointed out by Joan Robinson. She assumed their identity without explaining, however, that the latter depends on the equality of the capital coefficients. *The Rate of Interest and Other Essays* (London, 1952), pp. 92–6.

It should be pointed out that this close relation between γ and α' does not of course solve Fel'dman's classification problem.

instance), but it has no life of its own, so to speak, and is completely determined by the relative productive capacities of the two categories (see above, p. 229), because the underutilization of capital in either category is excluded by the assumed absence of any limits to production other than capital.

Though exaggerating the rigidities of the real world, Fel'dman's model contains an important element of truth: a closed economy without well-developed metal, machinery, and subsidiary industries (the complex of the so-called heavy industries) is unable to produce a sizable quantity of capital goods and thus to invest a high fraction of its income, however high its *potential* saving propensity may be. In Soviet economic thinking the former consideration has been predominant; in our recent literature the ability to save has been emphasized. Perhaps a synthesis, or more correctly, a return to a synthesis, is in order.[21]

Table III illustrates the behavior of α over time under two arbitrarily chosen sets of conditions. In both cases, α_0 is small as compared with γ. As expected, α rises over time and gradually approaches γ, but it remains relatively low for quite some time, in spite of the very high assumed rates of growth of investment given by $\frac{\gamma}{V_1}$ (10 and 17 per cent). Thus for some time, a country's *investment* can grow very rapidly even with a low average propensity to save. The latter does, however, determine the rate of growth of *income* as was shown on pp. 231–3, and a low α will of course result in a slowly growing income (see Table I). But a low α is not incompatible with a high rate of growth of investment for a period of time. Here may be found at least a partial explanation of their simultaneous existence in Soviet Russia, as found by Norman Kaplan, a phenomenon which has puzzled some economists, including myself.[22]

[21] The importance of the relationship between the capacity of capital goods industries and the current propensity to save is recognized by Moses Abramovitz in 'Economics of Growth,' Bernard F. Haley, ed., *A Survey of Contemporary Economics*, Vol. II (Homewood, Ill., 1952), pp. 155–6, and by Lowe, op. cit. This relationship was also the cornerstone of the so-called overinvestment business cycle theories, such as Hayek's, op. cit., and Gustav Cassel's *The Theory of Social Economy* (New York, 1924).

The inability of undeveloped countries to produce capital goods should not, however, be exaggerated. A good deal of construction can be carried on with fairly primitive methods.

[22] See Norman M. Kaplan, 'Capital Formation and Allocation,' and comments

If this application of Table III to the Soviet case may help to solve one problem, it immediately creates another: for in Table III α rises with time, while several of our estimates of the Soviet national product fail to show such a tendency. Thus according to Hoeffding, the ratio of gross investment to gross national product was 23.2 per cent in 1928, and according to Bergson and Heymann it stayed at 22.9

TABLE III.—THE BEHAVIOR OF α OVER TIME FOR GIVEN α_0, γ, AND V^*
$(V_1 = V_2 = 3)$

t	$\alpha_0 = .10$ $\gamma = .30$	$\alpha_0 = .20$ $\gamma = .50$
0	.100	.20
1	.107	.22
2	.114	.24
3	.121	.26
4	.128	.28
5	.136	.30
10	.173	.39
20	.236	.47
30	.273	.50
50	.296	.50

* Based on the expression $\alpha = \dfrac{\gamma}{(\gamma Y_0 - 1)e^{-\frac{\gamma}{V}t} + 1}$ derived from (1.5) and (1.10). The reader is reminded that $I_0 = 1$.

per cent in 1937, went down to 16.6 in 1940, and rose to 25.6 per cent in 1948 (all adjusted for turnover taxes).[23] And yet the Soviet experiment does resemble Fel'dman's model: the country started (in the

on his paper by Domar, Erlich, and Millikan in Abram Bergson, ed., *Soviet Economic Growth* (Evanston, Ill., 1953), pp. 37–100. I may add that my own comments expressed in terms of a *given* average propensity to save hardly helped to clarify the issue.

[23] Oleg Hoeffding, *Soviet National Income and Product in 1928* (New York, 1954), p. 46; Abram Bergson and Hans Heymann, Jr., *Soviet National Income and Product 1940–48* (New York, 1954), pp. 70–71. These estimates of the ratio of investment to national product are in gross (of depreciation) terms, while our present case is in net (permanent assets). A gross variant of Fel'dman's model would, however, indicate the same tendency as the net. See below, pp. 240–42.

nineteen-twenties) with a poorly developed capital goods industry and hence presumably with a low α_0. It set γ at a high (and according to Jasny, even increasing) level.[24] It did experience a very rapid rate of growth of investment. Why then did its α not rise with time?

Before we start looking for profound explanations, let us make sure we need them. Nineteen-forty was almost a war year, and 1948 a special reconstruction period. Excluding both we are left with only 1928 and 1937, and we do not yet know how typical either year was.[25] Next, we must remember that Fel'dman's model exaggerates the inability of an economy to transfer resources from one category to another: the Soviets invested a high fraction of their gross national product—23.2 per cent—as early as 1928. Finally, Soviet armament expenditures must have risen with the advent of the Nazis to power in Germany; if we add these expenditures to investment, the total as a fraction of gross national product does rise from 25.7 per cent in 1928 to 30.6 in 1937 and 32.2 per cent in 1940, a moderate but not a substantial increase.[26]

An attempt to interpret Soviet development in terms of a model as rigid and as simple as Fel'dman's is foolhardy; yet with all these qualifications, I am still puzzled by the failure of the Hoeffding-Bergson-Heymann estimates to show a rise in the fraction of product invested between 1928 and 1937. These estimates have been

[24] Naum Jasny, *The Soviet Economy during the Plan Era* (Stanford, Calif., 1951), p. 90.

[25] Hoeffding presents several estimates of the fraction of the Soviet gross national product invested for the period from 1925–26 to 1929–30 obtained by him directly from Soviet sources. These estimates, however, are so rough that he discouraged me from citing them. Hoeffding, op. cit. p. 82.

Francis Seton worked out an estimate of Soviet gross national product and its distribution for 1934 in market prices (unadjusted for turnover taxes). The fraction of gross product invested for that year he sets at 26.5 per cent, as compared with the corresponding Hoeffding and Bergson estimates for 1928 and 1937 at 20.8 and 19.2 per cent, respectively. 'The Social Accounts of the Soviet Union in 1934,' *The Review of Economics and Statistics*, Vol. 36 (Aug., 1954), p. 304. Hoeffding, op. cit. p. 22; Abram Bergson, *Soviet National Income and Product in 1937* (New York, 1953), p. 22.

[26] Sources are given in note 23. For our purposes, it is really not legitimate, except for a year or two, to add armaments to investment because the former are not supposed to increase productive capacity. It would be better to describe the situation in terms of a reduction in γ.

I should also remind the reader that the present model, including Table III, assumes a constancy of capital coefficients over time. We do not know enough about Soviet capital coefficients to judge whether this assumption is realistic. Its removal would require a reworking of the model.

adjusted for turnover taxes, though not for the presence of profits in consumer goods industries.[27] More important, the estimates, being in current prices, have been necessarily affected by the differential rates of technological progress, interpreted broadly, among the several sectors of the Soviet economy. According to Galenson, over the period of 1928–37, the average annual (compounded) rate of growth of labor productivity in iron ore mining was 13.7 per cent, in steel manufacture 10.6 per cent, in crude oil and gas 7.2 per cent, in coal mining 7.3 per cent, in automobiles 21.7 per cent, in tractors 20.4 per cent, in agricultural machinery 16.3 per cent, as compared with 5.1 per cent in sugar refining, 3.9 per cent in cotton cloth manufacturing, and an actual decline in productivity in shoe manufacturing.[28] However incomplete the picture derived from these estimates is, it does confirm the general impression which one derives from Soviet economic literature, namely that technological progress in capital goods industries has been much more rapid than in the rest of the Soviet economy. Hence, with the passage of time, a ruble spent on capital goods must have commanded greater real resources than one spent on consumer goods.[29] This hypothesis could be tested by a sector-by-sector deflation of the Soviet national product. If the hypothesis is true, the fraction of the product invested in real terms must have risen over time, even if it remained more or less constant in current prices.[30] A deflation of this type was made by Jasny, and it revealed that the ratio of net investment to net product did rise from 17.1 per cent in 1928 to 37.2 per

[27] The estimates are gross of subsidies which were paid mostly to capital goods industries; hence, the latter should show neither profit nor loss, at least on current account.

[28] Walter Galenson, *Labor Productivity in Soviet and American Industry* (New York, 1955), Table 28, p. 249. Crude oil and gas figures are for the period 1928–38; tractors and agricultural machinery—1932–36; automobiles—1932–37. There was also a decline in labor productivity in railroad locomotives and cars.

[29] This notion is reinforced by the profits made by consumer goods industries.

[30] Price changes resulting from differential rates of technological progress present a fascinating problem not only in relation to Soviet development but to that of any country. If one wants to know the fraction of a country's resources devoted to a given sector, should the answer be given in current or in constant prices? And if in the latter, what should be the deflation method? Many other interesting questions arise. Unfortunately, the relevant models presented in this volume (including Fel'dman's) are expressed in constant prices, and therefore are not helpful here.

Bergson and his associates are quite aware of this problem. See Bergson and Heymann, *op. cit.* note 20, pp. 106–8.

cent in 1937.[31] This piece of evidence taken by itself is of course insufficient to establish the applicability of Fel'dman's model; but it is comforting. At least until it is disproved by new evidence.

Case 2. Assets Subject to Wear

The purpose of this section is not to explore new problems in replacement and depreciation, but merely to show the close similarity between the results of a Fel'dman-type model and those of Essay VII. Following the latter, it is assumed here that assets retain their full productive capacity until their retirement at the end of m years. Fel'dman was evidently not aware that in a growing economy depreciation exceeds replacement and took their identity for granted.

LIST OF ADDITIONAL SYMBOLS

In order of their appearance.

m = length of life of capital assets;

G = annual rate of gross investment;

R = annual rate of replacement;

I^* = annual rate of net investment $(G - R)$, subscripts indicating the net investment allocated to the respective categories;

λ = fraction of total net investment allocated to Category 1;

U = marginal gross capital coefficient for the whole economy, subscripts indicating the capital coefficients of the respective categories;

r = annual relative rate of growth of G;

β' = gross marginal propensity to save (ratio of an increment in total gross investment to an increment in gross national product);

P = gross national product.

We shall assume that out of a given volume of gross investment G a required amount R is used for replacement of worn-out capital

---

[31] Jasny, op. cit., an enclosure entitled 'Errors and Omissions in Jasny's Monographs on the Soviet Union,' second page. He gives a great deal of data showing that inflation in consumer goods industries was very much greater than in producer's. *The Soviet Price System* (Stanford, Calif., 1951), pp. 17–22. His general methodology has, however, given rise to controversy. See Norman M. Kaplan, 'Arithmancy, Theomancy, and the Soviet Economy,' *The Journal of Political Economy*, Vol. 61 (Apr., 1953), pp. 93–116.

assets in both categories, and that the net investment so defined $(I^* = G - R)$ is then divided in the proportion of λ and $(1 - \lambda)$ between Categories 1 and 2 respectively.[32] Thus

$$(2.1) \qquad\qquad\qquad I^* = G - R,$$

$$(2.2) \qquad\qquad\qquad I_1^* = \lambda I^*,$$

and

$$(2.3) \qquad\qquad\qquad I_2^* = (1 - \lambda)I^*.$$

Following the reasoning of Case 1 (p. 230), we can write

$$(2.4) \qquad\qquad\qquad \frac{dG}{dt} = \frac{I_1^*}{U_1},$$

U_1, U_2, and U being the corresponding gross capital coefficients. From (2.1), (2.2), and (2.4),

$$(2.5) \qquad\qquad\qquad \frac{\frac{dG}{dt}}{G} = \frac{\lambda\left(1 - \dfrac{R}{G}\right)^{33}}{U_1}.$$

Assuming now, as we did in Essay VII, that

$$(2.6) \qquad\qquad\qquad G = e^{rt},$$

with $G_0 = 1$, and that this was also true for the preceding m years, so that

$$(2.7) \qquad\qquad\qquad R = e^{r(t-m)},$$

we obtain

$$(2.8) \qquad\qquad\qquad \frac{R}{G} = e^{-rm}.$$

The substitution of (2.8) into (2.5) then gives

$$(2.9) \qquad\qquad\qquad \frac{\frac{dG}{dt}}{G} = r = \frac{\lambda}{U_1}(1 - e^{-rm}),$$

[32] As an alternative, we could first divide G between the two categories in stated proportions, each category then allocating the required fraction of its share of investment to replacement and to the increase of its capital stock. With all parameters remaining constant, the two approaches give identical results.

[33] See note 31a, p. 170 of Essay VII.

an expression very similar to (8) of that essay, and likewise not yielding an explicit solution for r.

Following the procedure of Case 1, we can derive

$$(2.10) \qquad C = C_0 + \left(\frac{1-\lambda}{\lambda}\right)\frac{U_1}{U_2}(e^{rt} - 1),$$

$$(2.11) \qquad P = P_0 + \left[\left(\frac{1-\lambda}{\lambda}\right)\frac{U_1}{U_2} + 1\right](e^{rt} - 1).$$

The marginal *gross* propensity to save can be shown to be

$$(2.12) \qquad \beta' = \frac{dG}{dP} = \frac{\lambda U_2}{U_1 - \lambda(U_1 - U_2)},$$

and just as in Case 1, we find that if $U_1 > U_2$, $\lambda > \beta'$; but when $U_1 = U_2$

$$(2.13) \qquad\qquad\qquad \lambda = \beta'.$$

In the latter case, a fraction of net investment equal to the marginal gross propensity to save must be invested in Category 1 to meet the replacement requirements of both categories and to provide for growth.

Again following the method of Case 1 we can show that U is the weighted average of U_1 and U_2:

$$(2.14) \qquad\qquad U = \beta'U_1 + (1 - \beta')U_2.$$

All these expressions are so similar to the corresponding ones of Case 1 that no further elaboration is necessary. The magnitudes of the ratio $\frac{\lambda}{\beta'}$ can be read from Table II by substituting λ for γ, β' for α', and U_1 and U_2 for V_1 and V_2, respectively.

IV

To see the implications of Fel'dman's model for economic development, let us simplify our formulas as much as possible. For this reason, and also because I have nothing to add here to the replacement-depreciation problem, we shall disregard the latter, and treat capital assets as if they were permanent. In a rapidly growing economy, which Fel'dman had in mind, the fraction of gross investment allocated to replacement is small; so will be our error.[34]

[34] With $m = 30$ years and $r = 5$ per cent, $R/G = 22$ per cent; with the same

Our Case 1 (Permanent Assets) yielded the following results:

$$(1.5) \qquad\qquad I = e^{\frac{\gamma}{V_1}t},$$

$$(1.8) \qquad\qquad C = C_0 + \left(\frac{1-\gamma}{\gamma}\right)\frac{V_1}{V_2}(e^{\frac{\gamma}{V_1}t} - 1),$$

$$(1.10) \qquad Y = Y_0 + \left[\left(\frac{1-\gamma}{\gamma}\right)\frac{V_1}{V_2} + 1\right](e^{\frac{\gamma}{V_1}t} - 1),$$

all based on the assumption that $I_0 = 1$. In addition to these three expressions, we may have occasions to use some of their integrals (over time) or their respective rates of growth.

The examination of these three expressions reveals that I, C, and Y are all inverse functions of V_1 and V_2, a relationship which becomes obvious if $V_1 = V_2$. Fel'dman was much concerned with the magnitudes of his capital coefficients and treated them as variables rather than as constants. His diligence was great, but it made his work unreadable. He expected a great deal from a fall in the magnitudes of the coefficients, and argued that over the period 1924–25 to 1927–28 more was achieved from greater utilization of capital than from its expansion (Ib, p. 172). He was right in not being impressed with the widely held expectation that capital coefficients must rise with time (due to the rising organic composition of capital for a Marxist economist, and to the law of diminishing returns for a bourgeois one), because these expectations disregarded technological progress. On the other hand, he undoubtedly leaned too far in the other direction. His repeated references to American capital coefficients taken from an unnamed source did not show any downward trend (Ia, p. 158; Ib, pp. 170 and 176). His own analysis of data given in the first five-year plan (optimal version) indicated movement and variation in coefficients of specific industries, but the average for the whole economy remained virtually constant at 2.4 for every year from 1925–26 to 1932–33. Finally, he prepared two hypothetical versions of his own long-range plan. In the first, the

---

m, and $r = 10$ per cent, $R/G = 5$ per cent. See Essay VII, p. 162. Alternatively we can assume that assets are not permanent, but that depreciation is made good continuously and outside of the model.

Replacement of worn-out capital was a pressing and much discussed problem in Russia in the nineteen-twenties. (See Erlich's thesis given in note 2.) Fel'dman paid little attention to it, presumably because of his complete abstraction from immediate problems of his day and his preoccupation with long-term growth.

capital coefficient remained almost unchanged (at about 2.4) from 1926 to 1932 and then gradually rose to 3.3 in 1950, while the rate of growth of income first rose from 6.9 per cent in 1927 to 16.9 per cent in 1932 and then declined to 6.8 per cent by 1950. In the second —'The High Intensity Version'—the coefficient began to fall sharply in 1930 (about 2.0) and was stabilized at 1.4 over the period 1932 to 1950. The rate of growth of national income expected during the period 1935 to 1950 was a modest 35 per cent per year. The purpose of working out such contrasting versions was to illustrate the effect of the variation in the size of the capital coefficient on the rate of growth of national income (III, pp. 118–27).[35]

A planned society with a supposedly unlimited supply of labor (as assumed by Fel'dman) and free from cyclical disturbances might indeed utilize its capital stock more intensively than a capitalist one could. On the other hand, poor use of capital is a standard complaint in Soviet economic literature. We need not try to strike a balance between these forces here.[36] Whatever it might be, the determination of the magnitude of the capital coefficients is outside of Fel'dman's model, because he makes no attempt to relate it to any other variables, such as the durability of the assets, the length of the construction period, the supply of labor and of other factors, the magnitude, composition, and rate of growth of investment, and industrial structure. In this framework, a reduction in the size of the capital coefficients is always desirable. This is all that emerges from Fel'dman's lengthy illustrations and all that we can say about the capital coefficients here.

With capital coefficients being treated as given, the one and only variable which can be varied as an instrument of planning is our γ, the fraction of total investment allocated to Category 1 (capital goods industries). Since Fel'dman's model allows complete intra-category flexibility, γ can vary all the way from zero to one.[37]

[35] In all their examples, both Fel'dman and Kovalevskiĭ work with capital productivity—the reciprocal of the capital coefficient. I made the necessary recomputations in order to conform to our present usage. In essays III–V, I have used capital productivity myself.

[36] See Kaplan's paper and subsequent discussion given in note 22. That paper contains most interesting statistics on the magnitude and allocation of Soviet investment. See also Bergson and Heymann, op. cit. pp. 106–8.

[37] In a model with assets subject to wear, γ, being a fraction of the net invest-

The optimum size of γ (and it need not be constant) chosen by the planning authorities will depend on what they consider to be the purpose of economic development. This question is about as simple as that regarding the purpose of life itself, and I have no ready answer to either.[38] We are working here with a very limited model, too rigid in some respects and too flexible in others. It can be applied to only a few of the simplest objectives of economic development.

If the purpose of economic development lies in the maximization of investment or of national income (without differentiation between investment and consumption) at a point of time, or of their respective rates of growth, or of integrals over time, γ should be set as high as possible. This is always true for investment, and nearly always for income, the only exception being when V_1 greatly exceeds V_2, and even then for only a short period of time.[39] A high γ does not imply, however, any reduction in consumption. With capital assets assumed to be permanent, even $\gamma = 1$ would merely freeze consumption at its original level. If assets were subject to wear, consumption would be slowly reduced by failure to replace them. Finally, a transfer of resources from consumption to investment industries would reduce consumption still further. The latter possibility is, however, excluded from Fel'dman's model, and the former —assets subject to wear—is outside the present discussion.

Such an indifference between consumption and investment irrespective of the magnitude of γ (or of α) must be rare even among Soviet planners: after all, consumption standards affect the ability and the incentive of the populace to work and the willingness to obey. Fel'dman, who did not regard labor as a factor limiting production, had no room for such considerations, but he insisted time and again that consumption was the sole purpose of production,

---

ment, can be smaller than zero and larger than one if the wear of the assets in one category or another is not made good. This possibility is excluded in this paper.

[38] The theory of profit maximization raises similar questions; cf. Friedrich and Vera Lutz, *The Theory of Investment of the Firm* (Princeton, N. J., 1951).

[39] The derivation is given in the Appendix. For this exception to hold for income with $\gamma = .3$, $V_1 = 3$, and $t = 3$ years, V_1/V_2 must be (approximately) at least 1.8; if $t = 5$ years, V_1/V_2 must be not less than 3.5; with $t = 6$ years, not less than 5.8; when t reaches 8 years, the case becomes impossible. If we examined the integral of Y, rather than Y itself, V_1/V_2 could be somewhat larger.

the emphasis given to investment in his model being only temporary (Ia, pp. 150, 163; III, p. 102). He did not specify whether the variable to be maximized should be consumption at a point of time, or its rate of growth, or its integral over time; whether consumption should be discounted or not; and what value, if any, should be attached to the increasing capital stock as such, particularly in Category 1, so important during a war. On the whole, he was most concerned with the (relative) rate of growth of consumption, and desired a high γ with that end in mind. We shall consider here several possibilities: consumption at a point of time, its integral over a period of time, and its (relative) rate of growth; brief remarks will be made about the discount problem and about the value of the capital stock as such.

The examination of the expression (1.8) quickly reveals that γ has a dual effect on C. As the numerator of the exponent of $e^{\frac{\gamma}{V_1}t}$, it is related to C directly; as a member of the expression $\left(\dfrac{1-\gamma}{\gamma}\right)$, inversely. As γ increases, the latter falls very rapidly; thus with $\gamma = .1$, $\left(\dfrac{1-\gamma}{\gamma}\right) = 9$; when $\gamma = .2$, $\left(\dfrac{1-\gamma}{\gamma}\right) = 4$; a γ of .5 brings it down to 1. Over short periods of time C is dominated by $\left(\dfrac{1-\gamma}{\gamma}\right)$ and is therefore depressed by a high γ. As time goes on, the exponential $e^{\frac{\gamma}{V_1}t}$ will assert itself, and a high γ will eventually produce a large C.

When one variable (γ) has a dual effect on another (C), it is usually possible to find the magnitude of the former maximizing the latter. It is shown in the Appendix that γ maximizing C *at a given point* of time is given by the expression

$$(3.1) \qquad \gamma = 1 - \frac{1 - e^{-\frac{\gamma}{V_1}t}}{\frac{\gamma}{V_1}t},$$

and that this value of γ, being independent of V_2, varies inversely with V_1, and directly with t (it is a direct function of the ratio t/V_1); thus the longer the period in question, the higher the value of γ should be set. All this presupposes a constant γ over time. A variable γ would be a more flexible instrument.[39a]

As far as I know, the expression (3.1) cannot be solved explicitly for γ. Numerical results can be obtained by the simple device of taking a given value for $\frac{\gamma}{V_1} t$, finding the corresponding γ, and dividing the latter into $\frac{\gamma}{V_1} t$ to find t/V_1. Table IV gives the results.

TABLE IV.—THE OPTIMUM MAGNITUDE OF γ MAXIMIZING C AT A GIVEN POINT OF TIME*

$\frac{\gamma}{V_1} t$	γ	$\frac{t}{V_1}$	Implied t		
			with $V_1 = 3$	with $V_1 = 4$	with $V_1 = 5$
.01	.005	2.000	6.00	8.00	10.00
.02	.010	2.010	6.03	8.04	10.05
.03	.015	2.017	6.05	8.07	10.09
.04	.020	2.028	6.08	8.11	10.14
.05	.025	2.034	6.10	8.14	10.17
.10	.05	2.07	6.20	8.27	10.34
.20	.09	2.14	6.41	8.54	10.68
.30	.14	2.20	6.61	8.82	11.02
.40	.18	2.28	6.83	9.10	11.38
.50	.21	2.35	7.04	9.39	11.73
.75	.30	2.53	7.59	10.12	12.65
1.00	.37	2.72	8.15	10.87	13.59
2.00	.57	3.52	10.57	14.09	17.62

* Based on expression (3.1). The correspondence among the several columns is not exact because of rounding.

It reveals a most unhealthy sensitivity of γ to t/V_1. While t/V_1 ranges from 2.0 to 2.5, γ covers all the distance from practically nothing to 30 per cent. With $V_1 = 3$ and $t = 6$ years, the optimum γ is less than 1 per cent; but if the period is extended to 8 years, γ jumps to 37 per cent. A larger V_1 (such as 4 or 5) makes γ a bit

[39a] See note 43.

more stable, but not much. Since a planning horizon is a hazy notion at best, even if expressed in terms of one or more five-year plans, the maximization of consumption at some point of time provides no sensible clue to the optimum magnitude of γ.

To explain this mathematical puzzle, Chart I presents the actual behavior of C over time. The lower straight line corresponding to

CHART I.—THE BEHAVIOR OF CONSUMPTION OVER TIME FOR GIVEN
MAGNITUDES OF γ
$$(V_1 = V_2 = 3; C_0 = 9)$$

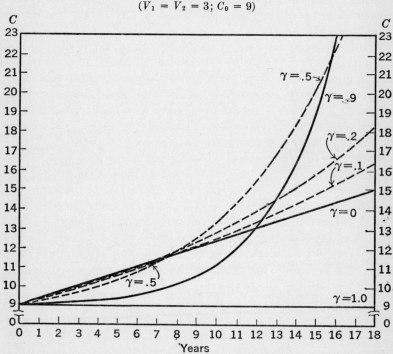

$\gamma = 1$ is horizontal: all investment being allocated to Category 1, consumption stays at its original level without any increase. This is an extreme and a misleading example, because even a slight reduction in γ (to 90 per cent) results in a rapid growth of C (the solid curve) after a few years. The $\gamma = 0$ straight line is more interesting: here all investment is directed to consumer goods industries (Category 2); hence the capacity of Category 1 remains constant, as does its output, i.e. the total stream of investment. Consequently the capacity of Category 2 increases, but only at a *constant absolute rate*. Its relative rate of growth declines with time.[40]

The dotted curves on Chart I correspond to several reasonable magnitudes of γ (10, 20, and 50 per cent), and as expected, the higher the γ, the smaller C is in the early years, and the more rapidly it grows thereafter. These curves are fairly close to each other and to the straight line $\gamma = 0$; they all intersect the latter within a surprisingly narrow period of time, in our case between 6 and 8 years. This explains why the maximization of C gave such an unstable magnitude of γ.

The message conveyed by Chart I is fairly clear: if the planning authorities have a short time horizon, they may just as well leave capital goods industries alone and stay on the line $\gamma = 0$. As their horizon expands, a strong effort to develop these industries should be made. Not much is gained by playing with small magnitudes of γ. If reality only corresponded to Fel'dman's model, the presence of so many undeveloped countries would be inexplicable.[41]

A large fraction of output invested produces such a rapid increase in consumption because a capital coefficient of 3 (without a lag) means a high return on investment in terms of output (but not necessarily in terms of profits). If V_1 rose to 4, the dotted curves would intersect the straight line $\gamma = 0$ in the 8–10 year range; a coefficient of 5 would move the latter to 10–12.7 years. But as these examples show, the range remains quite narrow, so that for any given V_1 the curves intersect the straight line $\gamma = 0$ more or

---

[40] A linear, but not constant, C given by $\gamma = 0$ is possible only because of the assumed absence of need for replacements. Otherwise, as the capacity of Category 2 expands, so will its replacement needs (though with a lag), and it will be impossible to satisfy them without allocating some investment to Category 1.

These qualifications are outside our present case with permanent assets.

[41] The introduction of time lags between investment and the resulting output dilutes this message, but not by much, unless unforeseen bottlenecks arise. Thus a lag of 2 or 3 years would reduce a 3 per cent annual rate of growth to some 2.8 per cent; a rate of growth of 10 per cent would be reduced to 8.4 and 7.9 per cent respectively—all this of course after the expiration of the initial lag period. The latter is not as long as it appears to be at first sight: roughly speaking, the average lag between the investment of resources into a project and its fruition is about one-half as long as the period between the beginning and the completion of the project.

less simultaneously and fairly independently of the magnitude of γ unless the latter becomes very high.[42]

The maximization of consumption at a point of time may not be a satisfactory objective of economic development because it implies an indifference to the behavior of consumption during the intervening period.[43] To remedy this defect, the integral of C over the whole period should be maximized instead. This approach, however, turns out to be no more helpful in determining the optimum magnitude of γ than the preceding one did. As shown on Chart II, the dotted ($\gamma = 50$ per cent) curve and the solid ($\gamma = 0$) one—now a quadratic, as an integral of a straight line—are so close together that there is no room for drawing the $\gamma = 10$ and $\gamma = 20$ per cent curves. (Note, however, the difference in scale between the two charts.) If drawn, all these curves would again intersect the $\gamma = 0$ one in a very narrow range, between 9 and 11 years, though the range itself is further away in time than it was on Chart I (6 and 8 years). For a country with a reasonably long time horizon, a high magnitude of γ is still worth while.

---

[42] The point of intersection of C with the straight line $\gamma = 0$ (more correctly $\underset{\gamma \to 0}{\text{Lim}} \; C$) is given by the equation

$$(3.2) \qquad \left(\frac{1-\gamma}{\gamma}\right) \frac{V_1}{V_2} \; (e^{\frac{\gamma}{V_1}t} - 1) = \frac{t}{V_2}.$$

V_2 cancels out and hence does not affect the result. The solution takes the form of

$$(3.3) \qquad \frac{\frac{\gamma}{V_1} t}{e^{\frac{\gamma}{V_1}t} - 1} = 1 - \gamma,$$

which cannot be solved for t explicitly; however, we can obtain approximate numerical solutions by first assuming given values for $\frac{\gamma}{V_1} t$, computing the left side of the equation which gives $1 - \gamma$; then finding the magnitudes of γ and dividing them into $\frac{\gamma}{V_1} t$. This gives the value of t/V_1, from which t can be computed for given values of V_1.

It should be made clear that the capital coefficient discussed above in the text is V_1, and not V_2.

[43] It is also fairly obvious that a strict adherence to this objective requires not a constant but a variable γ: it should equal zero in the last few years of the period, and by the same reasoning, it should be set high at the beginning. This is essentially a problem in calculus of variation which we shall not try to solve here.

CHART II.—THE BEHAVIOR OF THE INTEGRAL OF CONSUMPTION OVER
TIME FOR GIVEN MAGNITUDES OF γ
$(V_1 = V_2 = 3; C_0 = 9)$

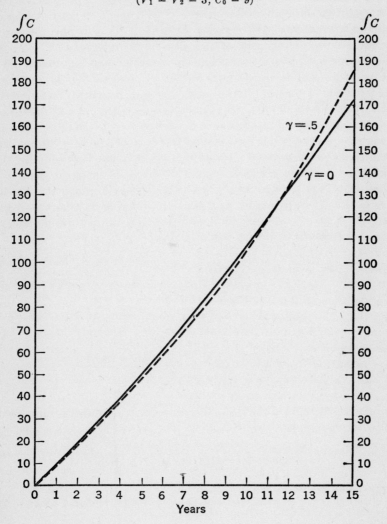

This conclusion will become even more forceful if some value is attached to the capital stock, possibly as a source of military security during the period, and as a source of future productive capacity after the end of the period.[44] The evaluation of these services, and particularly that of the security aspects of the capital stock, so important to Soviet planners, is not an easy task. Fortunately, we need not try to do it here, except to note once more that any positive value attached to these services will serve as an additional justification for increasing γ.

These refinements did not bother Fel'dman particularly. As mentioned before, to him the aim of economic development lay in the long-run maximization of consumption, and particularly of its (relative) rate of growth. As an objective of economic development, the latter can be misleading, because it abstracts from the absolute magnitude of C at a given point of time. Obviously, a slowly growing C can exceed a rapidly growing one, at least for some time, if it started from a higher level. This is not important for Fel'dman's model because the initial magnitude of C is the same for all time patterns. But the rate of growth of C is not constant over time, and as shown on Chart I, rapid growth at the beginning is achieved at the expense of slower growth later, and vice versa. Fel'dman could justify his disregard of these aspects of the model by his concern for the long run only. In the long run, which need not be very long, a higher γ will, as a rule, result in a more rapidly growing consumption.[45]

Nothing has been said so far about time preference. In taking the simple integral of consumption over time we have implicitly assumed that a ruble consumed in the future (in constant prices) is just as good as a ruble consumed today. Otherwise, some adjustment of future rubles must be made before they can all be added together. This is not the place to delve into the discount problem for which Fel'dman's model is unnecessarily rigid and complex. We need not

----

[44] Similar reasoning is commonly used in the case of an individual saver whose welfare function is made to consist of the stream of consumption, his stock of wealth at the end of the period (such as his life) which can presumably be converted then into consumption, and possibly a certain satisfaction from pure possession of the (increasing) stock of wealth during the period. The sum of these streams is usually discounted in time, a problem to which we shall turn presently.

[45] The larger V_1 is relative to V_2, the weaker this rule is.

even inquire whether the public, or in our case, the planning authorities, are endowed with the classical impatience to consume, so that confronted with two equally large integrals of consumption they would invariably prefer a declining stream to a constant or an ascending one.[46] In our model the stream of consumption is not constant; it grows (though it should be adjusted for the growth of population), and unless the planning authorities have very queer notions, a ruble of future consumption should be less valuable than that of the present simply because there will be more rubles to consume. Hence future consumption should be discounted before being compared with (or added to) present consumption, but just how this should be done is not obvious.[47]

It certainly makes no sense to discount the stream of consumption and the final stock of capital at what might be the implied rate of interest, because in the context of our model the latter would equal the reciprocal of the capital coefficient (i.e. the average productivity of investment, which equals the marginal), and the integral of such a discounted stream plus the discounted final stock of capital (if we deal with finite periods) will be the same, irrespective of the size of γ.[48] Besides, the rate of discount cannot be a constant. It should vary directly with the rate of growth of consumption and with the

[46] This question is ably handled by R. F. Harrod in his *Towards a Dynamic Economics* (London, 1948), Lecture Two. Besides Marshall, whom Harrod quotes, the reader is also referred to Irving Fisher's *The Rate of Interest* (New York, 1907). See also Paul A. Samuelson, 'Dynamics, Statics, and the Stationary State,' *The Review of Economic Statistics*, Vol. 25 (Feb., 1943), pp. 58–68.

It should be emphasized that the question raised in the text deals not with the preference for present as compared with future *income*—which I would expect most people to have—but with the preference for present over future *consumption*, which may or may not exist.

[47] The need for discount arises from the application of the law of diminishing marginal utility to consumption, and not necessarily because of mere passage of time. That a growing stream of consumption should be discounted on these grounds will, I believe, be accepted, and even insisted upon, by most economists. Yet we add individual incomes to obtain a national total without bothering about discount, even though we know quite well that, however difficult interpersonal welfare comparisons are, a small income contains more utility units per dollar, as it were, than a large one does.

[48] If the rate of discount is to equal the reciprocal of the capital coefficient, we must either operate with the over-all coefficient as the weighted average of V_1 and V_2 given by (1.15), or assume that $V_1 = V_2$. See the Appendix.

The capital coefficients were defined (p. 230) as marginal relative to capital; hence they are average relative to investment.

proportion of income saved, and thus be a direct function of γ and an inverse function of the capital coefficient. If the planning authorities gave us this function we could compute the optimum magnitude of γ, not necessarily constant in time, which would maximize this or that discounted objective. But the discount function, like a consumer preference map between apples and oranges, is highly subjective, and no amount of theorizing could enable *us* to tell the planning authorities what *their* discount function should be.[49] So having recognized its legitimate existence, we shall leave the discount function alone, perhaps with a face-saving remark that γ should be increased until the marginal rate of discount equals the marginal rate of return—an innocent but not a particularly helpful suggestion.

Fel'dman did not even mention the discount problem. Perhaps he was not aware of it, or thought it smacked of Wall Street. But perhaps he also felt that there was not much he could say about it. His task was to explain to the Soviet planners the basic principles of economic growth and to furnish them with several alternative patterns of development, depending on the magnitudes of γ and of the capital coefficients. It was up to the planners to choose the optimum path, depending on their own objectives, and on their evaluation of existing economic and political conditions and possibilities.[50] Such an evaluation of 'the state of the mind of the masses' was in a sense a search for a discount function, but what exactly would be gained by an attempt to formalize it?

V

It would be unfair to the reader to end my story without telling him about an event which took place in Russia in February and March, 1930, and which might serve as an epilogue to Fel'dman's model and perhaps not only to his. The event consisted of a meeting

[49] This does not imply that the planning authorities should not set some rate of discount of future inputs and outputs to enable their local agents to choose between investment alternatives with different time patterns.

[50] He was quite explicit: 'The politician will have to determine which patterns of growth of consumer goods capital and therefore of consumption are acceptable and desirable, and what magnitudes these rates of growth should reach. Technicians and statisticians should indicate what coefficients of effectiveness [the reciprocal of the capital coefficient] can be achieved in what time. Then the social engineer will be able to construct a plan for the development of the national economy.' Ib, p. 155.

held at the Institute of Economic Research of the Soviet State
Planning Commission at which N. A. Kovalevskiĭ, an important
official of that body and the then chief editor of the journal *Planned
Economy*, presented his report outlining the planned development
of the Soviet economy for the next decade or two.[51] It was based on
Fel'dman's model, though surprisingly enough Kovalevskiĭ used
not Fel'dman's two categories, but the propensity to save (fraction
of national income invested) and the over-all capital coefficient.
Perhaps he did this to simplify his (oral) presentation.[52] The vast
array of figures cited by him would indicate that a good deal of
detailed empirical work had now been built around Fel'dman's
model.

Here are some of Kovalevskiĭ's estimates of the future. The propensity to save was to rise from 20.1 per cent (probably in 1929)
to 37.7 per cent in 1930, thence to 45.3 and 46.4 per cent over the
next three years. Later it was to decline to 33 per cent in 1939–40,
and to some 31 per cent by 1944–45 (p. 129). The average capital
coefficient which began at 3.3 (about 1928) and fell to 2.7 in 1929–30
(as compared with the American figure which he estimated at 4.5),
was expected to decline gradually and reach its limiting magnitude
of some 1.5 at the end of the third five-year plan (pp. 130–32).
Endowed with these wonderful possibilities, the Soviet economy
was expected to lunge forward at an amazing speed, without, however, sacrificing current consumption; as a matter of fact, the latter
was supposed to rise by 15 per cent in 1930–31; by 31 per cent over
the next year; then make another jump of 44 per cent, and so on
(p. 129). The per capita American consumption level (evidently of
1929) was to be reached in ten years (about 1938) and tripled in
fifteen (p. 134).

Nor was the shift to heavy industry advocated in the report to be
accomplished at the expense of agriculture. Gross agricultural out-

[51] 'K postroeniiu general'nogo plana,' a discussion which took place at the
meetings of the Institute of Economic Research of the Gosplan of the USSR
on Feb. 25 and Mar. 5, 1930, and was published in *Planovoe Khoziaĭstvo*, Mar.,
1930, No. 3, pp. 117–209. This was not the first discussion of the General Plan.
See notes 3 and 56.

[52] It is also possible that by that time the planners had discovered the opera-
tional difficulties of Fel'dman's model. On the other hand, Kovalevskiĭ did refer
to relative magnitudes of Group A (producer goods) and Group B (consumer
goods), into which he divided Soviet industry. He did not make much use of
this division. Ibid. pp. 135, 139–40.

put estimated at 20 billion rubles (in constant 1927–28 prices) in 1929 was to rise to 70 billions at the end of the second five-year plan and to 140 billions at the end of the third (pp. 138–9).

Coming now to heavy industry, Kovalevskiĭ expected to have the following outputs at the end of the second five-year plan (about 1938 or so): coal—540 million tons (actual production in 1940—166 million tons); oil—about 127 million tons (1940—31 million tons); pig iron—78 million tons (1940—15 million tons); steel—82 million tons (1940—18.3 million tons).[53] While labor productivity was expected to grow at some 25 per cent per year, total output was to increase 19 times over 12 years (p. 128), and 'according to the most modest calculation, a ruble invested in the national economy now is transformed into some 14 rubles in 12 years. A ruble invested in industry or electrification grows even faster' (p. 118).

The discussion following Kovalevskiĭ's report was on the whole vague and general. There was plenty of dogmatic wrangling, many complaints about his disregard of social and human elements, such as the then intensified collectivization of the peasants, and even a suggestion (by R. E. Vaĭsberg, p. 148) that the forthcoming communist revolutions in other countries should have been taken into account. And although one discussant (A. Kon) quoted a statement by the well-known Soviet economist Strumilin that Kovalevskiĭ's method could give an output of iron equal to four times the volume of the earth (pp. 155–6), there was amazingly little said about the more practical aspects of Kovalevskiĭ's plan.

The rise of the Nazis to power in Germany, an event which Kovalevskiĭ could not have foreseen, diverted a part of Soviet output to armaments and presumably reduced the rate of growth of the Soviet economy after 1933 below what it might otherwise have been, but this event certainly could not explain away the fantasies of Kovalevskiĭ's plan. Perhaps its authors did not see that from a model like Fel'dman's almost any rate of growth could be derived on paper, provided the capital coefficients were low enough and the propensity to save (or γ) high enough. They certainly failed to realize that these parameters, and particularly the capital coefficients, were mere abstractions, useful (I trust) in theoretical work, but full of innumerable and well-hidden implications regarding the actual working of the economic mechanism, and that the whole

[53] Kovalevskiĭ, ibid. pp. 141–2. The actual production figures given in parentheses are from Bergson and Heymann, op. cit. p. 9.

problem of economic development lies not in the algebraic manipulations which Fel'dman carried out in such detail, but in overcoming the immense administrative, technological, and human obstacles which a rapid industrialization of a backward peasant economy was bound to create.[54]

There was also another reason which may explain the extreme optimism of Kovalevskiĭ's plan. Recognizing the backwardness of their country in comparison with advanced capitalist powers and being fearful that the 'capitalist encirclement' would finally erupt into an open aggression, Soviet planners felt an extreme sense of urgency in the industrialization of their economy. In 1929, a Soviet economist L. M. Sabsovich estimated that even if Soviet production increased at an annual rate of 10 per cent, thirty-five years would be required for it to reach the United States' 1929 output; allowing the latter an annual growth rate of 5 per cent, the Americans could not be overtaken in less than seventy years.[55] A similar thought was expressed by Fel'dman: 'Ten, a maximum of fifteen years—this is the schedule during which we must reconstruct all our productive relations within the country. The tempo must be such that the movement could be seen by every proletarian and peasant within and outside of our country with eyes to see' (II, p. 190). Those were typical sentiments.[56] From the insistence that this rapid progress had to be achieved to the belief that it could be achieved was but a short step, particularly among Soviet thinkers so imbued with the doctrine that human fate was in human hands.

[54] I could not judge from Kovalevskiĭ's report whether Fel'dman's model was at least adjusted for the presence of time lags. I suspect that such lags as could have been envisaged then would not have changed his conclusions substantially.

[55] L. M. Sabsovich, 'Gipoteza masshtabov produktsii osnovnykh otrasleĭ narodnogo khoziaĭstva SSSR v period general'nogo plana,' *Planovoe Khoziaĭstvo*, Jan., 1929, No. 1, pp. 54–103.

[56] Stalin declared: 'We are fifty or a hundred years behind the advanced countries. We must make good this distance in ten years. Either we do it, or they crush us.' 'The Tasks of Business Executives,' delivered at the First All-Union Conference of Managers of Socialist Industry, Feb. 4, 1931, and published in *Problems of Leninism* (Moscow, 1940), p. 366.

I don't intend to give the impression that everyone was as optimistic as Kovalevskiĭ. For instance, he was chided by G. M. Krzhizhanovskiĭ for paying insufficient attention to technological factors and advised to be more careful with mathematical derivations. But this was a suggestion, not a rebuke. 'K diskussii o genplane,' *Planovoe Khoziaĭstvo*, Feb., 1930, No. 2, pp. 7–21.

The General Plan was discussed in the Soviet literature of the period at great length. We are concerned with it here only in so far as it bears on Fel'dman's model. But it should make a fascinating study in itself.

To think otherwise was to lack faith in socialism. Could another plan, more realistic and practical but less exuberant than Kovalevskiĭ's, have satisfied the spirit of the times?

March 6, 1930, was the last public discussion of Kovalevskiĭ's plan reported in the *Planned Economy*. Soon afterward the journal was caught in the political storm raised by Stalin's struggle with the Right Opposition. The character of the journal began to change; frequent quotations from Stalin and diatribes against saboteurs appeared on its pages. Kovalevskiĭ was discharged as chief editor (middle of 1930), the editorial board was repeatedly reorganized, and in 1931–32 the journal suspended its publication for several months. When it reappeared in May, 1932, it was well on its way toward becoming a much more practical and down-to-earth, but also a much duller, periodical, a queer mixture of propaganda and economics, full of quotations from Stalin, party clichés, and invectives against enemies of socialism—a standard product of the Stalin era.

MATHEMATICAL APPENDIX

This section merely presents several derivations too long to be given in notes.

I. *Conditions Making* $\dfrac{\partial Y}{\partial \gamma} < 0$ *Possible* (to p. 245)

From (1.10),

$$(4.1) \qquad Y = Y_0 + \left[\left(\frac{1 - \gamma}{\gamma} \right) \frac{V_1}{V_2} + 1 \right] (e^{\frac{\gamma}{V_1}t} - 1);$$

$$(4.2) \qquad \frac{\partial Y}{\partial \gamma} = \frac{V_1}{V_2} \left[\left(\frac{1 - \gamma}{\gamma} \right) \frac{t}{V_1} e^{\frac{\gamma}{V_1}t} - \frac{e^{\frac{\gamma}{V_1}t} - 1}{\gamma^2} \right] + \frac{t}{V_1} e^{\frac{\gamma}{V_1}t}.$$

It can be easily deduced that $\dfrac{\partial Y}{\partial \gamma} < 0$ *if*

$$(4.3) \qquad \frac{V_1}{V_2} > \frac{\gamma}{\dfrac{1 - e^{-\frac{\gamma}{V_1}t}}{\dfrac{\gamma}{V_1}t} - (1 - \gamma)},$$

provided of course that the denominator is positive.

II. *The Magnitude of* γ *Maximizing C at a Point of Time* (to pp. 246–8)

From (1.8),

$$(5.1) \qquad C = C_0 + \left(\frac{1 - \gamma}{\gamma}\right) \frac{V_1}{V_2} (e^{\frac{\gamma}{V_1}t} - 1);$$

$$(5.2) \qquad \frac{\partial C}{\partial \gamma} = \frac{V_1}{V_2} \left[\left(\frac{1 - \gamma}{\gamma}\right) \frac{t}{V_1} e^{\frac{\gamma}{V_1}t} - \frac{e^{\frac{\gamma}{V_1}t} - 1}{\gamma^2} \right] = 0.$$

This can be quickly reduced to

$$(5.3) \qquad (1 - \gamma) \frac{\gamma t}{V_1} e^{\frac{\gamma}{V_1}t} = e^{\frac{\gamma}{V_1}t} - 1,$$

$$(5.4) \qquad \gamma = 1 - \frac{1 - e^{-\frac{\gamma}{V_1}t}}{\frac{\gamma}{V_1} t},$$

an expression independent of V_2.

Let

$$(5.5) \qquad \frac{t}{V_1} = x;$$

then

$$(5.6) \qquad \gamma = 1 - \frac{1 - e^{-\gamma x}}{\gamma x}.$$

We want to prove that $\frac{d\gamma}{dx} > 0$ for any $x > 0$.

$$(5.7) \qquad \frac{d\gamma}{dx} = - \frac{(\gamma x e^{-\gamma x} - 1 + e^{-\gamma x}) \left(\gamma + x \frac{d\gamma}{dx}\right)}{\gamma^2 x^2};$$

$$(5.8) \qquad \frac{d\gamma}{dx} = \frac{\gamma(1 - e^{-\gamma x} - \gamma x e^{-\gamma x})}{x(\gamma^2 x + \gamma x e^{-\gamma x} - 1 + e^{-\gamma x})}.$$

Consider

$$(5.9) \qquad N = 1 - e^{-\gamma x} - \gamma x e^{-\gamma x}.$$

If $\gamma x = 0$, $N = 0$;

$$(5.10) \qquad \frac{dN}{d(\gamma x)} = e^{-\gamma x} + \gamma x e^{-\gamma x} - e^{-\gamma x} = \gamma x e^{-\gamma x} > 0.$$

Hence, the slope of N is positive for $\gamma x > 0$, and therefore $N > 0$.[57]

---

[57] For an explanation of this method, see expressions (4.14) and (4.15) in the Mathematical Appendix to Essay VII.

Consider

(5.11) $$D = \gamma^2 x + \gamma x e^{-\gamma x} - 1 + e^{-\gamma x}.$$

From (5.6),

(5.12) $$\gamma^2 x = \gamma x - 1 + e^{-\gamma x}.$$

From (5.12) and (5.11),

(5.13) $$D = \gamma x - 2 + 2e^{-\gamma x} + \gamma x e^{-\gamma x}.$$

If $\gamma x = 0$, $D = 0$;

(5.14) $$\frac{dD}{d(\gamma x)} = 1 - e^{-\gamma x} - \gamma x e^{-\gamma x}.$$

If $\gamma x = 0$, $\dfrac{dD}{d(\gamma x)} = 0$;

(5.15) $$\frac{d^2 D}{d(\gamma x)^2} = e^{-\gamma x} + \gamma x e^{-\gamma x} - e^{-\gamma x} = \gamma x e^{-\gamma x} > 0.$$

Therefore, $\dfrac{dD}{d(\gamma x)} > 0$ for $\gamma x > 0$, and hence $D > 0$ for $\gamma x > 0$. Both N and D being positive,

(5.16) $$\frac{d\gamma}{dx} = \frac{d\gamma}{d\left(\dfrac{t}{V_1}\right)} > 0.$$

III. *The Discount Problem* (to pp. 252–4)

As indicated in note 48, we must either operate with the overall capital coefficient, as the weighted average of V_1 and V_2 given by (1.15), and then use α' as the marginal propensity to save, which in effect would give us a Keynesian model, or assume that $V_1 = V_2 = V$ and retain the formal structure of Fel'dman's model. The two methods give an identical result, which is almost intuitively obvious in any case. Let us retain Fel'dman's framework and assume that $V_1 = V_2 = V$.

From (1.8),

(6.1) $$C = C_0 + \left(\frac{1-\gamma}{\gamma}\right)(e^{\frac{\gamma}{V}t} - 1).$$

Since by assumption the rate of discount

(6.2) $$i = \frac{1}{V},$$

we obtain by straight integration

(6.3) $$\int_0^n Ce^{-it}dt = \frac{\left(C_0 - \frac{1-\gamma}{\gamma}\right)(1 - e^{-in})}{i} + \frac{1 - e^{(\gamma i - i)n}}{\gamma i}.$$

The stock of capital at the end of n years,

(6.4) $$K = K_0 + \int_0^n I\,dt = K_0 + \int_0^n e^{\gamma i t}dt = K_0 + \frac{e^{\gamma i n} - 1}{\gamma i},$$

and

(6.5) $$\text{Disc. } K = K_0 e^{-in} + \frac{(e^{\gamma i n} - 1)e^{-in}}{\gamma i}.$$

The present value of the integral of the discounted stream of consumption and the discounted final stock of capital is obtained by adding (6.3) and (6.5), and after a few simple manipulations we finally get

(6.6) $$\frac{Y_0(1 - e^{-in})}{i} + K_0 e^{-in},$$

because $$Y_0 = C_0 + I_0 = C_0 + 1.$$

The expression (6.6) is independent of γ.

If it so happens that the average and marginal capital coefficients are identical, so that

(6.7) $$Y_0 = \frac{K_0}{V} = K_0 i,$$

(6.6) is reduced to

(6.8) $$\frac{Y_0}{i},$$

that is, the present discounted value of the stream of consumption and of the final stock of capital equals the capitalized value of the present income, provided of course that $1/V = i$. This is a familiar result, which can also be obtained (and more simply) by making n infinitely large.

Index

A

Abramovitz, M., 236n.
Accelerated depreciation
  administrative aspects, 215
  the American system, 202–6,
    207n., 208–10, 216–20
  the British system, 202, 206–9,
    213n., 216, 220–21
  with carry-back and carry-over
    provisions, 196n., 203–5 *passim*, 212n., 213n., 215
  cyclical aspects, 213–14
  in economic literature, 195–6
  in existence, 195
  and the firm, 10, 204, 211–12, 214
  the Hybrid system, 202, 209–11,
    216, 222
  and income redistribution, 212–13
  with initial allowance, 207, 212–
    15 *passim*, 222
  as an interest-free loan, 195–6,
    204
  effect on investment, 196–7, 202,
    212
  restrictions on, 214–15
  and taxation, 196n., 212–13,
    215–16
  in undeveloped areas, 214
  with a variable write-off period,
    206
Acceleration principle, 94, 112
Ady, P. H., 195n.
Aftalion, A., 102–3
Alexander, S. S., 18
American Iron and Steel Institute,
  120
Amortization rate, *see* Foreign investment and lending
Andrews, P. W. S., 206n.
Anti-Keynesians, 103
Australia, 67–8
Austrians, 31
Ayres, C. E., **17**

B

Baran, P., 70n.
Barnes, L., 119
Bauer, O., 125
Baumol, W. J., 18
Benoit-Smullyan, E., 119n.
Berg, R. I., 154n.
Bergson, A., 159n., 223n., 237–**8**,
  239n., 244n., 256n.
Bodenhorn, G. D., 223n.
Bowley, A. L., 69
Brown, E. C., 196n., 198n.
Brunner, E., 206n.
Buchanan, N. S., 130n., 131n.
Buckatzsch, E. J. M., 195n.
Burchardt, F. A., 195n., 227n.
Business expectations and **growth**,
  120

C

Cairnes, J. E., 130
Canada, 67–8
Canada Year Book, 67
Capacity, *see* Productive capacity
Capital
  used to make more capital, 11,
    223–61 *passim*
  deepening of, 26, 77, 109–12,
    118
  as the factor of production, 7,
    88–9, 229, 233n.
  idle, effects of, 31, 79, 99, 113–15
  see also Investment
Capital accumulation
  in economic literature, 120–28
  effects of, 8, 32, 70, 72, 86–7,
    109–13
  excessive, 118, 122–5
  as a symptom of growth, 12
  and inflation, 115
  in the U. S., 88
  see also Investment

263

Capital coefficient
    and capital longevity, 172–80,
        187–94, 240–42
    explained, 110, 122–3, 168–9
    in Fel'dman's model, 228n., 230,
        235, 242–4, 255
    gross, and growth, 33, 167–80,
        187–94, 240–42
    and growth, 7, 31, 33, 249–50
    and investment productivity,
        168n.
    and technological progress, 243
    in the U. S. S. R., 160n., 172,
        243–4, 255
    in the U. S., 75n., 172n., 234n.
    see also Investment productivity
Capital-consumption ratio, 122–3
Capital durability, see Capital lon-
    gevity
Capital-income ratio as a function of
    growth, 76–7, 124
    see also Capital coefficient, In-
        vestment productivity
Capitalism, 122, 125
Capital longevity, 155, 197
    and capital coefficient, 172–80,
        187–94, 240–42
    and growth, 31, 169–80, 187–94,
        240–42
Capital losses, 77–9, 100
Capital productivity, see Investment
    productivity, Capital coeffi-
    cient
Capital-saving inventions, 7, 76n.
Capital stock
    net of depreciation, 219
    and investment, 76–8, 105, 123–4
Carroll, L., 83
Cassel, G., 17, 18n., 48n., 236n.
Catchings, W., 17, 18n., 103
Chase, S., 37n.
Clark, C., 67, 159n.
Cobb, C. W., 23
Cobb-Douglas production function,
    23–4
Coefficient of utilization, 77
Committee for Economic Develop-
    ment, 119, 196n.
Competition, 100
Concentration of income and wealth,
    and government investment,
    63

Consumption, as the aim of economic
    activity, 235, 246–54
Consumption function, 20–21
    see also Propensity to save
Cornfield, J., 28n.
Council of Economic Advisers, 116n.,
    132n.
Crawford, J. G., 67

D

Dahlgren, E., 69
Dartmouth College, 223n.
Davis, T. E., 20
Debt burden (tax rate)
    and the distribution of debt
        ownership, 37–8
    and reduction of the debt, 55–6
    and deficit financing, 36–8, 44
    defined, 37–9, 41
    and the growth of income, 45, 50,
        57, 64
    with constant income, 43–4, 46,
        55–6
    with income increasing at a con-
        stant absolute rate, 45–7, 55–6
    with income increasing at a con-
        stant relative rate, 47–51, 55–6
    and the price level, 40, 43n.,
        52n., 57, 58n., 86
    with variable fractions of income
        borrowed, 53–4, 56
    in the War Model, 51–6
Debt, national, 6, 35n., 47–9
Deficit financing
    and national debt, 36–8, 44
    and national income, 6, 39–40, 57
    and private investment, 101n.,
        133
    need for, 36
Demand and investment, 21–2
Depreciation
    accelerated, see Accelerated de-
        preciation
    declining balance method, 206–7
    explained, 9, 71, 84, 94, 155,
        166–7, 197
    and replacement, 9, 165–7, 180
    in the U. K., 206–9, 213n., 216,
        220–21
    see also Replacement-deprecia-
        tion ratio

Depreciation charges
    and economic stability, 164
    importance for growth, 176–7
    and changing prices, 164n., 179,
        198
    in several countries, 154, 164n.,
        180
Depreciation-investment ratio, 33,
        156–8, 161–2, 181–5, 198–201
    and investment financing, 159n.
    in a firm, 160, 198–201
    with two kinds of investment,
        156n., 182–5
    with changing prices, 163–6,
        185–7
    with constant prices, 181–2
    in the U. S. S. R., 154, 159–60
    in the U. K., 159n.
    in the U. S., 158–9, 161, 199–
        200
Depression, as a psychological phe-
        nomenon, 119
Dewhurst, J. F., 24n.
Discount function, 252–4, 260–61
Dobrovolsky, S. P., 196n.
Domar, E. D., 3n., 8n., 32n., 38n.,
        168, 195n., 237n.
Douglas, P. H., 23
Duesenberry, J. S., 21, 29, 70n.,
        116n., 166n., 170n.
Dupriez, L. H., 4n.

E

Economic development
    and accelerated depreciation, 214
    and capital goods capacity, 236
    and capital longevity, 171–2
    and growth models, 9–10, 256–7
    and inflation, 178–80
    objectives of, 245, 250, 252
Economic planning and the time
        horizon, 249–50
Economic processes, finality of, 30,
        32, 133, 166
Eisner, R., 168n., 195n., 196n., 212n.
Employment, 73, 85, 87, 98n., 99,
        101, 102n., 105
    see also Full employment
Engels, F., 224
Enke, S., 130n.
Equilibrium, dynamic, 30, 71, 75

Erlich, A., 167n., 223n., 224n., 237n.,
        243n.
Evans, G. H., 168n.
Evans, W. D., 28n.
Export-Import Bank, 134n.

F

Fabricant, S., 158n., 199n.
Federal Reserve Bulletin, 69, 136n.
Fel'dman, G. A., 10–11, 13, 223–61
        passim
Fel'dman's model
    permanent assets, 230–31
    assets subject to wear, 240–42
    capital coefficients, 228n., 230,
        235, 242–4, 255
    growth of consumption, 231–2,
        242–3, 248–52, 258–60
    discount problem, 252–4, 260–61
    empirical content of, 226–8
    foundations of, 225–9
    γ–investment fraction retained
        by capital goods category—de-
        fined, 229–30
    γ and marginal propensity to
        save, 233–5
    the role of γ, 244–54
    variable γ, 250n.
    and the General plan, 254–8
    rates of growth of main variables,
        231–2, 243
    immobility of resources, 229, 238
    growth of income, 231–2, 242–5,
        258
    treatment of inventories, 228n.
    growth of investment, 231–3,
        240–43, 245
    investment in undeveloped coun-
        tries, 236
    investment-output ratio, 229,
        235–40, 255
    and Keynesian models, 228,
        233–5
    long-range plans, 243–4
    treatment of Marx's scheme,
        226–8
    maximization problem, 245–52
    propensity to save, average, 229,
        235–40, 255
    propensity to save, marginal,
        233–5, 242

Fel'dman's model (*Cont.*)
    and reality, 11, 249, 254–8
    and the Soviet experiment, 228,
        237–40, 254–8
    time preference, 252–4
Fellner, W. J., 17, 18n., 26n., 116,
    123n., 168
Finality of economic processes, 30,
    32, 133, 166
Financial Statement (1953–54),
    H. M. S. O., 207n.
Financing, internal, 160, 198–201,
    219–20
Fisher, I., 102, 253n.
Ford, H., 224
Foreign economic policy, 129, 134
Foreign investment and lending
    as a continuous stream, 133
    similarity to domestic, 132
    in economic literature, 130–33
    equal installment method, 136,
        146, 152–3
    by the government, 133–4
    in the absence of growth, 137n.,
        142n.
    inflow-outflow ratio, 8–9, 32,
        130–53
    net value method, 132, 136–41,
        146–9
    objectives of, 129, 134
    original value method, 136,
        141–6, 149–52
    methods of repayment, 136n.,
        145–6
    revolving fund, 134
Foster, W. T., 17, 18n., 103
Frisch, R., 166n.
Full employment
    and growth, 14–15, 18, 71, 84,
        92
    output estimates, 71–2

G

Gaitskell, H., 207n.
Galenson, W., 239
Gaston, J. F., 195n., 196n., 202n.
Germany, 67–8
Gerschenkron, A., 160n.
Goldenberg, L., 69
Goldsmith, R. W., 172n.
Goldware, F. M., 129n.

Goode, R., 196n.
Government
    borrowing, *see* Deficit financing
    investment, 63
    receipts and expenditures, 20–21,
        60–61, 93, 115n.
Grant, E. L., 167n.
Great Britain, *see* United Kingdom
Greer, G., 37n.
Grossman, G., 10, 223n.
Groves, H. M., 196n.
Growing and stationary economies
    compared, 32–4
Growing firm, 196
Growth
    aims of, 5, 9
    and optimum allocation of re-
        sources, 30
    and the business cycle, 31, 34
    and capital coefficient, capital in-
        tensity, *see* Capital coefficient,
        Productivity of investment
    and capital longevity, 31, 169–80,
        187–94, 240–42
    and depreciation charges, 176–7
    and economic historians, 16
    and economic theory, 12–14,
        16–17, 30, 87–8
    equilibrium rate of, 6–8, 19, 34,
        71, 75, 89–92, 113–17, 128
    and the theory of a firm, 13, 30
    and full employment, 14–15, 18,
        71, 84, 92
    and inflation, 175, 178–80, 189,
        192–4
    insufficient, effects of, 77
    and the interest rate, 31
    paradoxes in, 4, 31, 120
    physical limitations to, 117–18,
        121, 125
    and the price level, 170–80,
        187–9, 191–4
    and the propensity to save, *see*
        Propensity to save
    and saving, 9–10, 107–8
    and technological progress, 7,
        59–60, 88, 101, 107–8, 118n.
    and time preference, 252–4
Growth models
    and aggregation, 19–20
    the α (capitalist) model, 175–80,
        190–94

Growth models (*Cont.*)
    the β model, 170–75, 179–80, 187–9
    and the consumption function, 20–21
    demand and capacity sides, 21–5
    and economic development, 9–10, 256–7
    and economic theory, 11–13, 18–19
    functions and limitations, 8, 11–13
    treatment of government, 20, 21
    in gross terms, 9, 33, 167–80, 187–94, 240–42
    and the input-output method, 27–9
    and investment, 20–21, 25–6
    and labor, 23–26
    Marxist, *see* Fel'dman's model
    and the production function, 7–8, 23–5
    with different average and marginal propensities to save, 233
Growth of national income
    actual compared with potential, 117–18
    effects on capital-output ratio, 76–7, 124
    and efficiency of production, 60–61
    and government expenditures, 60–61
    guaranteed, 79–81, 119–20
    and monetary factors, 57–8, 60, 64, 83–4, 92
    and population growth, 59–60
    and productive capacity, 57–8, 64
    and the profit rate, 62
    and new resources, 59–60
    in several countries, 67–9
    and technological progress, 59–60
    see also National income
Growth of national income in the U. S.
    in money terms, 35n., 58n.
    prospects, 5, 35n., 131–2
    real, per capita, 58–60, 68–9
    real, total, 35n., 58–60, 68–9
Growth rate
    alternative approaches, 96–7

Growth rate (*Cont.*)
    and capital longevity, *see* Capital longevity
    decreasing, 61–3
    special meaning in gross growth models, 169, 170n.
    and the productivity of investment, *see* Productivity of investment, Capital coefficient
    and the rate of profit, 200–201, 219–20
    and the propensity to save, *see* Propensity to save
Gunn, G. T., 23n.
Gurley, J. G., 13n.

H

Haavelmo, T., 11n.
Hagen, E. E., 24n., 88n.
Haley, B. F., 236n.
Hamberg, D., 8n.
Hansen, A. H., 36n., 37, 40n., 80n., 101n., 109n., 110, 112, 121, 154n.
Harris, S. E., 36n., 38n., 43n.
Harrod, R. F., 8n., 17, 18, 92n., 94n., 109n., 110, 112, 121, 168, 253n.
Hartley, R. W., 24n.
Harvard Economic Project, *see* Leontief, W. W.
Hawkins, D., 18
Hayek, F. A., 102, 228, 236n.
Heymann, H., Jr., 237–8, 239n., 244n., 256n.
Hicks, J. R., 17, 228
Hinshaw, R., 130n., 131
Hobson, J. A., 103–4
Hoeffding, O., 223n., 237–8
Hoffenberg, M., 28n.
Holland, D. G., 195n.
Hungary, 68–9
Hunter, H., 223n.

I

Ignatov, B., 227n.
Income, *see* National income, Growth of national income
Income distribution, 62
Income of non-bondholders, 43, 45–6, 51

Income Tax Act, 1952 and Finance Acts, etc., H. M. S. O., 207n.

Inflation
  and capital accumulation, 115
  and growth, 175, 178–80, 189, 192–4
  in peacetime, 98
  effect on replacement-depreciation ratio, 163–6, 185–7
  effect on replacement-investment ratio, 163–6, 185–7

Input-output method, 20, 27–9
  see also Leontief, W. W.

International Bank for Reconstruction and Development, 134n., 136n.

International investment and lending, *see* Foreign investment and lending

Inventories, 183–4, 228n.

Investment
  and accelerated depreciation, 196–7, 202, 212
  attitudes to, 106–7
  and capital stock, 76–8, 105, 123–4
  and deficit financing, 101n., 133
  defined, 26, 70
  and demand, 21–2
  -depreciation ratio, *see* Depreciation-investment ratio
  dual effect of, 6–7, 25, 34, 73, 84, 88–9, 97–101
  and dynamic changes, 112, 117
  effect on employment, 85, 101, 102n., 105
  and growth models, 20–21, 25–6
  and guaranteed growth of income, 79–81, 119–20
  and idle capital, 31, 79, 99, 113–15
  induced, 112, 119–20
  and the interest rate, 111
  financed from internal funds, 160, 198–201, 219–20
  in inventories, 183–4, 228n.
  used for further investment, 11, 223–61 *passim*
  and labor productivity, 24, 43, 46–7
  maximization of, 245

Investment (*Cont.*)
  and national income, *see* National income
  and productive capacity, 6, 26, 73–4, 85, 95–101
  post-war prospects, 36
  -replacement ratio, *see* Replacement-investment ratio
  and saving, 107
  spontaneous, 80, 112
  in the U. S. S. R., 159–60
  see also Capital

Investment function, 21

Investment-income ratio
  in several countries, 67–9
  in the U. S. S. R., 159–60, 172, 236–40, 255
  see also Propensity to save

Investment productivity
  diminution of, 43, 46–7, 62, 106
  estimates of, 116–17
  explained, 25–7, 47n.
  in specific projects (s), 7, 73, 89, 94–5, 111
  stability of, 26–7, 111
  total (σ), 7, 73–4, 89–90, 94–6
  divergence between total (σ) and specific (s), 76–81, 90, 95–6, 100–101, 107, 114n.
  see also Capital coefficient

J

Japan, 68–9

Japan Yearbook, 69

Jasny, N., 223n., 238–9, 240n.

Jaszi, G., 93n.

Junking process, 77–9, 80–81, 114–15

K

Kaldor, N., 110n., 121

Kalecki, M., 17, 72, 103, 110n., 121–2

Kaplan, N. M., 154n., 159–60, 172, 223n., 236, 240n., 244n.

Keirstead, B. S., 17

Kershaw, J. A., 154n.

Keynes, J. M., 5, 6, 8, 12n., 47n., 70, 73, 83, 87, 103–6, 137n., 154, 234

Keynesian era, 57

Keynesian model, 260

Keynesians, 19, 31, 82, 103, 109, 121
Keynesian system, 20, 72–3, 87, 92,
　105, 225n., 228
Kimmel, L. H., 166n.
Kirkpatrick, N. B., 24n., 88n.
Klein, L. R., 19n.
Knight, F. H., 109–10
Koch, K., 69
Kon, A., 256
Kovalevskiĭ, N. A., 224n., 229n.,
　244n., 255–8
Krzhizhanovskiĭ, G. M., 257n.
Kurihara, K. K., 225n.
Kuznets, S., 41, 42n., 58–9, 68–9, 75n.,
　88n., 100n., 158n., 159n., 172n.,
　199n., 226n.

L

Labor, as a factor of production, 7–8,
　23–6, 88
Labor force
　growth of, 7, 59–60, 78–9, 81, 88,
　96, 101, 107–8, 121, 125
　see also Employment, Full em-
　ployment
Labor productivity, 24, 43, 46–7, 72
Labor-saving devices, 7, 98n.
Lags (in time), 70, 84, 96, 102, 105,
　114, 249n., 257n.
Lange, O., 104
Lary, H. B., 130n.
Laursen, S., 70n.
Lenin, V. I., 224
Leontief, W. W., 8n., 17n., 20, 27n.,
　28–9, 116, 166n., 173, 234n.
Lerner, A. P., 37n., 38n., 43n.
Lindahl, E., 69
Loss offsets, 212n.
Lowe, A., 227n., 236n.
Lundberg, E., 17–18
Lutz, F. A., 130n., 131n., 245n.
Lutz, V., 245n.

M

McGurran, H. D., 34n.
Maclaurin's expansion, 188
Maffry, A., 131n.
Mahalanobis, P. C., 230n.
Malthus, T. R., 8
Mandeville, B. de, 8

Marginal efficiency of capital, 90, 106
Marshall, A., 17, 102, 130, 253n.
Marshall Plan, 129
Martin, R. F., 69
Marx, K., 5, 8, 12, 17, 43, 70, 71, 87,
　167n., 224, 225n., 227, 230
Marxists, 10, 17, 32, 109, 121, 133,
　225–6, 243
Marx's scheme, 11, 225–8, 255n.
Matolcsy, M., 69
May, G. O., 167n., 195n.
Mendershausen, H., 23n.
Metzler, L. A., 36n., 70n.
Mikesell, R. F., 130n.
Mill, J. S., 17
Millikan, M. F., 237n.
Model-builder, functions of, 12
Modigliani, F., 21
Monopoly, 100
The Monthly Review of Business Sta-
　tistics (Canada), 67
Multiplier, 36, 90–91, 96, 98, 107,
　112, 137n.
Multiplier effect, 6, 98, 101–7
Musgrave, R. A., 38n., 70n.

N

National Association of Manufac-
　turers, 133
National City Bank, 57n.
National income
　and government deficits, 6, 39–40,
　57
　and investment, 39–40, 42n., 43,
　46–7, 57, 73–5, 90, 97–8, 100,
　111–12, 236
　maximization of, 245
　and the propensity to save, 40
　see also Growth of national in-
　come
National Income and Expenditure of
　the United Kingdom 1946 to
　1950, Command Paper 8203,
　159n.
National Industrial Conference Board,
　58, 68–9
Natural resources, 59–60, 78–9, 81,
　88, 96, 101, 107
Neisser, H., 170n.
New Zealand, 68–9
New Zealand Official Yearbook, 69

Norton, P. T., 167n.
Notkin, A. I., 167n.
Nurkse, R., 227n.

O

Okun, B., 223n.
Oxford University Institute of Statistics, 195n.

P

Painter, M., 35n., 67, 70n.
Paradoxes of growth, 4, 31, 120
Patinkin, D., 164n.
Paul, R. E., 196n.
Penrose, E. T., 13n., 16n., 154n., 223n.
Perloff, H. S., 36n., 37n.
Pierson, J. H. G., 119n.
Pigou, A. C., 105n., 164n., 228
Pilvin, H., 8n.
The Planned Economy (Planovoe Khoziaĭstvo), 223, 255, 258
Population, *see* Labor force
Preobrazhenskiĭ, E., 225n.
President's Economic Report, 132n.
President's Report on the State of the Union, 132n.
Price changes, relative, 114
Price level
 assumed constancy of, 70, 85–6, 229
 and the debt burden, 40, 43n., 52n., 57, 58n., 86
 and growth, 85–6, 170–80, 187–9, 191–4
Production function, 7–8, 23–5
Productive capacity
 of capital assets, 168–9
 explained, 71–2, 94–5, 168–9
 and investment, 6, 26, 73–4, 85, 95–101
 and labor, natural resources, and technology, 88
 and growth of national income, 57–8, 64
 and replacement, 166–7
 see also Growth, Growth of national income, Growth rate
Profit rate, 32, 62, 200–201, 219–20
Profits, 200–201

Propensity to save
 average and marginal, 91, 233
 and the capital-output ratio, 124
 explained, 93–4, 169–70
 in Fel'dman's model, 229, 233–40, 242, 255
 under full employment, 115–16
 and government receipts and expenditures, 93, 115n.
 and growth, 7, 9, 33, 61–3, 167–80, 187–94, 240–42
 related to labor, natural resources, and technology, 78–9, 81, 96, 101, 107–8
 in the long run, 115–16
 proper magnitude, 100–101, 118–19
 in several countries, 67–9
 stability of, 111
 in the U. S., 41–2, 68, 75n., 100
 see also Investment-income ratio
Property income, 63
Prosperity and growth, 117

R

RAND Corporation, 154n., 159n., 160n.
Ratchford, R. U., 35n.
Reder, M. W., 70n.
Reeve, J. E., 172n.
Rentier, 6, 63
Replacement
 and accelerated depreciation, 202
 and depreciation, 9, 165–7, 180
 explained, 166–7
 and productive capacity, 166–7
 in the U. S. S. R., 243n.
Replacement-depreciation ratio, 9, 32–3, 160–67, 181–7
 in economic literature, 166
 with changing prices, 163–6, 185–7
 with constant prices, 160–63, 181–5
 in the U. S. S. R., 162–3
 in the U. S., 161
Replacement-investment ratio
 two kinds of investment, 182–5
 with changing prices, 163–6, 185–7

Replacement-investment ratio (*Cont.*)
    with constant prices, 160–63,
        181–5
    in the U. S. S. R., 162–3
    in the U. S., 161, 180
Research expenditures, 61
Robinson, J., 72, 226n., 235n.
Romanis, A. W., 195n.
Rostow, W., 16
Ruml, B., 36n.

S

Sabsovich, L. M., 257
Salant, W. S., 8, 129n., 132n.
Salera, V., 130n.
Samuelson, P. A., 36n., 94n., 112n.,
        253n.
Saving
    defined, 70–71
    and growth, 9–10, 107–8
    see also Propensity to save
Say's Law, 83, 102
Schelling, T. C., 17, 18n., 120n.
Schumpeter, J. A., 5n., 12n., 19, 31,
        112
Scitovsky, T., 70n., 97
Seton, F., 238n.
Shaw, E. S., 13n.
Sherrard, A., 70n.
σ effect, 98, 101–7
    see also Investment, dual effect
        of, Investment productivity
Simmons, E. J., 224n.
Simons, H. C., 109–10
Smelker, M., 70n.
Smelker, M. S., 70n.
Smith, A., 17
Snyder, C., 122–3
Solow, R. M., 8, 23n.
Soviet Russia, see U. S. S. R.
Soviet State Planning Commission,
        224
Stalin, J., 224, 257n., 258
Stationary state, 6, 14
Statisches Reichsamt (Germany), 67
Stern, E. H., 75n., 94n., 97, 109n.
Streeten, P. P., 195n.
Strumilin, S. G., 256
Survey of Current Business, 75n., 159n.
*Survey of Current Business Supple-
        ment*, 158n., 164n., 184n., 199n.

Sweden, 68–9
Sweezy, A. R., 119n.
Sweezy, P. M., 17, 18n., 110, 121,
        122–8, 223n., 225n., 228n.

T

Taxable income, 41, 56
Taxation, incentive, 36, 215–16
    see also Accelerated depreciation
Tax exemption of new firms, 195
Tax rate to service national debt, see
        Debt burden
Technological progress
    attitudes to, 106–7
    and capital coefficients, 243
    differential, 239–40
    and economic stability, 31–2
    and growth, 7, 59–60, 88, 101,
        107–8, 118n.
    and investment productivity, see
        Investment productivity
    and monopolies, 60
    and the propensity to save, 78–9,
        81, 96, 101, 107–8
    and unused capacity, 100
Terborgh, G., 158n., 166n., 168n.,
        196n., 206n.
Theorizing, the essence of, 22–3
Time horizon, 249–50
Time preference, 252–4
Tinbergen, J., 96n.
Tsiang, S. C., 18
Tsuru, S., 225n.

U

Underconsumptionist school, 109,
        120–21
Unemployment, 5, 107
    see also Employment, Full em-
        ployment
Union of Soviet Socialist Republics
    allocation of real and money
        product, 239–40
    attitudes to growth, 257–8
    attitudes to investment and tech-
        nological progress, 106–7
    capital coefficients, 160n., 172,
        243–4, 255
    capital use and replacement,
        243n., 244

Union of Soviet Socialist Republics
(*Cont.*)
depreciation-investment ratio,
154, 159–60
differential purchasing power,
239–40
economic thought, 223–4, 236
five-year plan, 224, 243
General plan, 224, 228n., 254–8
growth rates, 172, 236, 244,
255–6
as a source of ideas, 10
investment estimates, 159–60
investment-income ratio, 159–60,
172, 236–40, 255
labor productivity, 239
replacement, 243n.
replacement-depreciation ratio,
162–3
replacement-investment ratio,
162–3
differential technological progress, 239–40
see also Fel'dman's model
United Kingdom
American loan, 136n.
depreciation charges, 154
depreciation-investment ratio,
159n.
depreciation methods, 206–9,
213n., 216, 220–21
growth of national income, 67–9

United Kingdom (*Cont.*)
investment-income ratio, 67–9
United Nations Statistical Office,
159n.
U. S. Department of Commerce, 58,
68–9, 158n., 164n., 180
U. S. National Resources Committee,
61n.
U. S. National Resources Planning
Board, 61n.
U. S. Temporary National Economic
Committee, 154, 166n., 200n.

V

Vaïsberg, R. E., 256
Varga, S., 69
Vickrey, W., 196n.
Viner, J., 131

W

Wall Street Journal, 43
War financing, 52n.
Wicksellian tradition, 102
Worswick, G. D. N., 195n.
Wright, D. Mc., 17, 34

Y

Young, J. P., 131n., 132n.